I0124689

Johann J. Ignaz von Döllinger

The Pope and the Council

Johann J. Ignaz von Döllinger

The Pope and the Council

ISBN/EAN: 9783743322493

Manufactured in Europe, USA, Canada, Australia, Japa

Cover: Foto ©Thomas Meinert / pixelio.de

Manufactured and distributed by brebook publishing software
(www.brebook.com)

Johann J. Ignaz von Döllinger

The Pope and the Council

THE POPE

AND THE COUNCIL

BY JANUS

AUTHORIZED TRANSLATION FROM THE GERMAN

SECOND EDITION

RIVINGTONS

London, Oxford, and Cambridge

SCRIBNER, WELFORD AND CO., NEW YORK

1869.

EDINBURGH : T. CONSTABLE,
PRINTER TO THE QUEEN, AND TO THE UNIVERSITY.

TABLE OF CONTENTS.

CHAPTER III.

PAPAL INFALLIBILITY.

Table of Contents.

vii

NOTICE BY THE TRANSLATOR.

.

IT will be obvious at a glance to the reader, that this work emanates from Catholic authorship, and discusses the great religious crisis through which the Church and the world are now passing from a Catholic, though a "liberal Catholic," point of view. That it bears evidence of no common attainments and grasp of mind a very cursory examination will suffice to show. An English translation is offered to the public under the belief that there are very many in this country, as well Protestants as Catholics, who will gladly avail themselves of an opportunity of learning, on the most direct authority, how the grave questions which just now agitate the Church are regarded by the members of a school, morally if not numerically strong, within her pale, who yield indeed to none in their loyal devotion

to Catholic truth, but are unable to identify its interests
with the advance of Ultramontanism, or rather, who
cannot but recognise between the two an antithesis
which the Church history of the last thousand years
too eloquently attests, and to which present facts, no
less than past experience, give all the significance of a
solemn warning it would be worse than unwisdom to
ignore.

Two rival tendencies, alien alike in their principles
and their aims, which have long been silently developing themselves, are now contending for the mastery
within the bosom of the Church, like the unborn babes
in Rebekah's womb, and it is simply a truism to assert
that every section of our divided Christendom is inter-
ested in the result of the struggle. We live in an age
powerful beyond all that have gone before for good and for
evil, penetrated perhaps more deeply than controversial-
ists are willing to admit by Christian sentiment, but also
presenting in too many quarters a spectacle unprecedented in modern history, of fixed and deliberate anta-
gonism to the dogmas of the Christian creed. Not only
the world of sense, but of supernatural revelation, is

delivered over to the disputations of men. At such a moment, it is proposed, amid the fervid acclamations of one party, the earnest and sorrowful protests of another, the careless acquiescence or sullen indifference of a host of nominal believers, and the triumphant sneers of an amused but unbelieving outside world, to erect Papal Infallibility into an article—and' therefore inevitably the cardinal article—of the Catholic faith. Under a profound sense of the range and gravity of the issues involved this work was written, and with a similar feeling, which each day's experience only deepens, it has been translated. Man's necessity, we know, is God's opportunity, and even at the eleventh hour He may stretch forth His arm to save His menaced and afflicted Church. "Oculi omnium in Te sperant, Domine, et Tu das escam illorum in tempore opportuno."

We cannot, indeed, forget that two years elapsed before the œcumenical pretensions of the *Latrocinium* of Ephesus were formally superseded, and that for more than twenty the Church lay, technically at least, under the reproach of heresy inflicted on her by the Council of Rimini, to which St. Jerome gave expression in the

well-known words, " mundus miratus est se esse Aria-
num." Meanwhile, it behoves us to possess our souls
in patience, as knowing that the Church is greater than
any parties or individuals who for the moment may
usurp her functions and prostitute her awful name, and
that, come what will, truth must ultimately prevail.

It may be well to add that the substance of the
earlier portion of this volume appeared in a series of
articles on "The Council and the Civiltà," published
during last March in the *Allgemeine Zeitung*,[1] which
attracted very general attention on the Continent. But
the whole subject is here worked out in detail, and
with constant reference to the original authorities for
every statement that is dwelt upon.

[1] *See Allg. Z.* for March 10-15, 1869.

Sept. 10, 1869.

PREFACE.

THE immediate object of this work is to investigate by the light of history those questions which, we are credibly informed, are to be decided at the Œcumenical Council already announced. And as we have endeavoured to fulfil this task by direct reference to original authorities, it is not perhaps too much to hope that our labours will attract attention in scientific circles, and serve as a contribution to Ecclesiastical History. But this work aims also at something more than the mere calm and aimless exhibition of historical events ; the reader will readily perceive that it has a far wider scope, and deals with ecclesiastical politics, —in one word, that it is a pleading for very life, an appeal to the thinkers among believing Christians, a protest based on history against a menacing future, against the programme of a powerful coalition, at one time openly proclaimed, at another more darkly insinuated, and which thousands of busy hands are daily and hourly employed in carrying out.

We have written under a deep sense of anxiety in presence of a serious danger, threatening primarily the internal condition of the Catholic Church, and then—as is inevitable with what affects a corporation including 180 millions of men—destined to assume vaster dimensions, and take the shape of a great social problem, which cannot be without its influence on ecclesiastical communities and nations outside the Catholic Church.

This danger does not date from yesterday, and did not begin with the proclamation of the Council. For some twenty-four years the reactionary movement in the Catholic Church, which is now swollen to a mighty torrent, has been manifesting itself, and now it is preparing, like an advancing flood-tide, to take possession of the whole organic life of the Church by means of this Council.

We—and the plural must not here be understood figuratively, but literally—we confess to entertaining that view of the Catholic Church and her mission which its opponents designate by that much-abused term, so convenient in its vagueness for polemical purposes—*Liberal;* a term in the worst repute with all uncompromising adherents of the Court of Rome and of the Jesuits—two powers intimately allied,—and never mentioned by them without bitterness. We are of their opinion who are persuaded, *first,* that the Catholic Church, far from assuming an hostile and suspicious attitude towards the principles of political, intellectual, and religious freedom and independence of judgment, in so far as they are capable of a Christian interpretation, or rather are directly derived from the letter and spirit of the Gospel, ought, on the contrary, to be in positive accord with them, and to exercise a constant purifying and ennobling influence on their development; *secondly,* that a great and searching reformation of the Church is necessary and inevitable, however long it may be evaded.

To us the Catholic Church and the Papacy are by no means convertible terms, and therefore, while in outward communion with them, we are inwardly separated by a great gulf from those whose ideal of the Church is an universal empire spiritually, and, where it is possible, physically, ruled by a single monarch,—an empire of force and oppression, where the spiritual authority is aided by the secular arm in summarily suppressing every movement it dislikes. In a word, we reject that doctrine and idea of the Church which has for years been commended by the organ of the Roman Jesuits as alone true, as the sole remaining anchor of deliverance for the perishing human race.

It will more precisely indicate our point of view if we quote the words of a man regarded in his lifetime as the ornament and pride of the German clergy, the Cardinal and Prince Bishop Diepenbrock, who was himself the pupil of the ever-memorable Sailer, and shared his sentiments. Diepenbrock replied to the reforming suggestions of his friend Passavant, involving an alteration in the hierarchy, a softening of the sharp distinction between clergy and laity, a co-operation of the people in Church-government, and a transformation of the Roman Court, by saying that " only in this way can health be restored to the general body, and earthly conditions be elevated and ennobled, which is a task that Christianity must accomplish ; only thus, by developing and quickening the constitution and doctrine of the Church, can the questionings and aspirations this remarkable age of ours is everywhere seething with obtain their rest and satisfaction."

" It is true, indeed," he added, " that the *ultra* party

in the Church hopes to reach its goal by an opposite road. But such a return to the past is an impossibility in history. The Middle Ages are left behind once for all, and nothing but a *fata morgana* can make them hover like a possible future before the lively imagination of —— and his allies. The necessity of a complete renovation of the Church is already dawning on the vision of all who think without prejudice, while to the few only its nature and method are as clear as the thing itself. To speak out such ideas openly I hold to be a sort of duty of charity towards mankind."[1]

It would be easy to quote from the writings of Gügler, Görres, Eckstein, Francis Baader, and Möhler —to mention only the departed—a series of testimonies to prove that the most gifted and enlightened among German Catholics have entertained the same or kindred views.

Diepenbrock only lived to witness the first tentative approaches of that Ultramontanism which he has described. What appeared in his time as an isolated and half-unconscious tendency, has since grown up into a powerful party, with clearly ascertained objects, which has gained a firm footing through the wide ramifications

---

[1] See Letters published in Passavant's *Nachlass* (*Remains*), p. 87.

of the Jesuit Order, and enlists the energetic services of a constantly increasing body of fellow-labourers in the clergy educated at the Jesuit College in Rome.

As it had become necessary to assail this party, which carries on its plans either in ignorance of Church history or by deliberately falsifying it, we were obliged to distinguish the primacy as it existed in the ancient Church from its later form, and we could not therefore avoid bringing forward in this connexion a very dark side of the history of the Papacy. Every one who examines the internal relations of Church history will be constrained to acknowledge that, since the eleventh century, there has been no period of it on which a Christian student can dwell with unmixed satisfaction; and as he endeavours to get at the bottom of the causes underlying that unmistakable decay of Church life, constantly getting a deeper hold, and more widely spreading, he will always be brought back to the distortion and transformation of the Primacy as the ultimate root of the evil. If the Primacy is on the one hand a source of strength to the Catholic Church, yet on the other hand it cannot be denied that, when one looks at it from the standpoint of the ancient Church—from the Apostolic age till about 845,—the Papacy, such as it has become, presents the appearance of a disfiguring, sickly, and choking excrescence on the organization of the Church, hindering and decomposing the action of its vital powers, and bringing manifold diseases in its train. And now, when for many years preparations have been going on for effecting the final completion of the system which lies at the root of the present incongruities in the Church, and surrounding it with an impregnable bulwark by the doctrine of Infallibility, it becomes the duty of every one who wishes well to the Church and to society, to which it supplies an element of life, to try, according to the measure of his knowledge and working power, what can yet be done to ward off so fatal a catastrophe.

We do not conceal from ourselves that the charge of a radical aversion to the Papacy will be brought from more than one quarter against this book and its authors. Their number is legion at the present day, for whom the scriptural saying, " Meliora sunt vulnera diligentis quam fraudulenta oscula odientis," has no meaning, and who cannot comprehend how a man can at once love and honour an institution, and yet expose its weak points, denounce its faults, and purposely exhibit their mischievous results. In their opinion, things of the kind should be carefully hushed up, or only apologetically referred to. And for some time past this way of looking at matters has been designated "piety." It is therefore pious to believe gladly and readily fables and falsehoods which have been invented for certain ends connected with religion, or are clothed in a religious dress; it is pious either wholly to deny the injuries and abuses of the Church's life, and the perversities in her government, or, when this is impracticable, to do one's utmost to defend them, and to gain them the credit of being due to good motives, or, at least, of having a tolerable side. The absence of such a disposition is visited in ecclesiastical circles with the reproach of impiety—a reproach which, accordingly, our work is sure not to escape. But we do not acknowledge the justice of this view; we consider it, indeed, a commendable piety to maintain silence about the personal infirmities or errors of a man in high position, or even at the head of the Church, or at least to deal gently with them, but we think it a complete misapplication of the term when it is called a duty of piety to conceal or colour historical facts and faulty institutions. On the contrary, we believe our piety owes its first duties to the Divine institution of the Church and to the truth, and it is precisely this piety which constrains us to oppose, frankly and decisively, every disfigurement or disturbance either of the one or the other. And we hold it the more imperative on us to come forward, when not only hereditary evils are not to be got rid of, but are actually to be increased by new abuses, and that too at a time when the falling away from Christianity has become so general and cuts so deep—partly for this very reason, that, under the mass of rubbish it is overlaid with, its eternal, divine, and saving germ is hidden from the short-sighted gaze of the present generation. In proof that herein we are but acting in the spirit of the Church, we can appeal to sayings, the one of a Pope, the other of a highly-venerated saint. Innocent III. said, "Falsitas sub velamine sanctitatis tolerari non debet," and St. Bernard declares, "Melius est ut scandalum oriatur quam veritas relinquatur."

Every faithful Catholic is convinced—and to that conviction the authors of this book profess their adherence—that the primacy rests on Divine appointment. The Church from the first was founded upon it, and the Lord of the Church ordained its type in the person of Peter. It has therefore, from the necessity of the case, developed itself up to a certain point, but on this has followed, since the ninth century, a further development—artificial and sickly rather than sound and natural—of the Primacy into the Papacy, a transformation more than a development, the consequences of which have been the splitting up of the previously united Church into three great ecclesiastical bodies, divided and at enmity with each other. The ancient Church found the need of a centre of unity, of a bishop possessed of primatial authority, to whom the oppressed might turn, and by whose powerful intercession they might obtain justice. But when the presidency in the Church became an empire, when in place of the first bishop deliberating and deciding in union with his "brethren" on the affairs of the Church, and setting them the example of submission to her laws, was substituted the despotic rule of an absolute monarch, then the unity of the Church, so firmly secured before, was broken up. When we inquire for definite, fixed, and universally acknowledged rights, exercised equally throughout the whole Church during the first Christian centuries by the bishop of Rome, as holding the primacy, we seem to lose sight of him again, for of the privileges afterwards obtained or laid claim to by the Popes not one can be traced up to the earliest times, and pointed to as a right uninterruptedly and everywhere exercised.

But we meet with abundant facts which prove unmistakeably that the Roman bishops not only believed themselves to be in possession of a Divine right, and acted accordingly, but that this right was actually recognised by others. And if it was often affirmed, as by the Council of Chalcedon, that the Roman Church had received its privileges from the Fathers, we shall have to consider that the Primacy itself, the first rank among Churches, was not given to it by any Synod at any fixed time, but had always existed since the time of the Apostles, and that to any heathen who asked which among their Churches was the first and principal one, whose voice and testimony had the greatest weight and influence, every Christian would have answered at once that it was the Roman Church, where the two chief Apostles, Peter and Paul, sealed their testimony with their blood, just as Irenæus has expressed it.

But we shall be obliged to allow that the form which this Primacy took depended on the concessions of the particular local Churches, and was never therefore the same everywhere, acting within certain fixed limits prescribed by law. No one acquainted with Church history will choose to affirm that the Popes ever exercised a fixed primatial right, in the same way in Africa

as in Egypt, in Gaul as in Mesopotamia; and the
well-known fact speaks clearly enough for itself, that
throughout the whole ancient canon law, whether in
the collections preserved in the Eastern or the Western
Church, there is no mention of Papal rights, or any reference to a legally defined action of the bishop of Rome
in other Churches, with the single exception of the
canon of Sardica, which never obtained universally even
in the West.

A good illustration of this relation of the Primacy to
the Church is afforded by the Council of Chalcedon in
451. The position of Pope Leo, though he was not
present, is evidently a very high and influential one;
more honour was shown to him and his Church than
had been ever shown at any Synod to any other bishop,
and his legates presided with great authority at this
most numerous of the ancient assemblies of the Church.
Meanwhile matters came at last to a point, where the
Council maintained, and eventually, after long opposition on the side of Rome, carried out its own will against
the legates, and the instructions they had received
from Leo.[1]

[1] In the account of patristic teaching on the Roman primacy given
below (pp. 87 *sqq.*), there is no mention made of one important name, St.

In this book the first attempt has been made to give a history of the hypothesis of Papal Infallibility from its first beginnings to the end of the sixteenth century, when it appears in its complete form. That hypothesis, late as was the date of its invention, and though for a long time it met with strenuous opposition, will yet always have numerous adherents, if it is to remain for the future in its former condition of a mere theological opinion, for it is recommended by its convenience and facility of application. It seems to attain, by the shortest road, in the simplest way, and with least waste of time, what the ancient Church expended so much trouble upon, with so many appliances, and for so long a time. But, if once generally

Jerome's. As the omission might be considered intentional, we take this opportunity of making some remarks on him. His letters to Pope Damasus of 375 (*Opp.* ed. Vallarsi, i. 39), were written under the pressure of his distress in Syria from the charge of heresy; he was unwilling to use the received expression, "three hypostases," instead of "three persons," and was therefore accused of Sabellianism. He then urged the Pope, with courtly and high-sounding professions of unconditional submission to his authority, but, at the same time, in a strictly menacing tone, to pronounce upon this term in the sense needed for justifying him. In fact, he gave St. Cyril of Jerusalem, to whom he sent his profession of faith, as high a place as the Pope. But Cyril, with good ground, thought the case a suspicious one, and gave him no answer. St. Jerome's well-known saying, "Inter duodecim unus eligitur, ut capite constituto schismatis tolleretur occasio," gives the most pointed expression to the view then entertained by the faithful of the nature of the Primacy, only the notions current in our day of the privileges involved in this description of it are more extensive than was then the case.

accepted as a rule of faith, it becomes not only a soft cushion on which the wearied or perplexed mind, as well of the layman as of the theologian, may repose softly, and abandon itself to undisturbed slumber, but it also supplies to the intellectual world in religious matters what our steam conveyances and electrical wires supply to the material world in the saving of time and labour. Nothing could be more economical or better adapted to save study and intellectual toil even for Rome herself; for the inevitable result of the principle would speedily bring us to this point, that the essence of Infallibility consists in the Pope's signature to a decree hastily drawn up by a congregation or a single theologian. The remark has frequently been made that it is chiefly converts, with little theological cultivation, but plenty of youthful zeal, who surrender themselves in willing and joyful mental slavery to the infallible ruler of souls ; rejoicing and deeming themselves fortunate to have a master, visible, palpable, and easily inquired of. Christ seems to them so exalted and so distant, the Church so large and wide, so many-sided in its opinions, and so silent on many points people would like to know about. How much easier to get a dogmatic decision from a Pope by the proper amount of pressure ! We may call to mind, in this connexion, the decisions of Alexander VII. in favour of the newly discovered doctrine of attrition, the decrees of Clement XI. and Benedict XIII., and the powers which have thereby been called into operation.

But if raising the doctrine of Infallibility into an article of faith must, on the one hand, cripple all intellectual movement and scientific activity in the Catholic Church, it would, on the other hand, build up a new wall of partition, and that the strongest and most impenetrable of all, between that Church and the religious communities separated from her. We must renounce that dearest hope which no Christian can banish from his breast, the hope of a future reunion of the divided Churches both of the East and the West. For no one who is moderately acquainted with the history of the Eastern Church and of the Protestant bodies, will seriously hold it to be conceivable that a time can ever come in which even any considerable portion of these Churches will subject itself, of its own free-will, to the arbitrary power of a single man, stretched, as it would be, through the doctrine of Infallibility, even beyond its present proportions. Only when a universal conflagration of libraries had destroyed all historical documents, when Easterns and Westerns knew no more of their own early history than the Maories in New Zealand know of theirs now, and when, by a miracle, great nations had abjured their whole intellectual character and habits of thought, —then, and not till then, would such a submission be possible.

What was it that gave the Councils of Constance and Basle, in the fifteenth century, so constraining an authority and such a lasting influence on the condition of the Church ? It was the power of public opinion which backed them up. And if at this day a strong and unanimous public opinion, at once positive in its faith and firm in its resistance to the realization of the Ultra-montane scheme, were awakened and openly proclaimed in Europe, or even in Germany only, then, in spite of the utterances, so suggestive of gloomy forebodings, of the Bishops of Mayence, St. Pölten, and Mechlin, the present danger would happily pass away. We have attempted in this work to contribute to the awakening and direction of such a public opinion. It may, perchance, produce no more permanent effect than a stone thrown into the water, which makes a momentary ripple on the surface, and then leaves all as it was before ; but yet it may act like a net cast into the sea, which brings in a rich draught of fishes.

For many reasons no names of authors are placed on our title-page. We consider that a work so entirely made up of facts, and supporting all its statements by reference to the original authorities, must and can speak for itself, without needing any names attached to it. We are anxious that the reader's attention should be exclusively concentrated on the matter itself, and that, in the event of its evoking controversy, no opportunity should be given for transferring the dispute from the sphere of objective and scientific investigation of the weighty questions under review, conducted with dignity and calmness, into the alien region of venomous personal defamation and invective.

July **31, 1869.**

INTRODUCTION.

THE veil which has hitherto hung over the preparations and intention of the great General Council is already lifted.

The *Civiltà Cattolica* of 6th February published the following remarkable article, in the form of a communication from France :—"The liberal Catholics are afraid the Council may proclaim the doctrines of the Syllabus and the Infallibility of the Pope, but they do not give up the hope that it may modify or interpret certain statements of the Syllabus in a sense favourable to their own ideas, and that the question of Infallibility will either not be mooted or not decided. The true Catholics, who are the great majority of the faithful, entertain opposite hopes. They wish the Council to promulgate the doctrines of the Syllabus. In any case, the Council could put out in a positive form, and with the requisite developments, the negative statements of the Syllabus, and thereby quite set aside the misappre-

A

hensions which exist about some of them. Catholics will accept with delight the proclamation of the Pope's dogmatic infallibility. Every one knows that he himself is not disposed to take the initiative in a matter so directly concerning himself; but it is hoped that his infallibility will be defined unanimously, by acclamation, by the mouth of the assembled Fathers, under the inspiration of the Holy Ghost. Finally, many Catholics wish the Council to crown the many honours the Church has bestowed on the all-blessed Virgin by promulgating her glorious assumption into heaven as a dogma." It is said before, that "Catholics believe the Council will be of short duration, like the Council of Chalcedon (*i.e.*, that it will only last three weeks). It is believed that the Bishops will be so united on the main points, that the minority, however willing, will not be able to make any prolonged opposition."

In a later issue of the *Civiltà* similar wishes are put into the mouth of the Belgian Catholics, " who are not only devoted body and soul to the interests of the Church and the Holy See, but submit without hesitation to all doctrinal decisions of the Holy See." They hope, among other things, that the Council will once for all put an end to the division among Catholics, by striking a decisive blow at the spirit and doctrines of Liberalism, and that the doctrine of the Pope's infallibility and supremacy over a General Council will be defined. The Belgian correspondent is no less emphatic in repudiating the tolerably opposite desires of the so-called liberal Catholics. These, who number many of the younger clergy among their ranks, and who have not completely submitted to the teaching of the Encyclical and Syllabus, maintain that political questions do not belong to the Popes, and some of them have violently distorted the Encyclical and Syllabus in their own sense.[1] Their blindness, to say nothing worse, is so great, that they either expect opposite decisions to these, or an interpretation in their own sense.

We shall not be wrong in taking these correspondents' articles of the *Civiltà*, which are, perhaps, to be followed by others from other parts of the Catholic world, as something more than feelers merely to ascertain whether things are ripe for the dogmatic surprises already prepared. No! these zealots are not accustomed to pay the very slightest regard to the mental disposition of their age. In these communications

[1] [This seems to refer to the Pastoral of the Bishop of Orleans, Dupanloup.—Tr.]

about the wishes and hopes of Catholics, which take
the innocent form of petitions to the Holy See, we
have significant hints of what the Council is expected
to do; significant hints, first to the Bishops to acquaint
themselves with their duty, and abstain from useless
opposition; and next, to the rest of the Catholic world
to prepare itself for the approaching "announcements of
the Holy Ghost."

The *Civiltà*, written by Roman Jesuits, and commended some years ago in a Papal Brief as the purest
journalistic organ of true Church doctrine, may be
regarded as in some sense the *Moniteur* of the Court
of Rome. It is not too much to say that in all important questions its thoughts are identical with those
of the chief head, and of many other "heads," in Rome.
Its lofty tone and arrogant handling of all opponents
correspond to this official character. Its articles often
read like Papal Bulls spun out. One could not therefore desire a more trustworthy authority as to the aims
of Rome in convoking this Council.

Nor are other instructive signs wanting besides the
statements of the *Civiltà*. The Jesuits have been
active for some time past in founding confraternities
which bind themselves to hold and propagate Papal

Infallibility as an article of faith. For the same object the institution of Provincial Synods has been revived during the last ten years, under stringent and repeated exhortations from Rome. And it may be seen from the published acts of those held both in and out of Germany, that the question of Papal Infallibility and of the theses of the Syllabus has been laid before them. The Jesuit Schneemann reports that the Provincial Synods of Cologne, Colocsa, Utrecht, and those held in North America, have accepted Papal Infallibility.[1] He observes that " these Synodal affirmations of Papal Infallibility, revised at Rome, are important as showing that, though as yet no formal article of faith, it is in the eyes of Rome, and of the Bishops, an indubitable truth. For Provincial Synods are strictly forbidden to decide controverted points of belief." We may safely assume, on such good authority, that these decisions were not waited for at Rome, but were sent from Rome to the Provincial Synods for approval. The answers could have been known beforehand in the present state of things in the Church; they will be produced in the Council as proofs of the belief of the majority of Catholic Bishops, and to give the ap-

---

[1] *Literarischer Handweiser*, 1867, pp. 439 *seq.*

pearance of the definition of Papal Infallibility not being so exclusively the work of the Jesuits, an appearance Pius IX. was anxious to avoid in the case of the Immaculate Conception.   It appears, by a letter of Flir's from Rome, that he yielded quite unexpectedly in that case to Cardinal Rauscher's demand for striking out of the Bull some of the irrelevant proofs alleged, because, as he said, this must be endured, though a humiliation for Rome, that people might not say everything depended on the Jesuits.[1]

We know on good authority that the whole plan of the campaign for fixing the Infallibility dogma is already mapped out. An English Prelate—we could name him—has undertaken at the commencement of proceedings to direct a humble prayer to the Holy Father to raise the opinion of his infallibility to the dignity of a dogma. The Jesuits and their Roman allies hope that the majority of the Bishops present, who have been already primed for the occasion, will accede by acclamation to this petition, and the Holy Father will gladly yield to

---

[1] *Briefe aus Rom* (Innsbruck, 1864), p. 25:—"The Holy Father has found this criticism of a stranger (viz. Rauscher) very unpleasant, and said—'Questa è una mortificazione per Roma, ma è bisogno di soffrirla, affinchè non si dica, che tutto sia dipendente dai Gesuiti." [Flir was Rector of the German Church at Rome, and Auditor of the Rota. His Letters are reviewed in the *Saturday Review* for May 28, 1864.—Tr.]

the pressure coming on him spontaneously, and, as it were, through a sudden and irresistible inspiration from on high, and so the new dogma will be settled at one sitting, without further examination, as by the stroke of a magician's wand. As the Roman people are told after a Conclave, *Habemus Papam*, on the evening of this memorable sitting the news will go forth to the whole Catholic world, *Habemus Papam infallibilem.* And before this newly risen and bright sun of divine truth, all the ghosts of false science and forms of modern civilisation will be scared away for ever.

Meanwhile, to keep to the articles of the *Civiltà* already quoted, it is clear from them that the Council is summoned chiefly for the purpose of satisfying the darling wishes of the Jesuits and that part of the *Curia* which is led by them.

We propose to examine these theories in the following order:—first we shall take the Syllabus and what concerns it; then we shall briefly discuss the new dogma about Mary; and lastly we shall set the dogma of Papal Infallibility in the light of history.

CHAPTER I.

THE articles of the Syllabus—such, we are told, is one of the urgent wishes of true Catholics—are to be defined by the Council in the form of positive dogmas. The Church will thus be enriched with a considerable number of new articles of faith, hitherto unheard of or abundantly contradicted; but when once Papal Infallibility has become matter of faith, this will be only the first fruits of a far richer harvest in the future. The extent of the Catholic Church will thereby be gradually narrowed, perhaps till it presents the spectacle once offered to the world by a Pope, Peter de Luna, Benedict XIII., who from his castle of Peniscola condemned the whole of Christendom which refused to acknowledge him, and finally, when the Council of Constance had solemnly deposed him (1417), and the number of his adherents was reduced to a few individuals, declared—"The whole Church is assembled in

Peniscola, not in Constance, as once the whole human race was collected in Noah's ark." But this will give them little concern ; nay, the more the educated classes are forced out of the Church, the easier will it be for Loyola's steersmen to guide the ship, and reduce the true flock that still remains in it to more complete subjection. Catholicism, hitherto regarded as a universal religion, would, by a notable irony of its fate, be transformed into the precise opposite of what its name and notion imports. As the assembled Bishops are to exercise their power of formulating dogmas on the contents of the Syllabus, they have only to set their conciliar seal on a work already prepared to their hand by the Vienna Jesuit, Schrader.[1] He has already turned the negative statements of the Syllabus into affirmatives, and so we can, without trouble, anticipate the decisions of the Council on this matter. And, as it is to last only three weeks, from and after 29th December 1869 the Roman Catholic world will be enriched by the following truths, and will have to accept, on peril of salvation, the following principles :—

(1.) The Church has the right of employing external

---

[1] *Der Pabst und die modernen Ideen.* Heft II. Die Encyclica. Wien, 1865.

coercion; she has direct and indirect temporal power, *potestatem temporalem* as distinguished from *spiritualem,* or, in ecclesiastical language, power of civil and corporal punishment.[1] Schrader himself intimates that this is meant when he says, " It is not only minds that are under the power of the Church." [2] His fellow-Jesuit, Schneemann, speaks out clearly and roundly enough on this point : " As the Church has an external jurisdiction she can impose temporal punishments, and not only deprive the guilty of spiritual privileges. . . . The love of earthly things, which injures the Church's order, obviously cannot be effectively put down by merely spiritual punishments. It is little affected by them. If that order is to be avenged on what has injured it, if that is to suffer which has enjoyed the sin, temporal and sensible punishments must be employed." Among these Schneemann reckons fines, imprisonment, scourging, and banishment, and he is but endorsing an article in the *Civiltà, Del potere coattivo della Chiesa,* which maintains the necessity of the Church visiting her opponents with

---

[1] The Syllabus condemns the following propositions : " Ecclesia vis inferendæ potestatem non habet, neque potestatem ullam temporalem, directam aut indirectam " (24). " Præter potestatem episcopatui inhærentem, alia ei attributa est temporalis potestas a civili imperio vel expresse vel tacite concessâ, revocanda propterea, cum libuerit, a civili imperio " (25).

[2] *Der Pabst,* p. 64.

fines, fasts, imprisonment, and scourging, because without this external power the Church could not last to the end of the world. She herself is to fix the limits of this power, and he is a rebel against God who denies it. Schneemann does not conceal his grief that the present world is so far gone from the apprehension and application of these wholesome truths : "We see that the State does not always fulfil its duties towards the Church according to the divine idea, and, let us add, cannot always fulfil them, through the wickedness of men. And thus the Church's rights in inflicting temporal punishment and the use of physical force are reduced to a minimum."[1]

It was from the spirit here manifested that Pius IX. in 1851 censured the teaching of the canonist Nuytz in Turin, because he allowed only the power of spiritual punishment to the Church.[2] And in the Concordat made in 1863 with the Republics of South America, it

---

[1] Schneemann's *Die kirchliche Gewalt und ihre Träger* forms vol. vii. of the *Stimmen aus Maria Laach* (Freiburg, 1867). The passages quoted are from pp. 18, 41. The article of the *Civiltà* referred to appeared in 1854, vol. vii. p. 603. It is said expressly of the Church that against those "che ricusano la soggezione dello spirito, operi per via di castighi temporali, multandoli nelle sostanze, maurandoli con privazioni e digiuni, affligendoli con carcere e battiture." The other references to the *Civiltà* are from vol. viii. pp. 42, 279-282.

[2] The works censured are *Juris Ecclesiastici Instit.* and *In Jus Eccles. Univ. Tractat.*

is laid down in Article 8 that the civil authorities are absolutely bound to execute every penalty decreed by the spiritual courts. In a statement addressed by Pius IX. to Count Duval de Beaulieu, published in the *Allgemeine Zeitung* of November 13, 1864, the power of the Church over the government of civil society, and its direct jurisdiction in temporal matters, is expressly guarded.

It follows that they are greatly mistaken who suppose that the Biblical and old Christian spirit has prevailed in the Church over the mediæval notion of her being an institution with coercive power to imprison, hang, and burn. On the contrary, these doctrines are to receive fresh sanction from a General Council, and that pet theory of the Popes—that they could force kings and magistrates, by excommunication and its consequences, to carry out their sentences of confiscation, imprisonment, and death—is now to become an infallible dogma. It follows that not only is the old institution of the Inquisition justified, but it is recommended as an urgent necessity in view of the unbelief of the present age. The *Civiltà* has long since described it as "a sublime spectacle of social perfection;"[1] and the two recent

---

[1] In 1855, vol. i. p. 55, the Inquisition is called "un sublime spettacolo della perfezione sociale."

canonizations and beatifications of inquisitors, following in rapid succession, gain in this connexion a new and remarkable significance.

(2.) According to Schrader's affirmative statement of the twenty-third proposition of the Syllabus, the Popes have never exceeded the bounds of their power or usurped the rights of princes.[1] All Catholics must for the future acknowledge, and all teachers of civil law and theology must maintain, that the Popes can still depose kings at their will, and give away whole kingdoms and nations at their good pleasure.

When, for instance, Martin IV. placed King Pedro of Aragon under excommunication and interdict for making good his hereditary claim to Sicily after the rising of the Sicilians against the tyranny of Charles I. (in 1282), and then promised indulgences for all their sins to those who fought with him and Charles against Pedro, and finally declared his kingdom forfeit, and made it over for a yearly tribute to Charles of Valois—a step which cost the two kings of France and Aragon their life, and the French the loss of an army,[2]—this was not,

[1] The Syllabus condemns the following proposition (23), "Romani Pontifices et Concilia Œcumenica a limitibus suæ potestatis recesserunt, jura Principum usurparunt." Cf. Schrader, *ut sup.* p. 63.

[2] See Raynald. *Annal. Eccles.* (ed. Mansi), vol. iii. pp. 183-4. The Bull of Martin IV. against Peter of Aragon runs thus : "Regnum Aragoniæ cæter-

as the world in its false enlightenment has hitherto supposed, a violent usurpation, but the application of a divine right which every Pope still possesses in full, though prudence may require that for the moment, and perhaps for some time to come, they should let it lie dormant, and adopt meantime a waiting attitude.

Pope Clement IV., in 1265, after selling millions of South Italians to Charles of Anjou for a yearly tribute of eight hundred ounces of gold, declared that he would be excommunicated if the first payment was deferred beyond the appointed term, and that for the second neglect the whole nation would incur interdict, *i.e.*, be deprived of sacraments and divine worship.[1]

asque terras Regis ipsius exponentes, ut sequitur, ipsum Petrum regem Aragonum eisdem regno et terris regioque honore sententialiter, justitiâ exigente, privamus; et privantes exponimus eadem occupanda Catholicis, de quibus et prout Sedes Apostolica duxerit providendum, in dictis regno et terris ejusdem Ecclesiæ Romanæ jure salvo." The Pope required of Charles of Anjou, "quingentas libras parvorum Turonensium" as Papal tribute, and for this consideration had a crusade preached against Peter, with the following promise (1283): "Omnibus Christi fidelibus qui contra Regem Aragoniæ nobis, Ecclesiæ vel Regi Siciliæ astiterint, si eos propterea in conflictu mori contigerit, illam peccatorum suorum, de quibus corde contriti et ore professi fuerint, veniam indulgemus quæ transfretantibus in terræ sanctæ subsidium consueverit." It is noteworthy that Martin IV. compelled several German churches (Liége, Metz, Verdun, Basle) to pay a tenth of all ecclesiastical property to France for carrying on this war. When Rudolph of Hapsburg reclaimed vigorously against so unheard of a demand, Martin's successor, Honorius IV., exhorted him "to submit patiently to the exaction out of reverence for the Papal See." Raynald. *ut sup.* pp. 600-1.

[1] Raynald. p. 162. "Quod si in secundo termino infra subsequentes

Nevertheless, the Bishops of the future Council are to make it an article of faith that the Pope did not thereby exceed the limits of his power; in other words, that he could at his mere caprice, and for purely political or pecuniary ends, deprive millions of innocent men of what, according to the teaching of the Church, are the necessary means of salvation.

(3.) If the Council executes the programme of the *Civiltà*, it will also undertake a correction of the hitherto prevalent estimate of history. We now read in all historical books and systems of Church law that the immunities of the clergy (*e.g.*, the *privilegium fori*, the unrestricted right of acquiring property, and exemption from civil functions) were gradually conceded to the Church by the Roman emperors and later kings, and have therefore a civil origin. This will be characterized as heresy.[1]

Those also will become guilty of heresy who write or teach that the extravagant pretensions of the Popes contributed to the separation of the Eastern and Western Churches, though this may be discovered in official

duos menses eundem censum sine diminutione quâlibet non persolveritis, totum regnum ac tota terra predicta ecclesiastico erunt supposita interdicto."

[1] The Syllabus condemns the prop. (30), "Ecclesiæ et personarum ecclesiasticarum immunitas a jure civili ortum habuit."

documents from the twelfth to the sixteenth century, and the avowals of a number of contemporary authorities.[1]

In prospect of such decrees all Catholic writers on Law or History should be urgently advised to publish their works before 30th December 1869 ; for from thenceforward, " magnus ab integro sæclorum nascitur ordo," and only Jesuits or their pupils will be called or qualified, without savour of heresy, to write on secular or Church history, civil law, politics, canon law, etc. There will at least be required for literary and academical work a flexibility and elastic versatility of spirit and pen hitherto confined to journalism.

(4.) Still more dangerous will be the questions of freedom of conscience, and persecution, when once the propositions of the Syllabus are made articles of faith, according to the will of the Jesuits and the Bishops acting under their guidance.

The Syllabus condemns the whole existing view of the rights of conscience and religious faith and profession : it is a wicked error to admit Protestants to equal political rights with Catholics, or to allow Protestant

---

[1] It condemns proposition 38, " Divisioni Ecclesiæ in Orientalem atque Occidentalem Romanorum Pontificum arbitria contulerunt."

immigrants the free use of their worship ;[1] on the contrary, to coerce and suppress them is a sacred duty, when it has become possible, as the Jesuit Fathers and their adherents teach. Till then, Schneemann[2] says, the Church will, of course, act with the greatest prudence in the use of her temporal and physical power, according to altered circumstances, and will not therefore at present adopt her entire mediæval policy.

The inevitable result of this is to propagate, from generation to generation, lies, hypocrisy, and deceit by wholesale; but that is the lesser evil. For freedom of opinion and worship produces, according to the Syllabus, profligacy and the pest of indifferentism. That, too, is to become an article of faith, and the future commentators on the decrees of the Council will have to confirm its truth by reference to the actual condition of the nations which have these liberties. They will point to the Germans, the English, the French, and the Belgians

---

[1] It condemns prop. 77, " Ætate hâc nostrâ non amplius expedit religionem Catholicam haberi tanquam unicam statûs religionem, cæteris quibuscunque cultibus exclusis ;"—prop. 78, "Hinc laudabiliter in quibusdam Catholici nominis regionibus lege cautum est, ut hominibus illuc immigrantibus liceat publicum proprii cujusque cultûs exercitium habere ;" —prop. 79, " Enimvero falsum est civilem cujusque cultûs libertatem, itemque plenam potestatem omnibus attributam quaslibet opiniones cogitationesque palam publiceque manifestandi, conducere ad populorum mores animosque facilius corrumpendos ac indifferentismi pestem propagandam."

[2] Schneemann, *ut supra,* p. 30.

B

as the most profligate of men, while the Neapolitans, Spaniards, and inhabitants of the Roman States, with whom the exclusive system flourishes, or did till quite lately, are a brilliant model of virtue among all nations of the earth.   To speak seriously, the contest inaugurated by the Encyclical of 1864 will have to be carried out with the free use of every available Church weapon,—a contest against the common sentiment and moral sense of every civilized people, and all the institutions that have grown out of them.

It is but a few years since Ketteler, Bishop of Mayence, in a widespread work praised by all the Catholic journals of the day, undertook to show the moderation, tolerance, and self-restraint of the Catholic Church in its relations with the State and the separate Churches.   He insists that the Church so thoroughly respects freedom of conscience as to repudiate all outward coercion of those beyond her pale as immoral and utterly unlawful; that nothing is further from her mind than to employ any physical force against those who, as being baptized, are her members; that she must leave it entirely to their own freest determination whether they will accept her faith; and that it is absurd for Protestants to suppose they have any need to

fear a forcible conversion, etc. etc.[1]   How far these statements can be verified by history is indeed very doubtful.

Meanwhile the Bishop is instructed by the Syllabus
and its commentator, Schrader, that he has fallen into
that forbidden liberalism which is, according to the
Roman view, one of the grossest errors of the day, and
that it was by special indulgence of Rome that his
book was not put on the Index.   What a light this
throws on the condition of the Church, and what an
unworthy mental slavery the Roman Jesuit party
threatens foreign Catholics with is thus made clear
enough !   An illustrious bishop speaks, amid universal
applause, without a syllable of dissent from his fellow-
bishops, on those grave questions, upon the right answer to which the legal position and beneficial action of
the Church in our days in large measure depends.   And
now, a few years afterwards, the Pope, without indeed
naming him, condemns his doctrine, and the very people
who applauded the bishop's book applaud the Encyclical
with yet profounder homage, and are convinced that
what they took for white is black.   Ketteler, who knows
well enough that the main object of the Syllabus is to
exalt principles at first only applied to the condition

---

[1] *Freiheit, Autorität, und Kirche,* Mainz, 1862.

and circumstances of a particular country into universal articles of faith, tried to save himself by the pitiful evasion that these articles of the Syllabus do not contain a general principle, but only one applicable to certain countries, especially Spain.[1] It appears, then, that our bishops, our theologians and preachers, and our people, did not know what the true doctrine of the Catholic Church is, but only those monks and monsignori, especially the Jesuits, who compose the Roman Congregations, and who have now for the first time since the Encyclical of Gregory XVI. opened the hitherto jealously closed fountains of knowledge. And thus the singular fact has come to light that the Catholic nations have for a long time been thoroughly heterodox, and that their appointed teachers have helped on the error, and sworn to Constitutions moulded in utterly vicious principles and laid under ban of Rome.

(5.) The Syllabus closes with the notorious assertion that "they are in damnable error who regard the reconciliation of the Pope with modern civilisation as possible or desirable."[2]

Every existing Constitution in Europe, with the sole

---

[1] *Deutschland nach dem Kriege*, Mainz, 1867, cap. 12.

[2] The Syllabus condemns prop. 80, " Romanus Pontifex potest ac debet cum progressu cum liberalismo et cum recenti civilisatione sese reconciliare et componere."

exception of Russia and the Roman States, is an outgrowth of this modern civilisation. Freedom of religious profession, worship, and teaching, freedom of political rights and duties before the law,—these, with the people's right of taxing themselves, and taking a part in legislation and municipal self-government, are the dominant principles and ideas which interpenetrate all existing Constitutions, and they are so closely connected, and so sustain each other, that where some of them are conceded, the rest inevitably follow. But an opposite course has been steadily pursued in the Church for centuries, especially since the pseudo-Isidorian decretals; the hierarchical system has become more and more built up into an unlimited oligarchical absolutism, and a constantly growing and encroaching bureaucratic centralization has killed out all the old Church-life in its harmonious disposition and synodal self-government, or turned it into a mere empty form.

Thus Church and State are like two parallel streams, one flowing north, the other south. The modern civil Constitutions, and the efforts for self-government and the limitation of arbitrary royal power, are in the strongest contradiction to Ultramontanism, the very kernel and ruling principle of which is the consolidation of absolutism in the Church. But State and Church are intimately connected; they act and react on one another, and it is inevitable that the political views and tendencies of a nation should sooner or later influence it in Church matters also.

Hence the profound hatred, at the bottom of the soul of every genuine ultramontane, of free institutions and the whole constitutional system. The *Civiltà* not long since gave pointed utterance to it :—" Christian States have ceased to exist; human society is again become heathen, and is like an earthly body with no breath from heaven. But with God nothing is impossible; he can quicken the dry bones, as in Ezekiel's vision. The political power, parliaments, voting urns, civil marriages, are dry bones. The universities are not only dry, but stinking bones, so great is the stench that rises from their deadly and pestilential teaching. But these bones can be recalled to life if they hear God's word and receive His law, which is proclaimed to them by the supreme and infallible doctor, the Pope."[1]

Let us remember that the noble mother of European Constitutions, the English Magna Charta, was

[1] Vol. iii. pp. 265 *seq.*, 1868. " Ossa, non pur aride, ma fetenti le università, tanto è il puzzo, che n'esce di dottrine corrompitrici e pestiferi."

visited with the severest anger of Pope Innocent III., who understood its importance well enough. He saw therein a contempt for the Apostolic See, a curtailing of royal prerogatives, and a disgrace to the English nation; he therefore pronounced it null and void, and excommunicated the English barons who obtained it.[1] We may readily do Pius IX. and his Jesuit counsellors, who are notoriously the authors of the Encyclical and Syllabus, the justice of admitting that they have done in 1864 what Innocent in 1215 was prophet enough to consider for the interests of the Church. What was then a weak and tender sapling has grown, in spite of the curse of the most powerful of all the Popes, into a mighty tree, overshadowing half the world, and is blest with bloom-

---

[1] The Bull (Aug. 15, 1215) runs thus :—"Nos tantæ indignitatis audaciam dissimulare nolentes, in apostolicæ sedis contemptum, regalis juris dispendium, Anglicanæ gentis opprobrium et grave periculum totius negotii crucifixi (quod utique immineret, nisi per auctoritatem nostram revocarentur omnia, quæ a tanto Principe cruce signato totaliter sunt extorta, etiam ipso volente illa servari): ex parte Dei omnipotentis, Patris et Filii, et Spiritus sancti, auctoritate quoque beatorum Petri et Pauli Apostolorum ejus, ac nostra, de communi fratrum nostrorum consilio, compositionem hujusmodi reprobamus penitus et damnamus ; sub interminatione anathematis prohibentes, ne dictus Rex eam observare præsumat, aut Barones cum complicibus suis ipsam exigant observari : tam chartam quam obligationes seu cautiones, quæcunque pro ipsa vel de ipsa sunt factæ, irritantes penitus, aut cassantes, ut nullo unquam tempore aliquam habeant firmitatem."—Rymer, *Fœdera,* etc. (ed. Clarke), i. p. 135. Innocent sent a similar document to the English barons, and when they took no heed of it the ban and interdict followed.

ing children and children's children. And so, too, its latest offspring, the Austrian Constitution,—which a far feebler successor of Innocent has stigmatized as an " unspeakable abomination" (*infanda sane*),—may rest in peace, and appeal confidently to the world's verdict on the world's history. And the more so, since this very successor was not ashamed, a year or two ago, to have the question asked in London, whether he too might not find a residence in the motherland of those " demoralizing" laws of freedom.

Rome has shown herself no less hostile to the French than to the English Constitution. In 1824, Leo XII. addressed a letter to Louis XVIII., pointing out the badness of the French Constitution, and urgently pressing him to expunge from the charter those articles which savoured of liberalism.[1] When Charles X. tried to change the Constitution by the ordinances of July 1830, every one gave the blame to his episcopal advisers, and especially his confessor, Cardinal Latil. The fall of the Bourbons was the result. Soon after the establishment of the new Belgian Constitution in 1832, Gregory XVI. issued his famous Encyclical, recently used and confirmed by Pius IX., which pronounces freedom of

[1] See Artaud de Montor, *Hist. Leo XII.* (Paris, 1843), vol. i. p. 234 *seq.*

conscience an insane folly, and freedom of the press a pestiferous error, which cannot be sufficiently detested. The immediate consequence was the rise of a liberal party in Belgium, at internecine feud with the Catholic party. The contest still goes on, after nearly forty years; the schism has grown ever wider and deeper, and the hatred fiercer between them, and, as Ultramontanism makes every understanding or compromise between them impossible, the political controversy has merged in a systematic attacking and undermining of all positive religion. The Belgian Catholics have never been able to meet the reproach of being necessarily enemies to a Constitution condemned as wicked by the Pope, and that all their assurances of loyalty and conscientious respect for the fundamental law of the country are mere hypocrisy. And thus, with all the religiousness of the people, the liberal and anti-religious party is constantly gaining ground, while the Catholic party, divided against itself by the split between ultramontanes and liberals (*i.e.*, Catholics true to the Constitution), is no longer competent to form any available Cabinet. The attempt of the Congress of Malines in 1863 was wrecked; the Syllabus has pronounced sentence of death on its programme, so eloquently set forth by

Montalembert, for reconciling the Church with civil freedom.

In the United States, Catholics cannot form a political party. There, too, as an American bishop has assured us, their situation is most unfavourable as regards political influence and admission to office, because it is always cast in their teeth by Protestants that they find their principles in Papal pronouncements, and cannot therefore honestly accept the common liberties and obligations of a free State, but always cherish an *arrière pensée* that if ever they become strong enough they will upset the Constitution.

In Italy, the Papal Government has used every effort to deter Austria and the other Italian sovereigns from granting parliamentary and free municipal institutions. The documents proving this are to be seen in print. The Roman Court declared that it could not suffer even the very mildest forms of parliamentary government in its neighbourhood, on account of the bad example.[1]

---

[1] Prince Schwarzenberg reported this in 1850 to Baron Hügel in Florence. As the document is not well known north of the Alps, we give the passage. The whole letter will be found in a book printed by Gennarelli at Florence in 1862—" *Le Dottrine civili e religiose della Corte di Roma,*" p. 72. It says, in reference to the Tuscan Constitution of 1848, " Le gouvernement pontifical avoue, que ses repugnances à cet égard se fondent aussi sur des motifs, qui lui sont plus particuliers. Il ne cherche nullement à dissimuler, que, forcé comme il est, à devoir reconnoître et pro-

The mild and just Grand-Duke Leopold of Tuscany was compelled against his will, under pressure from Rome, to abolish that article of the Constitution which asserted the equality of all citizens before the law, without distinction of religion, because the Pope declared that it could not be promulgated " *tutâ con-scientiâ.*"[1] Under the same influence the Jewish physicians in Tuscany were first in 1852 forbidden to practise, as they had long been allowed to do. Who can wonder, after this, at the hatred of the Italians towards the Papacy as it now is, or think any permanent peace possible between Italy and such a hierarchy as this?

That the Bavarian Constitution, with its equality of religious confessions, and of all citizens before the law, is looked on with an evil eye at Rome, is sufficiently shown by the constant reproaches of the *Curia* since

clamer tout régime parlementaire comme directement menaçant pour le libre exercice du pouvoir spirituel, il ne sauroit voir sans alarme se propager et se consolider autour de lui non seulement des principes constitutionnels imposés originairement par la révolution, *mais encore des formes représentatives plus mitigées,* dont la contagion lui semble non moins inévitable et désastreuse dans l'intérieur des états," etc. In other words, " Our absolutist system, supported by the Inquisition, the strictest censorship, the suppression of all literature, the privileged exemption of the clergy, and arbitrary power of bishops, cannot endure any other than absolutist governments in Italy."

[1] Gennarelli, *ut supra,* pp. 78, *seq.*

1818.[1] And finally, the Austrian Constitution has
drawn on itself the curse of the Vatican.   In the Allo-
cution of 22d June 1868 we read—

" By our apostolic authority we reject and condemn
the above-mentioned (new Austrian) laws in general,
and in particular all that has been ordered, done, or
enacted in these and in other things against the rights
of the Church by the Austrian Government or its subordinates; by the same authority we declare these laws
and their consequences to have been, and to be for the
future, null and void (*nulliusque roboris fuisse ac fore*).
We exhort and adjure their authors, especially those
who call themselves Catholics, and all who have dared
to propose, to accept, to approve, and to execute them,
to remember the censures and spiritual penalties incurred
ipso facto, according to the apostolical constitutions and
decrees of the Œcumenical Councils, by those who violate
the rights of the Church."

By this sentence the whole legislature and executive
of Austria is placed under ban, with the Emperor Francis
Joseph at its head, and the Austrians may be thankful
that the whole territories of the empire are not placed

[1] See, for these, *Concordat und Constitutions Eid der Kathol. in Bayern*
(Augsburg, 1847), pp. 244 *seq.*

under interdict, according to the earlier precedent put in practice the last time against Venice (1606).

Pius IX. condemns the Austrian Constitution for making Catholics bury the bodies of heretics in their cemeteries where they have none of their own, and he considers it "abominable" (*abominabilis*), because it allows Protestants and Jews to erect educational institutions. He seems to have quite forgotten that similar laws have long prevailed elsewhere without opposition from Rome.

If the will of the *Civiltà* is accomplished, the Bishops will solemnly condemn, by implication, next December, the Constitutions of the countries they live in, and the laws which they, or many of them, have sworn to observe, and will bind themselves to use all their efforts for the abolition of those laws and the overthrow of the Constitutions. This will not, of course, be so openly stated; the *Civiltà* and its allies will say, what has often been said since 1864, that the Church must observe for a time a prudent economy, and must so far take account of circumstances and accomplished facts, as, without any modification of her real principles, to pay a certain external deference to them. The Bishops do well to endure the lesser evil, as long as open resist-

ance would lead to worse consequences, and prejudice
the interests of the Church. But this submission, or
rather silence and endurance, is only provisional, and
simply means that the lesser evil must be chosen in
preference to a contest with no present prospect of
success.

As soon as the situation changes, and there is a
hope of contending successfully against free laws, the
attitude of the bishops and clergy changes too. Then,
as the Court of Rome and the Jesuits teach, every oath
taken to a Constitution in general or to particular laws
loses its force. The oft-quoted saying of the apostle,
that we must obey God rather than man, means, in the
Jesuit gloss, that we must obey the Pope, as God's
representative on earth, and the infallible interpreter of
His will, rather than any civil authority or laws. Therefore Innocent X., in his Bull of 20th November 1648,
" *Zelus domûs Dei*," which condemns the Peace of West-
phalia as " null and void, and of no effect or authority
for past, present, or future," expressly adds, that no one,
though he had sworn to observe the Peace, is bound
to keep his oath.[1]   It was chiefly those conditions

---

[1] The passage referred to runs as follows :—" Motu proprio, ac ex certâ
scientiâ et maturâ deliberatione nostris, deque Apostolicœ potestatis

of the Westphalian Peace which secured to Protestants the free exercise of their religion, and admission to civil offices, that filled the Pope, as he said, with profound grief (*cum intimo doloris sensu*). And this sentence was adhered to, for in 1789 Pius VI. declared that the Church had never admitted the Westphalian Peace, "*Pacem Westphalicam Ecclesia nunquam probavit.*" Thus again in 1305, Pius VII., in writing to his nuncio at Venice, upholds the punishments imposed by Innocent III. for heresy, viz., confiscation of property for private persons, and the relaxation of all obligations of tribute and subjection to heretical princes; and he only regrets that we are fallen on such evil days, and the Bride of Christ is so humbled, that it is neither possible to carry out, nor even of any avail to recall, these holy maxims, and she cannot exercise a righteous severity against the enemies of the faith.[1]

These "holy maxims," then, are allowed for a while

plenitudine, prædictos alterius seu utriusque Pacis hujusmodi articulos cæteraque in dictis Instrumentis contenta . . . . ipso jure nulla, irrita, invalida, injusta, damnata, reprobata, inania, viribusque et effectu vana omnia fuisse, esse et in perpetuo fore; neminemque ad illorum et cujus libet eorum etiamsi juramento vallata sint, observantiam teneri . . . . decernimus et declaramus."—*Magnum Bullar. Roman.* t. v. p. 466 seq. Luxemb. 1727.

[1] The Italian text of the letter is given in *Essai sur la Puissance Temp. des Papes* (Paris, 1818), vol. ii. p. 320.

to lie dormant, though, according to the Jesuit plan of
the campaign, they are to be raised at the approaching
Council to the dignity of irreversible dogmas through
the assertion of Papal Infallibility. Better times must
be waited for, when the Church (that is, the Court of
Rome) shall be raised once more from the dust, and
seated on the throne of her universal, world-wide, spiritual sovereignty.

But here "the true Catholics" are divided into two
parties. The one party, which is sufficiently educated
to understand something of the spirit and tendencies of
the age, cherishes no illusions as to the possibility, or
at least the near approach, of a thousand years' reign
of absolute Papal dominion, and therefore despairs of
humanity, which in its scornful blindness has rejected
its last anchor of hope. The age we live in is the dark
age of Antichristian dominion, the age of wailing and
woe which is to precede the appearance of the bodily
Antichrist for two years and a half, after which comes
the end of all things and the general judgment. This
party was represented in Bavaria by a learned and
influential ecclesiastic, now dead, who gave it expression in a pastoral of the present Cardinal Reisach.[1] It

---

[1] [Windischmann, Vicar-General of Cardinal Reisach when Archbishop

simply means : As history does not go our way, there shall be no more history, or, in other words, the world must come to an end, because our system is not carried out. As their wisdom is at fault, they presume the wisdom of Providence is exhausted also! Men of this school think a Council so near the end of the world superfluous, or at best only last warning, given to men rather in wrath than in mercy.

The other party, and the Jesuits at their head, see in the Council the last star of hope, and expect that, when Papal Infallibility and the articles of the Syllabus have been proclaimed, mankind will bow down its proud neck, like the royal Sicambrian, Clovis, and will burn what it adored before, and adore what it burnt.

A holy bishop, Francis of Sales, often expressed his dislike of writings which deal with political questions, such as the indirect power of the Pope over princes, and thought with good reason that, in an age when the Church has so many open enemies, such questions should not be mooted.[1] But St. Francis of Sales is no authority for the Jesuits.

of Munich, one of the few very learned men modern Ultramontanism has produced.—Tr.]

[1] *Œuvres*, xi. 406.

CHAPTER II.

THE NEW DOGMA ABOUT MARY.

IN comparison with the principles involved in sanctioning the Syllabus, the new dogma proposed about Mary is harmless enough. No one indeed can comprehend the urgent need for it only a few years after Pius IX. has solemnly proclaimed the Immaculate Conception as a revealed truth. But there never seems to be enough done for the glorification of Mary. It is worth while, however, to take note of this second exhibition of the characteristic contempt of the Jesuits for the tradition of the ancient Church.

Neither the New Testament nor the Patristic writings tell us anything about the destiny of the Holy Virgin after the death of Christ. Two apocryphal works of the fourth or fifth century—one ascribed to St. John, the other to Melito, Bishop of Sardis—are the earliest authorities for the tradition about her bodily assump-

tion.[1] It is contained also in the pseudo-Dionysius;
he and Gregory of Tours brought it into the Western
Church.[2] But centuries passed before it found any
recognition. Even the Martyrology of Usuard, used in
the Roman Church in the ninth century, confined itself
to the statement that nothing was known of the manner
of the holy Virgin's death and the subsequent condition of her body : " Plus eligebat sobrietas Ecclesiæ cum
pietate nescire, quam aliquid frivolum et apocryphum
inde tenendo docere."[3] If this floating tradition too is
made into a dogma under Jesuit inspiration, it may
easily be foreseen that the Order—*l'appétit vient en
mangeant*—will bestow many a jewel hereafter on the
dogma-thirsting world, out of the rich treasures of its
traditions and pet theological doctrines. There is, for
instance, the doctrine of *Probabilism*, which lies quite
as near its heart as the Syllabus and Papal Infallibility,
and which has stood it in such excellent stead in practice.[4] What a glorious justification it would be for an
Order which has been so widely blamed, if the Council

---

[1] Εἰς τὴν Κοίμησιν τῆς ὑπεραγίας Δεσποίνης, and *De Transitu Mariæ.*
[2] *De Nom. Div.* 3. *De Glor. Mart.* i. 4.
[3] Usuard, *Martyrol.* 18 Kal. Sept.
[4] [The lax system of Jesuit casuistry exposed in the *Provincial Letters*
of Pascal. Innocent XI. condemned some of the extremer forms of it.
—Tr.]

were to be so accommodating as to set its seal to this doctrine too as an article of faith !

We know that the Order expects another important service from the Council, viz., that the gymnasia and schools of higher education should be placed in its hands, as being specially called and fitted for the work, and that the Bishops should engage, wherever they have the power, to hand over these establishments to the Fathers of the Society. It is therefore extremely desirable, nay necessary, that that ever-gaping wound in the reputation of the Order—its moral system— should be healed by a decree of the Council.

CHAPTER III.

§ I.—*Ultramontanism.*

IT is the fundamental principle of the Ultramontane view that when we speak of the Church,
its rights and its action, we always mean the Pope, and
the Pope only. "When we speak of the Church, we
mean the Pope," says the Jesuit Gretser, at the beginning of the seventeenth century, Professor at Ingold-
stadt, and one of the most learned theologians of the
Order. Taken by itself, as the community of believers,
clergy, and bishops, the Church, according to Cardinal
Cajetan—the classical theologian of the Roman Court
—is the slave (*serva*) of the Pope. Neither in its whole
nor its parts (National Churches) can it desire, strive
for, approve, or disapprove, anything not in absolute
accordance with the Papal will and pleasure. In an

article of the *Civiltà,* entitled "The Pope the Father of the Faithful," we read as follows :—

"It is not enough for the people only to know that the Pope is the head of the Church and the Bishops ; they must also understand that their own faith and religious life flow from him ; that in him is the bond which unites Catholics to one another, and the power which strengthens and the light which guides them ; that he is the dispenser of spiritual graces, the giver of the benefits of religion, the upholder of justice, and the protector of the oppressed. And still this is not enough ; it is further requisite to refute the accusations directed against the Pope by the impious and the Protestants, and to show how serviceable the Papacy and the Pope have at all times been to civil society, to the Italian people, to families, and to individuals, even in regard to their temporal interests."[1]

---

[1] *Civ.* 1867, vol. xii. pp. 86 *seq.* — "Non basta che il popolo sappia essere (il Papa) il capo della chiesa e dei vescovi : bisogna che intenda da lui derivare la propria fede, da lui la propria vita religiosa, in lui risiedere il vincolo che unisce insieme i cattolici, la forza che li convalida, la guida che li dirige : lui essere il dispensiere delle grazie spirituali, lui il promotore dei beneficii che la religione impartisce, lui il conservatore della giustizia, lui il protettore degli oppressi. Né ciò solo basta ; si richiede di più che dileguinsi le accuse lanciate contro del Papa dagli empii e dai protestanti, e che dimostrisi quanto benefico alle società civili, ai popoli italiani, alle famiglie e agli individui, eziandio in ordine agl' interessi temporali sia stato in ogni tempo il Papato e il Papa."

It was St. Jerome's reproach to the Pelagians that, according to their theory, God had, as it were, wound up a watch once for all, and then gone to sleep because there was nothing more for Him to do.   Here we have the Jesuit supplement to this view.   God has gone to sleep because in His place His ever wakeful and infallible Vicar on earth rules, as lord of the world, and dispenser of grace and of punishment.   St. Paul's saying, " In him we live, and move, and are," is transferred to the Pope.   Few even of the Italian canonists of the fifteenth century could screw themselves up to this point, those greedy place-hunters and sycophants, who were blamed even in Rome as mainly responsible for the corruption of the Church caused by the Popes.   Under the lead of the new Order of the sixteenth century all hitherto said and done for the exaltation of the Papal dignity was thrown into the background.   We owe it to Bellarmine and other Jesuits that in some documents the Pope is expressly designated " Vice-God."   The *Civiltà*, too, after asserting that all the treasures of divine revelation, of truth, righteousness, and the gifts of God, are in the Pope's hand, who is their sole dispenser and guardian, comes to the conclusion that the Pope carries on Christ's work on earth, and is in relation to us what Christ would be if He was still visibly present to rule His Church.[1] It is but one step from this to declare the Pope an incarnation of God.[2]

Ultramontanism, then, is essentially Papalism, and its starting-point is that the Pope is infallible in all doctrinal decisions, not only on matters of faith, but in the domain of ethics, on the relations of religion to society, of Church to State, and even on State institutions, and that every such decision claims unlimited and unreserved submission in word and deed from all Catholics. On this view the power of the Pope over the Church is purely monarchical, and neither knows nor tolerates any limits. He is to be sole and absolute master; all beside him are his plenipotentiaries and servants, and are, in fact, whether mediately or immediately, the mere executors of his orders, whose powers

[1] Vol. iii. p. 259, 1868. "I tesori di questa revelazione, tesori di verità, tesori di giustizia, tesori di carismi, vennero da Dio depositati in terra nelle mani di un uomo, che ne è solo dispensiero e custode . . . quest' uomo è il Papa. Ciò evidentemente è racchiuso nella sua stessa appellazione di Vicario di Christo. Imperocchè se egli sostiene in terra le veci di Christo, vuol dire che egli continua nel mondo l'opera di Christo ; ed è rispetto a noi ciò che sarebbe esso Christo, se per sè medesimo e visibilmente quaggiù governasse la chiesa."

[2] [Compare with this Pusey's *Eirenicon,* p. 327 : "One recently returned from Rome had the impression that 'some of the extreme Ultramontanes, if they do not say so in so many words, imply a quasi-hypostatic union of the Holy Ghost with each successive Pope.' The accurate writer who reported this to me observed in answer, ' *This seems to me to be Llamaism.*'" —Tr.]

he can restrict or cancel at his pleasure. On Ultramontane principles the Church is in a normal and flourishing condition in proportion as it is ruled, administered, supervised, and regulated, down to the minutest details, in all its branches and national boundaries, from Rome. Rome is to act as a gigantic machine of ecclesiastical administration, a Briareus with a hundred arms, which finally decides everything, which reaches everywhere with its denunciations, censures, and manifold means of repression, and secures a rigid uniformity. For the Church-ideal of the Ultramontanes is the *Romanizing* of all particular Churches, and above all the suppression of every shred of individuality in National Churches.[1] Nay, more, they consider it the conscientious duty of all nations to mould themselves, to the utmost of their power, into the specifically clerico-Italian fashion of thinking and feeling. How should they not, when the *Civiltà* says roundly, "As the Jews were formerly God's people, so are the Romans under the New Covenant. They have a supernatural dignity" ?[2]

[1] ["Romanism," "Romanize," etc., are used by German writers not as synonymous terms with Roman Catholicism, etc., but for the Romanist or Ultramontane party in the Roman Catholic Church.—Tr.]

[2] Vol. iii. p. 11, 1862. "Sopranaturale essendo il fine, per cui Iddio conserva lo stato Romano, sopranaturale in qualche modo si vedrà essere la dignità di questo popolo." These praises of the so-called Roman people, which no longer exists—for the population of Rome is a mere fluctuating

The Ultramontane knows nothing higher than the breath and law of Rome. For him Rome is an ecclesiastical address and inquiry-office, or rather a standing oracle —the *Civiltà* calls the Pope *summum oraculum,*—which can give at once an infallible solution of every doubt, speculative or practical. While others are guided in their judgment on facts and events by the moral and religious sentiment developed in their Church-life, with Ultramontanes the authority of Rome and the typical example of Roman morals and customs are the embodiment of the moral and ecclesiastical law. If Jewish parents are forcibly robbed of their child in Rome, that he may be brought up a Christian, the Ultramontane finds it quite in order that natural human rights should yield to the ordinances of Rome, however late devised, although theologians used to maintain that in this case the law of Nature is the law of God, and therefore above any mere human and ecclesiastical ordinance. If the Inquisition still proclaims excommunication in the States of

medley of Italians, and especially Italian clerics, from all parts of the Peninsula—seem to be phrases brought up from a former age. Thus, for example, in 1626, Carrerio, Provost and Professor at Padua, says, "The Italians are exalted above all nations by the special grace of God, who gives them in the Pope a spiritual monarch, who has put down from their thrones great kings and yet mightier emperors, and set others in their place, to whom the greatest kingdoms have long paid tribute, as they do to no other, and who dispenses such riches to his courtiers that no king or emperor has ever had so much to give."

the Church against every son and daughter if they omit
to denounce their parents, and get them put into prison
for using flesh or milk on a fast-day, or reading a book
on the Index, the Romanist is prepared to justify this
too. If the Roman Government, by its lottery, openly
conducted by priests, fosters the passion for gambling,
and produces the ruin of whole families, the *Civiltà*
composes an apology for the lottery, although Alexander VII. and Benedict XIII. forbade it under pain of excommunication. If in Rome, clergymen (the so-called
preti di piazza) stand in the public places till some one
hires them for a mass, this gives no more offence to the
Romanist than the sale of indulgence-bills ; and so the
Roman commissionaires, after showing visitors the various sights of the place, finally point out this spectacle to
them. He thinks it at least very excusable that the very
utmost is got out of dispensations and indulgences as a
mine of pecuniary profit ; that, for instance, the indulgences of " privileged altars" are sold to certain churches
at a scudo apiece, thus giving occasion to the grossest
superstition about the delivery of souls from Purgatory ; that certain marriage dispensations are granted to
the wealthy for a high price, which are denied to the
poorer ; that some kinds of matrimonial causes are car-

ried to Rome, against the express stipulation of treaties, and the citizens thereby subjected to protracted and costly processes,—as happened not long since in a German State, when this new encroachment seemed to the local bishops so strong a case, that they made energetic representations at Rome on the subject, which resulted in the demand being given up for a while, and the question being allowed to be settled on the spot.

Rome on her part omits no means of confirming the whole Catholic world in this clerico-Italian manner of thinking and feeling. More than nine-tenths of the Roman congregations and tribunals are composed of Italians, and they regulate everything through their precepts and decisions, spun out into the minutest and most frivolous detail, and issued in the name of the Pope. Every breath of religious life is to be drawn by Italian rule. Bishoprics out of Italy are to be filled, as far as possible, by men who have got the Catholic mind in Rome, or who at least have been trained by the Jesuits or their pupils.

The more questions any country or diocese refers to Rome—the more dispensations, indulgences, altar privileges, consecrated objects, and the like, it receives from Rome—the more presents of money it sends there,—so much the higher praise it gets for piety and genuine Catholic sentiment. What is called Catholicity can only be attained in the eyes of the Court of Rome by every one translating himself and his ideas, on every subject that has any connexion with religion, into Italian. If, in points where the Italian form or view, or practice or manner of devotion, conflicts with their national feeling, or is being forced into the place of what is native and suits them better, Germans or Frenchmen or Englishmen repudiate the foreign use, they are said to be on a wrong road, they are not " genuine Catholics," but only liberal Catholics ; for so the Society of Jesus distinguishes what we should call " Ultramontane," or simply " Catholic."

§ II.—*Consequences of the Dogma.*

The root of the whole Ultramontane habit of mind is the personal infallibility of the Pope, and accordingly the Jesuits declare it to be the wish of true Catholics that this dogma should be defined at the forthcoming Council. If this desire is accomplished, a new principle of immeasurable importance, both retrospective and prospective, will be established—a principle which, when once irrevocably fixed, will extend its dominion

over men's minds more and more, till it has coerced
them into subjection to every Papal pronouncement in
matters of religion, morals, politics, and social science.
For it will be idle to talk any more of the Pope's
encroaching on a foreign domain ; he, and he alone,
as being infallible, will have the right of determining
the limits of his teaching and action at his own good
pleasure, and every such determination will bear the
stamp of infallibility.   When once the narrow adherence
of many Catholic theologians to the ancient tradition
and the Church of the first six centuries is happily
broken through, the pedantic horror of new dogmas
completely got rid of, and the well-known canon of St.
Vincent, " Quod semper, quod ubique, quod ab omnibus,"
which is still respected here and there, set aside—then
every Pope, however ignorant of theology, will be free
to make what use he likes of his power of dogmatic
creativeness, and to erect his own thoughts into the
common belief, binding on the whole Church.   We say
advisedly, " however ignorant he may be of theology,"
for the Jesuit theologians have already foreseen this
contingency as being not an unusual one with Popes,
and one of them, Professor Erbermann of Mayence, has
observed—" A thoroughly ignorant Pope may very well

be infallible, for God has before now pointed out the
right road by the mouth of a speaking ass."[1] But,
after Infallibility has been made into a dogma, whoever
dares to question the plenary authority of any new
article of faith coined in the Vatican mint, will incur,
according to the Jesuits, excommunication in this world
and everlasting damnation in the next. Councils will
for the future be superfluous; the Bishops will no
doubt be assembled in Rome now and then to swell
the pomp of a Papal canonization or some other grand
ceremony, but they will have nothing more to do with
dogmas. If they wish to confirm a Papal decision,
itself the result of direct Divine inspiration—as, *e.g.*,
the Council of Chalcedon, after careful examination,
sanctioned the dogmatic letter of Pope Leo I.,—this
would be bringing lanterns to aid the light of the noonday sun. The form hitherto used by the Bishops in
subscribing the doctrinal decisions of Councils, *definiens
subscripsi*, would for the future be a blasphemy.

Papal Infallibility, once defined as a dogma, will give
the impulse to a theological, ecclesiastical, and even

[1] *Irenic Cathol.* (Mogunt. 1645), cap. vi. p. 97 : " Quomodo hinc infertur,
nos fidem salutemque nostram ab unico tali homine suspendere et non
potius ab eo, qui novit etiam per asinum loquentem dirigere iter nostrum."

political revolution, the nature of which very few—and least of all those who are urging it on—have clearly realized, and no hand of man will be able to stay its course. In Rome itself the saying will be verified, " Thou wilt shudder thyself at thy likeness to God."

In the next place, the newly-coined article of faith will inevitably take root as the foundation and corner-stone of the whole Roman Catholic edifice. The whole activity of theologians will be concentrated on the one point of ascertaining whether or not a Papal decision can be quoted for any given doctrine, and in labour-ing to discover and amass proof for it from history and literature. Every other authority will pale beside the living oracle on the Tiber, which speaks with plenary inspiration, and can always be appealed to.

What use in tedious investigations of Scripture, what use in wasting time on the difficult study of tradition, which requires so many kinds of preliminary know-ledge, when a single utterance of the infallible Pope may shatter at a breath the labours of half a lifetime, and a telegraphic message to Rome will get an answer in a few hours or a few days, which becomes an axiom and article of faith ? On one side the work of theolo-gians will be greatly simplified, while on the other it becomes harder and more extensive. A single comma in a single Bull (of Pius V. against Baius) has before now led to endless disputes, because it is doubtful whether it should precede or follow certain words, and the whole dogmatic meaning of the Bull depends on its position. But the dispute, which has gone on three centuries, can never be settled now, not even by examining the original document at Rome, which is written, according to the old custom, without punctuation. And how will it be in the future? The Rabbis say, " On every apostrophe in the Bible hang whole mountains of hidden sense," and this will apply equally to Papal Bulls; and thus theology, in the hands of the Ultramontane school, which will alone prevail, promises to become more and more Talmudical.

To prove the dogma of Papal Infallibility from Church history nothing less is required than a complete falsification of it. The declarations of Popes which contradict the doctrines of the Church, or contradict each other (as the same Pope sometimes contradicts himself), will have to be twisted into agreement, so as to show that their heterodox or mutually destructive enunciations are at bottom sound doctrine, or, when a little has been subtracted from one dictum and added to the other, are not really contradictory, and mean the same thing. And here future theologians will have to get well indoctrinated in the Rabbinical school; and indeed they will find a good deal of valuable matter ready to their hand in the Jesuit casuists. These last, meantime, will be their best teachers in the skilful manipulation of history. They never had any particular difficulty in manufacturing Church history; they have already performed the most incredible feats in that line. Not to speak now of their zeal for the discovery and dissemination of apocryphal tales of miracles and lives of saints, of which the Catholic world owes to them so many, we will merely refer here to their huge falsification of Spanish Church-history. They have provided Spain with a wholly new history, in accordance with the interests of their Order, as well as the national wish, and the dogma of the Immaculate Conception; and this could only be accomplished by the Jesuit, Roman De la Higuera, inventing chronicles and archæological records, with the necessary appurtenance of relics, the genuineness of which had to be proved by a miracle brought forward for this express purpose.

§ III.—*Errors and Contradictions of the Popes.*

It is necessary for illustrating the question of Infallibility to recall some of the historical difficulties it is beset with.

Innocent I. and Gelasius I., the former writing to the Council of Milevis, the latter in his epistle to the Bishops of Picenum, declared it to be so indispensable for infants to receive communion, that those who die without it go straight to hell.[1] A thousand years later the Council of Trent anathematized this doctrine.

It is the constant teaching of the Church that ordination received from a bishop, quite irrespectively of his personal worthiness or unworthiness, is valid and indelible. Putting aside Baptism, the whole security of the sacraments rests on this principle of faith, and re-ordination has always been opposed in the Church as a crime and a profanation of the sacrament. Only in Rome, during the devastation which the endless wars of Goths and Lombards inflicted on Central Italy, there was a collapse of all learning and theology, which disturbed and distorted the dogmatic tradition. Since the eighth century, the ordinations of certain Popes

[1] S. Aug. *Opp.* ii. 640; *Concil. Coll.* (ed. Labbé), iv. 1178.

began to be annulled, and the bishops and priests ordained by them were compelled to be re-ordained. This occurred first in 769, when Constantine II., who had got possession of the Papal chair by force of arms, and kept it for thirteen months, was blinded, and deposed at a Synod, and all his ordinations pronounced invalid.

But the strongest case occurred at the end of the ninth century, after the death of Pope Formosus, when the repeated rejection of his ordinations threw the whole Italian Church into the greatest confusion, and produced a general uncertainty as to whether there were any valid sacraments in Italy. Auxilius, who was a contemporary, said that through this universal rejection and repetition of orders (" ordinatio, exordinatio, et superordinatio") matters had come to such a pass in Rome, that for twenty years the Christian religion had been interrupted and extinguished in Italy. Popes and Synods decided in glaring contradiction to one another, now for, now against, the validity of the ordinations, and it was self-evident that in Rome all sure knowledge on the doctrine of ordination was lost. At the end of his second work, Auxilius, speaking in the name of those numerous priests and bishops whose ecclesiastical status was called in question by the decisions of Stephen VII. and Sergius III., demanded the strict investigation of a General Council, as the only authority capable of solving the complication introduced by the Popes.[1]

But the Council never met, and the dogmatic uncertainty and confusion in Rome continued. In the middle of the eleventh century the great contest against Simony, which was then thought equivalent to heresy, broke out, and the ordinations of a simoniacal bishop were pronounced invalid. Leo IX. re-ordained a number of persons on this ground, as Peter Damiani relates.[2] Gregory VII., at his fifth Roman Synod, made the invalidity of all simoniacal ordinations a rule, and the principle, confirmed by Urban II., that a simoniacal bishop can give nothing in ordination, because he has nothing, passed into the *Decretum* of Gratian.[3]

In these cases it is obvious that doctrine and practice were most intimately connected. It was only from their holding a false, and, in its consequences, most injurious, notion of the force and nature of this sacrament, that the Popes acted as they did, and if they had then been generally considered infallible, a hopeless

---

[1] Mabillon, *Analecta* (Paris, 1723), p. 39.
[2] Petri Damiani *Opusc.* p. 419.
[3] Caus. i. Q. 7. c. 24.

confusion must have been introduced, not only into Italy, but the whole Church.

In contrast to Pope Pelagius, who had declared, with the whole Eastern and Western Church, the indispensable necessity of the invocation of the Trinity in Baptism, Nicolas I. assured the Bulgarians that baptism in the name of Christ alone was quite sufficient, and thus exposed the Christians there to the danger of an invalid baptism. The same Pope declared confirmation administered by priests, according to the Greek usage from remote antiquity, invalid, and ordered those so confirmed to be confirmed anew by a bishop, thereby denying to the whole Eastern Church the possession of a sacrament, and laying the foundation of the bitter estrangement which led to a permanent division.[1]

Stephen II. (III.) allowed marriage with a slave girl to be dissolved, and a new one contracted, whereas all previous Popes had pronounced such marriages indissoluble.[2] He also declared baptism, in case of necessity, valid when administered with wine.[3]

Celestine III. tried to loosen the marriage tie by declaring it dissolved if either party became heretical. Innocent III. annulled this decision, and Hadrian VI.

---

[1] *Concil. Coll.* (ed. Labbé), vi. 548.   [2] *Ib.* vi. 1650.   [3] *Ib.* vi. 1652.

called Celestine a heretic for giving it. This decision
was afterwards expunged from the MS. collections of
Papal decrees, but the Spanish theologian Alphonsus
de Castro had seen it there.[1]

The Capernaite doctrine, that Christ's body is sen-
sibly (*sensualiter*) touched by the hands and broken by
the teeth in the Eucharist—an error rejected by the
whole Church, and contradicting the impassibility of
His body,—was affirmed by Nicolas II. at the Synod of
Rome in 1059, and Berengar compelled to acknowledge
it. Lanfranc reproaches Berengar with afterwards wanting to make Cardinal Humbert, instead of the Pope,
responsible for this doctrine.[2]

Innocent III., in order to exhibit the Papal power in
the fullest splendour of its divine omnipotence, invented
the new doctrine that the spiritual bond which unites
a bishop to his diocese is firmer and more indissoluble
than the " carnal" bond, as he called it, between man
and wife, and that God alone can loose it, viz., translate
a bishop from one see to another. But as the Pope is
the representative of the true God on earth, he and he
alone can dissolve this holy and indissoluble bond, not

---

[1] *Adv. Hor.* (ed. Paris), 1565. Cf. Melch. Canus, p. 240.
[2] Lanfranc, *De Euch.* c. 3 (ed. Migne), p. 412.

by human but divine authority, and it is God, not man, who looses it.[1] The obvious and direct corollary, that the Pope can also dissolve the less firm and holy bond of marriage, Innocent, as we have seen, overlooked, for he solemnly condemned Celestine III.'s decision on that point; and thus he unwittingly involved himself in a contradiction. Many canonists have accepted this as the legitimate consequence of his teaching.

Innocent betrayed his utter ignorance of theology, when he declared that the Fifth Book of Moses, being called Deuteronomy, or the Second Book of the Law, must bind the Christian Church, which is the second Church.[2] This great Pope seems never to have read Deuteronomy, or he could hardly have fallen into the blunder of supposing, *e.g.*, that the Old Testament prohibitions of particular kinds of food, the burnt-offerings, the harsh penal code and bloody laws of war, the prohibitions of woollen and linen garments, etc., were to be again made obligatory on Christians. And as the Jews were allowed in Deuteronomy to put away a wife who displeased them, and take another, Innocent ran the risk

---

[1] Decretal "*De Transl. Episc.*," c. 2, 3, 4. This was to introduce a new article of faith. The Church had not known for centuries that resignations, depositions, and translations of bishops, belonged by divine right to the Pope.

[2] Decretal "*Qui filii sint legitimi,*" c. 13.

of falling himself into a greater error about marriage than Celestine III.

Great light is thrown on this question by the history of the alternate approbations and persecutions of the Franciscan Order by the Popes.

Nicolas III., in the decretal *"Exiit qui seminat,"* gave an exposition of the rule of St. Francis, and affirmed the renunciation of all personal or corporate property to be holy and meritorious ; that Christ Himself had taught, and by His example confirmed it, and also the first founders of the Church. The Franciscans therefore were to have the use only, not the possession, of property ; the possession he adjudged to belong to the Roman Church. He expressly added that this exposition of the rule of St. Francis was to have permanent force, and, like every other constitution or decretal, to be used in the schools and literally interpreted. He forbade, under pain of excommunication, all glosses against the literal sense. There can be no shadow of doubt that Nicolas meant in this decree to issue a solemn decision on a matter of faith. It is not addressed to the Franciscan Order only, but to the schools (*i.e.*, universities) and the whole Church.

Clement V., in the decretal *" Exivi de Paradiso,"*

renewed the ordinance assigning the property of Franciscans to the Roman Church ; and John XXII., in the Bull " *Quorundam,*" declared this ordinance of Nicolas III. and Clement V. to be salutary, clear, and of force. But no sooner did John come into conflict with the Order, partly in his attempts to limit their ludicrous excesses in the exhibition of Evangelical poverty, partly from the strong denunciations of the corruption of the Papal Court, and loud demands for a reformation in the Church, which issued from the bosom of the Franciscan Order, than he began gradually, and as far as he could without prejudicing his authority, to undermine the constitution of Nicolas III. First, he removed the excommunication for all non-literal interpretations of the Franciscan rule, and then attacked certain of its details. Meanwhile the strife grew fiercer ; the " Spirituals," in union with Louis of Bavaria, began to brand John as a heretic, and he, in a new Bull, declared the distinction between use and possession impossible, neither serviceable for the Church nor for Christian perfection, and finally rejected the doctrine of his predecessor, that Christ and the Apostles were in word and deed patterns of the Franciscan ideal of poverty, as heretical, and hostile to the Catholic faith.

And thus the perplexing spectacle was afforded the Church of one Pope unequivocally charging another with false doctrine. What Nicolas III. and Clement V. had solemnly commended as right and holy, their successor branded, as solemnly, as noxious and wrong. The Franciscans repeated the charge of heresy against John XXII. with the more emphasis, "since what the Popes had once defined in faith and morals, through the keys of wisdom, their successors could not call in question."[1] John condemned the writings of D'Olive, and several more of their theologians, and handed over the whole community of the "Spirituals," or Fratricelli, as the advocates of extreme poverty were called, to the Inquisition. Between 1316 and 1352, 114 of them were burnt,—martyrs to their misconception of Evangelical poverty and Papal infallibility; for they were among the first champions of that theory, then still new in the Church. After long and bitter persecutions, Sixtus IV. at last made some satisfaction to the "Spirituals," by letting the works of their prophet and theologian, D'Olive, be re-examined, and, in contradiction to the sentence of John XXII., declared orthodox. Later Popes resumed possession of the property of the Franciscans, which John had repudiated.

---

[1] Cf. Bossuet, *Defens. Declarat.*—*Œuvres*, xviii. pp. 339 *seq.* Liége, 1768.

One of the most comprehensive, dogmatic documents ever issued by a Pope is the decree of Eugenius IV. " to the Armenians," dated 22d November 1439, three months after the Council of Florence was brought to an end by the departure of the Greeks.   It is a confession of faith of the Roman Church, intended to serve as a rule of doctrine and practice for the Armenians, on those points they had previously differed about.   The dogmas of the Unity of the Divine Nature, the Trinity, the Incarnation, and the Seven Sacraments, are expounded, and the Pope moreover asserts that the decree thus solemnly issued has received the sanction of the Council, that is, of the Italian bishops whom he had detained in Florence.

If this decree of the Pope were really a rule of faith, the Eastern Church would have only four sacraments instead of seven; the Western Church would for at least eight centuries have been deprived of three sacraments, and of one, the want of which would make all the rest, with one exception, invalid.   Eugenius IV. determines in this decree the form and matter, the substance, of the sacraments, or of those things on the presence or absence of which the existence of the sacrament itself depends, according to the universal doctrine of the Church. He gives a form of Confirmation which never existed in one-half of the Church, and first came into use in the other after the tenth century. So again with Penance. What is given as the essential form of the sacrament was unknown in the Western Church for eleven hundred years, and never known in the Greek. And when the touching the sacred vessels, and the words accompanying the rite, are given as the form and matter of Ordination, it follows that the Latin Church for a thousand years had neither priests nor bishops— nay, like the Greek Church, which never adopted this usage, possesses to this hour neither priests nor bishops, and consequently no sacraments except Baptism, and perhaps Marriage.[1]

It is noteworthy that this decree—with which Papal Infallibility or the whole hierarchy and the sacraments of the Church stand or fall—is cited, refuted, and appealed to by all dogmatic writers, but that the adherents of Papal Infallibility have never meddled with it. Neither Bellarmine, nor Charlas, nor Aguirre, nor Orsi,

[1] Cf. Denzinger, *Enchirid. Symbol. et Definit.* (Wirceb. 1854), pp. 200 *seq.* But Denzinger, in order to conceal the purely dogmatic character of this famous decree, *has omitted the first part, on the Trinity and Incarnation,* which is given in Raynaldus's *Annals,* 1439. [The same conspicuously untenable explanation was adopted in the *Dublin Review* for January 1866.—Tr.]

nor the other apologists of the Roman Court, troubled themselves with it.

After the Papal claim to infallibility had taken a more definite shape at Rome, Sixtus v. himself brought it again into jeopardy by his edition of the Bible. The Council of Trent had pronounced St. Jerome's version authentic for the Western Church, but there was no authentic edition of the Latin Bible sanctioned by the Church. Sixtus v. undertook to provide one, which appeared, garnished with the stereotyped forms of anathema and penal enactments. His Bull declared that this edition, corrected by his own hand, must be received and used by everybody as the only true and genuine one, under pain of excommunication, every change, even of a single word, being forbidden under anathema.

But it soon appeared that it was full of blunders, some two thousand of them introduced by the Pope himself. It was said the Bible of Sixtus v. must be publicly prohibited. But Bellarmine advised that the peril Sixtus had brought the Church into should be hushed up as far as possible; all the copies were to be called in, and the corrected Bible printed anew, under the name of Sixtus v., with a statement in the Preface that the errors had crept in through the fault of the

compositors and the carelessness of others. Bellarmine
himself was commissioned to give circulation to these
lies, to which the new Pope gave his name, by compos-
ing the Preface. In his Autobiography this Jesuit and
Cardinal congratulates himself on having thus requited
Sixtus with good for evil; for the Pope had put his
great work on Controversies on the Index, because he
had not maintained the direct, but only the indirect,
dominion of the Pope over the whole world. And now
followed a fresh mishap. The Autobiography, which was
kept in the archives of the Roman Jesuits, got known
in Rome through several transcripts. On this Cardinal
Azzolini urged that, as Bellarmine had insulted three
Popes and exhibited two as liars, viz., Gregory XIV.
and Clement VIII., his work should be suppressed and
burnt, and the strictest secrecy inculcated about it.[1]

§ IV.—*The Verdict of History.*

Some explanation is imperatively needed of the strange
phenomenon, that an opinion according to which Christ

[1] For, thought Azzolini, what shall we say, if our adversaries infer
" Papa potest falli in exponenda Ecclesiæ S. Scripturâ "—the Pope can err
in expounding Scripture—nay hath erred, " non solum in exponendo sed
in eâ multa perperam mutando," not only in expounding it, but in making
many wrong changes in the text ?— *Voto nella causa della Beatif. del Card.
Bellarm.* (Ferrara, 1761), p. 46.

has made the Pope of the day the one vehicle of His inspirations, the pillar and exclusive organ of Divine truth, without whom the Church is like a body without a soul, deprived of the power of vision, and unable to determine any point of faith—that such an opinion, which is for the future to be a sort of dogmatic Atlas carrying the whole edifice of faith and morals on its shoulders, should have first been certainly ascertained in the year of grace 1869, but is from henceforth to be placed as a primary article of faith at the head of every catechism.

For thirteen centuries an incomprehensible silence on this fundamental article reigned throughout the whole Church and her literature. None of the ancient confessions of faith, no catechism, none of the patristic writings composed for the instruction of the people, contain a syllable about the Pope, still less any hint that all certainty of faith and doctrine depends on him. For the first thousand years of Church history not a question of doctrine was finally decided by the Pope. The Roman bishops took no part in the commotions which the numerous Gnostic sects, the Montanists and Chiliasts, produced in the early Church, nor can a single dogmatic decree issued by one of them be found during the first four centuries, nor a trace of the existence of any.

Even the controversy about Christ kindled by Paul of Samosata, which occupied the whole Eastern Church for a long time, and necessitated the assembling of several Councils, was terminated without the Pope taking any part in it. So again in the chain of controversies and discussions connected with the names of Theodotus, Artemon, Noetus, Sabellius, Beryllus, and Lucian of Antioch, which troubled the whole Church, and extended over nearly 150 years, there is no proof that the Roman bishops acted beyond the limits of their own local Church, or accomplished any dogmatic result. The only exception is the dogmatic treatise of the Roman bishop Dionysius, following a Synod held at Rome in 262, denouncing and rejecting Sabellianism and the opposite method of expression of Dionysius of Alexandria. This document, if any authority had been ascribed to it, was well fitted in itself to cut short, or rather strangle at its birth, the long Arian disturbance; but it was not known out of Alexandria, and exercised no influence whatever on the later course of the controversy. It is only known from the fragments quoted afterwards by Athanasius.

In three controversies during this early period the Roman Church took an active part,—the question about Easter, about heretical baptism, and about the peni-

E

~ tential discipline.   In all three the Popes were unable to
~ carry out their own will and view and practice, and the
~ other Churches maintained their different usage without its leading to any permanent division.   Pope Victor's
attempt to compel the Churches of Asia Minor to adopt
the Roman usage, by excluding them from his communion, proved a failure.

The dispute about the stricter or milder administration of penance, and as to whether certain heinous sins
should exclude from communion for life, lasted a long
time in the Church of Rome, as elsewhere.   There is
no trace found of any attempt to force other Churches
to adopt the principles received at Rome ; and even in
the fourth century, the Spanish Synod of Elvira established rules differing widely from the Roman.   This
difference had an intimate relation to dogma.

The dispute about heretical baptism, in the middle of
the third century, had a still more clearly dogmatic character, for the whole Church doctrine of the efficacy and
conditions of sacramental grace was involved.   Yet the
opposition of Pope Stephen to the doctrine, confirmed
at several African and Asiatic Synods, against the
validity of schismatical baptism, remained wholly inoperative.   Stephen went so far as to exclude those

Churches from his communion, but he only drew down sharp censures on his unlawful arrogance. Both St. Cyprian and Firmilian of Cesarea denied his having any right to dictate a doctrine to other bishops and Churches. And the other Eastern Churches, too, which were not directly mixed up in the dispute, retained their own practice for a long time, quite undisturbed by the Roman theory. Later on, St. Augustine, looking back at this dispute, maintains that the pronouncement of Stephen, categorical as it was, was no decision of the Church, and that St. Cyprian and the Africans were therefore justified in rejecting it ; he says the real obligation of conforming to a common practice originated with the decree of a great (*plenarium*) Council, meaning the Council of Arles in 314.[1]

In the Arian disputes, which engaged and disturbed the Church beyond all others for above half a century, and were discussed in more than fifty Synods, the Roman See for a long time remained passive. Through the long episcopate of Pope Silvester (314-335) there is no document or sign of doctrinal activity, any more than

---

[1] Aug., *De Bapt. contr. Donat.*, *Opp.* (ed. Benedict.) ix. pp. 98-111. The advocates of Papal Infallibility are obliged to give up St. Augustine. Orsi formally rebukes him, and Bellarmine (*De Eccles.* i. 4) thinks he perhaps spoke a falsehood.

from all his predecessors from 269 to 314. Julius and Liberius (337-366) were the first to take part in the course of events, but they only increased the uncertainty. Julius pronounced Marcellus of Ancyra, an avowed Sabellian, orthodox at his Roman Synod; and Liberius purchased his return from exile from the Emperor by condemning Athanasius, and subscribing an Arian creed. " Anathema to thee, Liberius!" was then the cry of zealous Catholic bishops like Hilary of Poitiers. This apostasy of Liberius sufficed, through the whole of the middle ages, for a proof that Popes could fall into heresy as well as other people.

Later on, and especially after the unfortunate issue of the Synods of Milan, Sirmium, Rimini, and Seleucia, when men's confidence in this method of securing sound definitions was greatly shaken, and St. Jerome wrote that the world was amazed to find itself Arian—then, if ever, we might expect that Christians and Churches would resort in their perplexity from all parts of the empire to the Roman See for aid and counsel, as the one anchor of salvation and rock of orthodoxy; but nothing of the kind took place; so far from it, that in all the treatises and discussions consequent on the Synods of Rimini and Seleucia in 359, the Pope's name

s never once mentioned. The first sign of life he gave
was some years afterwards, when he adopted the procedure of the Synod of Alexandria against the bishops
who fell at Rimini.[1]

During all the fourth century Councils alone decided
dogmatic questions. If the Bishop of Rome was ever
appealed to for a decision, it was understood that he
was desired to call a Synod to decide the point at issue.
At the second Œcumenical Council in 381, which decreed
the most important definition of faith since the Nicene,
by first formulizing the doctrine of the Holy Ghost, the
Church of Rome was not represented at all; only the
decrees were communicated to it as to other Churches.
Two Roman Synods, under Damasus, about 378, did
indeed anathematize certain errors without naming their
authors; but Pope Siricius (384-398) declined to pronounce on the false doctrine of a bishop (Bonosus),
when requested to do so, on the ground that he had no
right, and must await the sentence of the bishops of the
province, " to make it the rule of his own."[2] He condemned the teaching of Jovinian, which originated in
Rome itself, but only through the means of a Synod.

A greater share fell to the Popes in the Pelagian con-

[1] *Epist. Pontif.* (ed. Const.) p. 448. [2] *Ib.* p. 679.

troversies, which chiefly concerned the West, than in previous ones. Innocent I., when invoked by the Africans, after five years of disputing, had sanctioned the decrees of their two Synods of Milevis and Carthage (417), and pronounced a work of Pelagius heretical, so that St. Augustine said, in a sermon, " The matter is now ended."[1] But he deceived himself, for the strife was only fairly begun, and it was not ended till many years later, by the decision of the Œcumenical Council of Ephesus in 431. Meanwhile Pope Zosimus spoke on the Pelagian doctrine in a very different fashion from his immediate predecessor, Innocent. He bestowed high commendation on the profession of faith of Celestius, who was accused before him of the heresy, though it contained an open denial of Original Sin, and severely rebuked the African bishops, who had made the complaint, for accusing so orthodox a person of heresy. It was only after they had addressed an energetic letter to Zosimus, telling him that they adhered to their decision, and that he was mistaken, and after they had again anathematized the teaching of Pelagius and Celestius, at a Council held at Carthage, that the Pope assented to their judgment.

[1] *Sermo* 131, c. 10. *Opp.* (ed. Antwerp) v. 449.

But St. Augustine's saying, quoted above, has been alleged in proof of his accepting Papal Infallibility, which, in dealing with the baptismal controversy, he so often and so pointedly repudiates. Such a notion was utterly foreign to his mind. The Pelagian system was in his eyes so manifest and deadly an error (*aperta pernicies*), that there seemed to him no need even of a Synod to condemn it.[1] The two African Synods, and the Pope's assent to their decrees, appeared to him more than enough, and so the matter might be regarded as at an end. That a Roman judgment in itself was not conclusive, but that a "*Concilium plenarium*" was necessary for that purpose, he had himself emphatically maintained; and the conduct of Pope Zosimus could only confirm his opinion.

A new chapter in the dogmatic action of the Popes opens with the year 430, which was the starting-point of the controversies on the Incarnation and the relation of the two natures in Christ, which lasted on to the close of the seventh century. Pope Celestine's condemnation of Nestorius was superseded by the Emperor's convoking a General Council at Ephesus in 431, where it was submitted to examination, and approved. When the Euty-

---

[1] *Contr. Ep. Pelag.* i. 4, c. ult.

chian controversy arose, the letter of Leo the Great to Flavian appeared in 449, and this was the first dogmatic writing of a Pope which found acceptance both in East and West, but not until it had been examined at the Council of Chalcedon. Leo himself acknowledged that his treatise could not become a rule of faith till it was confirmed by the bishops.[1]

Pope Vigilius was less happy in the dispute about the "Three Chapters"—the writings of Theodore, Theodoret, and Ibas, which were held to be Nestorian,—which he first pronounced orthodox in 546, then condemned the next year, and thus again reversed this sentence in deference to the Western bishops, and then came into conflict with the Fifth General Council, which excommunicated him. Finally, he submitted to the judgment of the Council, declaring that he had unfortunately been a tool in the hands of Satan, who labours for the destruction of the Church, and had thus been divided from his colleagues, but God had now enlightened him.[2] Thus he thrice contradicted himself: first he anathematized those who condemned the Three Chapters as erroneous; then he anathematized those who held them to be orthodox,

---

[1] Leonis *Ep. ad Episc. Gall.* See Mansi, *Concil.* vi. 181.
[2] See his letter to the Patriarch Eutychius. Cf. De Marca, *Dissert.* (Paris, 1669), p. 45.

as he had just before himself held them to be ; soon after
he condemned the condemnation of the Three Chapters ;
and lastly, the Emperor and Council triumphed again
over the fickle Pope. A long schism in the West was
the consequence. Whole National Churches—Africa,
North Italy, Illyria—broke off communion with the
Popes, whom they accused of having sacrificed the
faith and authority of the Council of Chalcedon by
condemning the Three Chapters. Pelagius I., Vigilius's
successor, whose orthodoxy was on this ground suspected by the Frankish king, Childebert, and the bishops
of Gaul, never dreamt of claiming immunity from
error, but excused himself in all directions. He laid
before Childebert a public profession of his faith, and
declared himself, before the bishops of Tuscany, ready
to give to every one an account of his faith.

Often and earnestly as the Popes exhorted separated
bishops and Churches to return to communion with
Rome, they never appealed to any peculiar authority or
exemption from error in the Roman See.

The Monothelite controversy, growing out of the as-
sertion that Christ had not two wills, a human and a
Divine, but one Divine will only, led to the General
Synod of Constantinople in 680. At the beginning of

the controversy, Pope Honorius I., when questioned by three Patriarchs, had spoken entirely in favour of the heretical doctrine in letters addressed to them, and had thereby powerfully aided the new sect. Later on, in 649, Pope Martin, with a Synod of 105 bishops from Southern and Central Italy, condemned Monothelism. But the sentence of a Pope and a small Synod had no binding authority then, and the Emperor Constantine found it necessary to summon a General Council to settle the question. It was foreseen that Pope Honorius I., who had hitherto been protected by silence, must share the fate of the other chief authors of the heresy at this Council. He was, in fact, condemned for heresy in the most solemn manner, and not a single voice, not even of the Papal legates who were present, was raised in his defence. His dogmatic writings were committed to the flames as heretical. The Popes submitted to the inevitable; they subscribed the anathema, and themselves undertook to see that the "heretic" Honorius was condemned in the West as well as throughout the East, and his name struck out of the Liturgy. This one fact—that a Great Council, universally received afterwards without hesitation throughout the Church, and presided over by Papal legates, pronounced the dogmatic decision of a Pope heretical, and anathematized him by name as a heretic—is a proof, clear as the sun at noonday, that the notion of any peculiar enlightenment or inerrancy of the Popes was then utterly unknown to the whole Church. The only resource of the defenders of Papal Infallibility, since Torquemada and Bellarmine, has been to attack the Acts of the Council as spurious, and maintain that they are a wholesale forgery of the Greeks. The Jesuits clung tenaciously to this notion till the middle of the last century. Since it has had to be abandoned, the device has been to try and torture the words of Honorius into a sort of orthodox sense. But whatever comes of that, nothing can alter the fact, that at the time both Councils and Popes were convinced of the fallibility of the Pope.

A century later, Pope Hadrian I. vainly endeavoured to get the decrees of the second Nicene Council on Image Worship, which he had approved, received by Charles the Great and his bishops. The great assembly at Frankfort in 794, and the Caroline books, rejected and attacked these decrees, and Hadrian did not venture to offer more than verbal opposition. In 824 the bishops assembled in synod at Paris spoke without

remorse of the "absurdities" (*absona*) of Pope Hadrian,
who, they said, had commanded an heretical worship
of images.[1]

No less light is thrown on the relations of Western
bishops to the Pope by the Predestinarian controversy
occasioned by the monk Gottschalk, and prolonged for
ten years at Synods and in various writings. The first
prelates of the day, Hincmar, Rhabanus, Amulo, Pru-
dentius, Wenilo, and others, took opposite sides, Synod
contended against Synod, and there seemed no possibility of coming to an agreement. Yet it never occurred
to any one to appeal to the Pope's sentence, ready as he
was to interpose in the affairs of the Frankish Church;
only at the last Gottschalk himself made an unsuc-
cessful attempt to get his hard fate mitigated by the
Pope.

Up to the time of the Isidorian decretals no serious
attempt was made anywhere to introduce the neo-
Roman theory of Infallibility. The Popes did not dream
of laying claim to such a privilege. Their relation to
the Church had to be fundamentally revolutionized,
and the idea of the Primacy altered, before there could
be any room for this doctrine to grow up; after that it

---

[1] Mansi, *Concil.* xiv. 415 *seq.*

developed itself by a sort of logical sequence, but very
slowly, being at issue with notorious historical facts.

§ V.—*The Ancient Constitution of the Church.*

To get a view of the enormous difference in the position and action of the Primacy, as it was in the Roman
Empire, and as it became in the later middle ages, it is
enough to point out the following facts :—

(1.) The Popes took no part in convoking Councils.
All Great Councils, to which bishops came from different countries, were convoked by the Emperors, nor
were the Popes ever consulted about it beforehand. If
they thought a General Council necessary, they had to
petition the Imperial Court, as Innocent did in the
matter of St. Chrysostom, and Leo after the Synod of
449 ;[1] and then they did not always prevail, as both
the Popes just named learnt by experience.

(2.) They were not always allowed to preside, per-
sonally or by deputy, at the Great Councils, though no
one denied them the first rank in the Church. At
Nice, at the two Councils of Ephesus in 431 and 449,
and at the Fifth General Council in 553, others presided; only at Chalcedon in 451, and Constantinople in

---

[1] [The " Latrocinium" of Ephesus.—Tr.]

680, did the Papal legates preside. And it is clear that the Popes did not claim this as their exclusive right, from the conduct of Leo I. in sending his legates to Ephesus, although he knew that the Emperor had named, not him, but the bishop of Alexandria, to preside.

(3.) Neither the dogmatic nor the disciplinary decisions of these Councils required Papal confirmation, for their force and authority depended on the consent of the Church, as expressed in the Synod, and afterwards in the fact of its being generally received. The confirmation of the Nicene Council by Pope Silvester was afterwards invented at Rome, because facts would not square with the newly devised theory.

(4.) For the first thousand years no Pope ever issued a doctrinal decision intended for and addressed to the whole Church. Their doctrinal pronouncements, if designed to condemn new heresies, were always submitted to a Synod, or were answers to inquiries from one or more bishops. They only became a standard of faith after being read, examined, and approved at an Œcumenical Council.

(5.) The Popes possessed none of the three powers which are the proper attributes of sovereignty, neither the legislative, the administrative, nor the judicial. The Council of Sardica, in 343, gave them, indeed, a handle for the attempt to usurp the latter. Here it was decreed for the first time, and as a personal privilege to the then Pope, Julius, that he should be authorized to appoint judges for a bishop in the second instance to hear the cause on the spot, with the assistance of a Roman legate, and, in the event of a further appeal, to pronounce sentence himself. But this regulation was received neither by the Eastern Church nor the African, never observed by the former, and steadily rejected by the latter, and it never came into full force anywhere till after the Isidorian decretals were fabricated. The African bishops wrote to Pope Boniface I., in 419, " We are resolved not to admit this arrogant claim."[1]

The Popes at that time made no attempt to exercise legislative power. For a long time, according to their own statement, no canons but those of the first Nicene Council obtained in the West, in the East only the canons of Eastern Synods. Declarations or ordinances issued by Popes in reply to questions of particular bishops could not be regarded as general laws of the

---

[1] *Epist. Pontif.* (ed. Coust.), p. 113 :—" Non sumus jam istum typhum passuri."

Church, for the simple reason that they were only known to particular bishops and Churches. The spread of the Dionysian writings, with the second part composed of Papal documents, after the sixth century, began gradually to pioneer the way for the notion that certain decretals of the Roman bishops had the force of law, but their authority was still limited, as in the Spanish Church, to those issued by Roman Synods, or else was made dependent on their express acceptance by National Churches. Even if the Popes had attempted at that time to exercise a formal government over the Church, the thing was a sheer impossibility. Government cannot be carried on by occasional Synods, and there was no other means of governing. The Popes would have required a court, a system of clerical officials, congregations, and the like, but nothing of the kind was remotely dreamt of. The Roman clergy were organized just like every other; for all the offices and functions undertaken later, and still discharged by the court, there was then neither need nor occasion.

(6.) Nobody thought of getting dispensations from Church laws from the Roman bishops, nor was a single tax or tribute paid to the Roman See, for no court as yet existed. To make laws which could be dispensed for money would have appeared both a folly and a crime. The power of the keys, or of binding and loosing, was universally held to belong to the other bishops just as much as to the bishop of Rome.

(7.) The bishops of Rome could exclude neither individuals nor Churches from the communion of the Church Universal. They could withdraw their own Church from communion with particular bishops or Churches, and they often did so, but this in nowise affected their relation to other bishops or Churches, as was shown, among other instances, by the long Antiochene schism from 361 to 413. And, on the other hand, if they admitted into their own communion one excommunicated by other Churches, this did not bring him into communion with any other Church.

(8.) For a long time nothing was known in Rome of definite rights bequeathed by Peter to his successors. Nothing but a care for the weal of the Church, and the duty of watching over the observance of the canons, was ascribed to them. Only after the Sardican Council, and in reliance solely on it, or the Nicene, which was designedly confounded with it, was a right of hearing appeals laid claim to. Innocent I. himself (402-417), who tried to give the widest extent to the Sardican canon, and

F

claimed, on the strength of it, a right to interpose in all graver Church questions, grounded his claim entirely on "the Fathers" and the Synod. So, too, with Zosimus (417-418),—it was the Fathers who had given the See of Rome the privilege of final decision in appeals.[1] But soon afterwards, at the Council of Ephesus, the Roman legates declared that Peter, to whom Christ gave the power of binding and loosing, lives and judges in his successors.[2] No one put forward this plea more frequently or more energetically than Leo I. But when the Council of Chalcedon declared, in its famous twenty-eighth canon, that it was the Fathers who adjudged the primacy to Rome, and that too on account of the political dignity of the city, Leo did not venture to contradict them, though he strenuously resisted the main purport of the canon, which raised the See of Constantinople to the first rank after the Roman, and to equal rights. It was not the degradation of the Roman See, but only the injury done to the Eastern Patriarchs and the Nicene canon, which, according to his own assurance, was the ground of his refusing his assent to the canon of Chalcedon.[3] He

---

[1] Mansi, *Concil.* iv. 366. [2] *Ib.* iv. 1296.

[3] The sixth Nicene canon, referring to the rights of the Roman See over part of the Italian Church, had given the same rights to the bishops of Alexandria and Antioch over their own Patriarchates.

had, indeed, some years before, induced the Emperor
Valentinian III. to issue an edict in favour of the See of
Rome, which subjected all the bishops of the then very
reduced Western empire (strictly only those of Italy and
Gaul) to the Pope, and which, had it obtained full force,
would have changed the whole constitution of the Western Church. This edict names, besides the canon of
Sardica, and the greatness of the city, " the merit of St.
Peter," as the first ground for so comprehensive a power,
which the bishops were to be compelled by the imperial
officers to bow to. But when Leo had to deal with
Byzantium and the East, he no longer dared to plead this
argument,—which would alone have proved the hated
twenty-eighth canon of Chalcedon to be null and void,
—but preferred to appeal to the Nicene Council, utterly
untenable as his inferences from the sixth canon must
have appeared to the Greeks. The opposition of his
successors was equally fruitless. The canon took full
effect, and from that day to this has determined the
form and constitution of the Eastern Church, and its
view of the prerogatives of Rome.

(9.) What was afterwards called the Papal system,
when first proclaimed in words only, was repudiated
with horror by that best and greatest of Popes, Gregory

the Great. On this theory the Pope has the plenitude of power, all other bishops are only his servants and auxiliaries, from him all power is derived, and he is concurrent ordinary in every diocese. So Gregory understood the title of "Œcumenical Patriarch," and would not endure that so "wicked and blasphemous a title" should be given to himself or any one else.[1]

(10.) There are many National Churches which were never under Rome, and never even had any intercourse by letter with Rome, without this being considered a defect, or causing any difficulty about Church communion. Such an autonomous Church, always independent of Rome, was the most ancient of those founded beyond the limits of the empire, the Armenian, wherein the primatial dignity descended for a long time in the family of the national apostle, Gregory the Illuminator. The great Syro-Persian Church in Mesopotamia, and the western part of the kingdom of the Sassanidæ, with its thousands of martyrs, was from the first, and always remained, equally free from any influence of Rome. In its records and its rich literature we find no trace of the arm of Rome having reached there. The same holds good of the Ethiopian

---

[1] Lib. v. *Ep*. 18 *ad Joann;* Lib. viii. *Ep*. 30 *ad Eulog*. etc.

or Abyssinian Church, which was indeed united to the See of Alexandria, but wherein nothing, except perhaps a distant echo, was heard of the claims of Rome. In the West, the Irish and the ancient British Church remained for centuries autonomous, and under no sort of influence of Rome.

If we put into a positive form this negative account of the position of the ancient Popes, we get the following picture of the organization of the ancient Church :— Without prejudice to its agreement with the Church Universal in all essential points, every Church manages its own affairs with perfect freedom and independence, and maintains its own traditional usages and discipline, all questions not concerning the whole Church, or of primary importance, being settled on the spot. The Church is organized in dioceses, provinces, patriarchates (National Churches were added afterwards in the West), with the bishop of Rome at the head as first Patriarch, the Centre and Representative of unity, and, as such, the bond between East and West, between the Churches of the Greek and the Latin tongue, the chief watcher and guardian of the, as yet very few, common laws of the Church,—for a long time only the Nicene; but he does not encroach on the rights of patriarchs, metropolitans, and bishops. Laws and articles of faith, of universal obligation, are issued only by the whole Church, concentrated and represented at an Œcumenical Council.

§ VI.—*The Teaching of the Fathers.*

What has now become a rule in dogmatic works—to give a separate "treatise" or "locus" to the Pope—came in with Aquinas, the first theologian who, on grounds to be explained presently, made the doctrine of the Pope a formal part of dogmatic theology, *i.e.*, of the Scholastic, and it thus dates from 1274. Since then every doctrinal treatise has its section on the "Primacy," and since Melchior Canus (about 1550) more especially, but in a shorter form with Aquinas, a discussion of the Pope's authority in matters of faith. With the Jesuit theologians (compare, *e.g.*, among living writers, Passaglia, Schrader, Weninger, etc.), the monarchical authority and magisterial power of the Pope is the chief article on which all the rest depends, and which comes before all in weight and fundamental significance. And rightly so, if the Pope is infallible in his decisions; for then every authority in the Church, that of Councils included, is a mere derivation from his, and all certainty of faith rests ultimately on him and his divine prerogative of being the vehicle of a permanent Divine inspiration. Every Christian must say: "I believe this or that article of faith, because I believe in the Pope's infallibility, and because the Pope has decided it, or has ratified the decision and teaching of others."

And now compare with this the silence of the ancient Church. In the first three centuries, St. Irenæus is the only writer who connects the superiority of the Roman Church with doctrine; but he places this superiority, rightly understood, only in its antiquity, its double apostolical origin, and in the circumstance of the pure tradition being guarded and maintained there through the constant concourse of the faithful from all countries. Tertullian, Cyprian,[1] Lactantius, know nothing of special Papal prerogative, or of any higher or supreme right of deciding in matter of doctrine. In the writings of the Greek doctors, Eusebius, St. Athanasius, St. Basil the Great,[2] the two Gregories,

---

[1] On the famous interpolation in Cyprian's *De Unit. Eccles.* see later.

[2] St. Basil (*Opp.* ed. Bened. iii. 301, *Epp.* 239 and 214) has expressed most strongly his contempt for the writings of the Popes, "those insolent and puffed up Occidentals, who would only sanction false doctrine." He says he would not receive their letters if they fell from heaven. He was provoked by the support given at Rome to the open Sabellianism of Marcellus and the unsettling of the Antiochene Church.

and St. Epiphanius, there is not one word of any prerogatives of the Roman bishop. The most copious of
the Greek Fathers, St. Chrysostom, is wholly silent on
the subject, and so are the two Cyrils; equally silent are
the Latins, Hilary, Pacian, Zeno, Lucifer, Sulpicius, and
St. Ambrose. Even the Roman writer Ursinus (about
440), in defending the Roman view of re-baptism,
avoids—perhaps cannot venture upon any appeal to
—the authority of the Roman Church, as final, or even
of especial weight![1]

St. Augustine has written more on the Church, its
unity and authority, than all the other Fathers put
together. Yet, from all his numerous works, filling ten
folios, only one sentence, in one letter, can be quoted,
where he says that the principality of the Apostolic
Chair has always been in Rome,[2]—which could, of
course, be said then with equal truth of Antioch,
Jerusalem, and Alexandria. Any reader of his Pastoral
Letter to the separated Donatists on the Unity of the
Church, must find it inexplicable, on the Jesuit theory,
that in these seventy-five chapters there is not a single

---

[1] That he is the author is clear from the all but contemporary statement
of Gennadius, and the oldest MS. See Bennettis, *Privilegia R. P. Vin-
dicata* (Romæ, 1756), ii. 274.

[2] *Ep.* 43, *Opp.* (Antwerp), ii. 69.

word on the necessity of communion with Rome as the
centre of unity. He urges all sorts of arguments to
show that the Donatists are bound to return to the
Church, but of the Papal Chair, as one of them, he
knows nothing. So again with the famous *Commoni-
torium* of St. Vincent of Lerins, composed in 434. If
the view of Roman infallibility had existed anywhere
in the Church at that time, it could not have been
possibly passed over in a book exclusively concerned
with the question of the means for ascertaining the
genuine Christian doctrine. But the author keeps to
the three notes of universality, permanence, and consent, and to the Œcumenical Councils. Even Pope
Pelagius I. praises St. Augustine for "being mindful
of the divine doctrine which places the foundation of
the Church in the Apostolical *Sees*, and teaching that
they are schismatics who separate themselves from the
communion of these Apostolical *Sees*."[1] This Pope (555-
560), then, knows nothing of any exclusive teaching
privilege of Rome, but only of the necessity of adhering in disputed questions of faith to the Apostolical
Churches—Alexandria, Antioch, and Jerusalem, as well
as Rome.[2]

[1] Mansi, *Concil.* ix. 716.   [2] *Ib.* ix. 732.

Moreover, we have writings or statements about the ranks of the hierarchy in the ancient Church, and the Papal dignity is never named as one of them, or mentioned as anything existing apart in the Church. In the writings of the Areopagite, composed at the end of the fifth century, on the hierarchy, only bishops, presbyters, and deacons are mentioned. In 631, the famous Spanish theologian, Isidore of Seville, describes all the grades of the hierarchy, and divides bishops into four ranks— Patriarchs, Archbishops, Metropolitans, and Bishops. Gratian incorporated this long chapter from Isidore into his *Decretum,* strange as it must have appeared to him that the first and highest office should not be named at all. As late as 789 the Spanish Abbot Beatus gives the same account; he too knows no higher office in the Church than Patriarchs, of whom he calls the Roman the first.[1]

There is another fact the infallibilist will find it impossible to explain. We have a copious literature on the Christian sects and heresies of the first six centuries,—Irenæus, Hippolytus, Epiphanius, Philastrius, St. Augustine, and, later, Leontius and Timotheus, have left us accounts of them to the number of eighty, but

[1] Beati *Comment. in Apoc.* (Madr. 1770), p. 99.

not a single one is reproached with rejecting the Pope's authority in matters of faith, while Aërius, *e.g.*, is reproached with denying the episcopate as a grade of the hierarchy. Had the *mot d'ordre* been given for centuries to observe a dead silence on this, in the Ultramontane view, *articulus stantis vel cadentis Ecclesiæ?*

All this is intelligible enough, if we look at the patristic interpretation of the words of Christ to St. Peter. Of all the Fathers who interpret these passages in the Gospels (Matt. xvi. 18, John xxi. 17), *not a single one applies them to the Roman bishops as Peter's successors.* How many Fathers have busied themselves with these texts, yet not one of them whose commentaries we possess—Origen, Chrysostom, Hilary, Augustine, Cyril, Theodoret, and those whose interpretations are collected in catenas,—has dropped the faintest hint that the primacy of Rome is the consequence of the commission and promise to Peter! Not one of them has explained the rock or foundation on which Christ would build His Church of the office given to Peter to be transmitted to his successors, but they understood by it either Christ Himself, or Peter's confession of faith in Christ; often both together. Or else they thought Peter was the foundation equally with all the other

Apostles, the Twelve being together the foundation-stones
of the Church (Apoc. xxi. 14).   The Fathers could the
less recognise in the power of the keys, and the power
of binding and loosing, any special prerogative or lordship of the Roman bishop, inasmuch as—what is obvious to any one at first sight—they did not regard a
power first given to Peter, and afterwards conferred in
precisely the same words on all the Apostles, as anything peculiar to him, or hereditary in the line of Roman
bishops, and they held the symbol of the keys as meaning just the same as the figurative expression of binding
and loosing.[1]

Every one knows the one classical passage of Scripture on which the edifice of Papal Infallibility has been
reared : " I have prayed for thee, that thy faith fail not :
and when thou art converted, confirm thy brethren."[2]
But these words manifestly refer only to Peter person-
ally, to his denial of Christ and his conversion ; he is
told that he, whose failure of faith would be only of

---

[1] Döllinger might therefore have spared himself the trouble of trying to
show that the power of the keys differs from the power of binding and
loosing, so that the former extended over the whole Church, and passed
to Peter's successors (*First Age of the Church*, pp. 29, 30, 2d ed.)   This
contradicts all the patristic interpretations, and the exegetical tradition
of the Church.

[2] Luke xxii. 32.

short duration, is to strengthen the other Apostles, whose faith would likewise waver. It is directly against the sense of the passage, which speaks simply of faith, first wavering, and then to be confirmed in the Messianic dignity of Christ, to find in it a promise of future infallibility to a succession of Popes, just because they hold the office Peter first held in the Roman Church. No single writer to the end of the seventh century dreamt of such an interpretation; all without exception—and there are eighteen of them—explain it simply as a prayer of Christ that his Apostle might not wholly succumb, and lose his faith entirely in his approaching trial. The first to find in it a promise of privileges to the Church of Rome was Pope Agatho in 680, when trying to avert the threatened condemnation of his predecessor, Honorius, through whom the Roman Church had lost its boasted privilege of doctrinal purity.

Now, the Tridentine profession of faith, imposed on the clergy since Pius IV., contains a vow never to interpret Holy Scripture otherwise than in accord with the unanimous consent of the Fathers—that is, the great Church doctors of the first six centuries, for Gregory the Great, who died in 604, was the last of the Fathers; every bishop and theologian therefore breaks his oath when he interprets the passage in question of a gift of infallibility promised by Christ to the Popes.

§ VII.—*Forgeries.*

At the beginning of the ninth century no change had taken place in the constitution of the Church as we have described it, and especially none as to the authority for deciding matters of faith. When the Frankish bishops came to Leo III., he assured them that, far from setting himself above the Fathers of the Council in 381, who made the additions to the Nicene Creed, he did not venture to put himself on a par with them, and therefore refused to sanction the interpolation of *Filioque* into the Creed.[1]

But in the middle of that century—about 845—arose the huge fabrication of the Isidorian decretals, which had results far beyond what its author contemplated, and gradually, but surely, changed the whole constitution and government of the Church. It would be difficult to find in all history a second instance of so successful, and yet so clumsy a forgery. For three centuries past it has been exposed, yet the principles it introduced and brought into practice have taken such

[1] *Concil. Gall.* (ed. Sirmondi) ii. 256.

deep root in the soil of the Church, and have so grown into her life, that the exposure of the fraud has produced no result in shaking the dominant system.

About a hundred pretended decrees of the earliest Popes, together with certain spurious writings of other Church dignitaries and acts of Synods, were then fabricated in the west of Gaul, and eagerly seized upon by Pope Nicolas I. at Rome, to be used as genuine documents in support of the new claims put forward by himself and his successors. The immediate object of the compiler of this forgery was to protect bishops against their metropolitans and other authorities, so as to secure absolute impunity, and the exclusion of all influence of the secular power. This end was to be gained through such an immense extension of the Papal power, that, as these principles gradually penetrated the Church, and were followed out into their consequences, she necessarily assumed the form of an absolute monarchy subjected to the arbitrary power of a single individual, and the foundation of the edifice of Papal Infallibility was already laid—first, by the principle that the decrees of every Council require Papal confirmation; secondly, by the assertion that the fulness of power, even in matters of faith, resides in the Pope alone, who

. is bishop of the universal Church, while the other bishops are his servants.

Now, if the Pope is really the bishop of the whole Church, so that every other bishop is his servant, he, who is the sole and legitimate mouth of the Church, ought to be infallible. If the decrees of Councils are invalid without Papal confirmation, the divine attestation of a doctrine undeniably rests in the last resort on the word of one man, and the notion of the absolute power of that one man over the whole Church includes that of his infallibility, as the shell contains the kernel. With perfect consistency, therefore, the pseudo-Isidore makes his early Popes say: "The Roman Church remains to the end free from stain of heresy."[1]

Formerly all learned students of ecclesiastical antiquity and canon-law—men like De Marca, Baluze, Coustant, Gibert, Berardi, Zallwein, etc.—were agreed that the change introduced by the pseudo-Isidore was a substantial one, that it displaced the old system of Church government and brought in the new. Modern writers have maintained that the compiler of the forgery only meant to codify the existing state of things, and

---

[1] *Ep. Lucii* in Hinschius' ed. of Decretals, p. 179. Cf. p. 206. The same statement is put into the mouth of Marcus and Felix I.

give it a formal status, and that the same development would have taken place without his trick.[1] The truth is :—

First, Before his fabrication many very efficacious forgeries had won a gradual recognition at Rome since the beginning of the sixth century ; and on them was based the maxim that the Pope, as supreme in the Church, could be judged by no man.

Secondly, The Isidorian doctrine contradicted itself, for it aimed at two things which were mutually incompatible,—the complete independence and impunity of bishops on the one hand, and the advancement of Papal power on the other. The first point it sought to effect by such strange and unpractical rules that they never attained any real vitality, while, on the contrary, the principles about the power of the Roman See worked their way, and became dominant under favourable circumstances, but with a result greatly opposed to the views of Isidore, by bringing the bishops into complete subjection to Rome. But that the pseudo-Isidorian principles eventually revolutionized the whole constitution of the Church, and introduced a new system in

---

[1] So Walter, Phillips, Schulte, Pachmann, among canonists, and Döllinger in his *Church History* (ii. 41-43), on grounds betraying a very imperfect knowledge of the decretals.

G

place of the old,—on that point there can be no controversy among candid historians.

At the time when the forged decretals began to be
widely known, the See of Rome was occupied by Nicolas I. (858-867), a Pope who exceeded all his predecessors in the audacity of his designs. Favoured and
protected by the break-up of the empire of Charles the
Great, he met East and West alike with the firm resolu-
tion of pressing to the uttermost every claim of any one
of his predecessors, and pushing the limits of the Roman
supremacy to the point of absolute monarchy. By a bold
but non-natural torturing of a single word against the
sense of a whole code of law, he managed to give a turn
to a canon of a General Council, excluding all appeals
to Rome, as though it opened to the whole clergy in East
and West a right of appeal to Rome, and made the Pope
the supreme judge of all bishops and clergy of the whole
world.[1] He wrote this to the Eastern Emperor, to the
Frankish king, Charles, and to all the Frankish bishops.[2]
And he referred the Orientals, and so sharp-sighted a

---

[1] Canon 17 of Chalcedon, which speaks of appeals to the "primas
dioceseos," *i.e.*, one of the Eastern patriarchs, not a civil ruler, as Baxmann
thinks (*Politik der Päbste*, ii. 13). Nicolas said the singular meant the
plural, "dioceseon," and that the "primate" meant the Pope,—a notion
which would not seem worth a reply in Constantinople.

[2] Mansi, *Concil.* v. 202, 688, 694.

man as Photius, to those fabrications fathered on Popes
Silvester and Sixtus, which were thenceforth used for
centuries, and gained the Roman Church the oft-repeated
reproach from the Greeks, of being the native home of
inventions and falsifications of documents. Soon after,
receiving the new implements forged in the Isidorian
workshop (about 863 or 864), Nicolas met the doubts
of the Frankish bishops with the assurance that the
Roman Church had long preserved all those documents
with honour in her archives, and that every writing of
a Pope, even if not part of the Dionysian collection of
canons, was binding on the whole Church.[1] In a Synod
at Rome in 863 he had accordingly anathematized all
who should refuse to receive the teaching or ordinances
of a Pope.[2] If, indeed, all Papal utterances were a
rule for the whole Church, and all decrees of Councils
dependent on the Pope's good pleasure,—as Nicolas
asserted on the strength of the Isidorian forgery,—then
there would be but one step further to the promulgation
of Papal Infallibility, though it has been long delayed.
It was thought enough to repeat from time to time that
the Roman Church keeps the faith pure, and is free from
every stain.

[1] Mansi, *Concil.* xv. 695.   [2] Harduin, *Concil.* v. 574.

Nearly three centuries passed before the seed sown produced its full harvest. For almost two hundred years, from the death of Nicolas I. to the time of Leo IX., the Roman See was in a condition which did not allow of any systematic acquisition and enforcement of new or extended rights. For above sixty years (883-955) the Roman Church was enslaved and degraded, while the Apostolic See became the prey and the plaything of rival factions of the nobles, and for a long time of ambitious and profligate women. It was only renovated for a brief interval (997-1003) in the persons of Gregory V. and Silvester II., by the influence of the Saxon emperor. Then the Papacy sank back into utter confusion and moral impotence; the Tuscan Counts made it hereditary in their family; again and again dissolute boys, like John XII. and Benedict IX., occupied and disgraced the Apostolic throne, which was now bought and sold like a piece of merchandise, and at last three Popes fought for the tiara, until the Emperor Henry III. put an end to the scandal by elevating a German bishop to the See of Rome.

With Leo IX. (1048-1054) was inaugurated a new era of the Papacy, which may be called the Hildebrandine. Within sixty years, through the contest with kings, bishops, and clergy, against simony, clerical marriage, and investiture, the Roman See had risen to a height of power even Nicolas I. never aspired to. A large and powerful party, stronger than that which two hundred years before had undertaken to carry through the Isidorian forgery, had been labouring since the middle of the eleventh century, with all its might, to weld the States of Europe into a theocratic priest-kingdom, with the Pope as its head. The urgent need of reform in the Church helped on the growth of the spiritual monarchy, and again the purification of the Church seemed to need such a concentration and increase of ecclesiastical power. In France this party was supported by the most influential spiritual corporation of the time, the Congregation of Cluny. In Italy, men like Peter Damiani, Bishop Anselm of Lucca, Humbert, Deusdedit, and above all Hildebrand,—who was the life and soul of the enterprise,—helped on the new system, though some of them, as Damiani and Hildebrand, differed widely both in theory and practice.

It has not perhaps been sufficiently observed that Gregory VII. is in fact the only one of all the Popes who set himself with clear and deliberate purpose to introduce a new constitution of the Church, and by new means.

He regarded himself not merely as the reformer of the Church, but as the divinely commissioned founder of a wholly new order of things, fond as he was of appealing to his predecessors. Nicolas I. alone approaches him in this, but none of the later Popes, all of whom, even the boldest, have but filled in the outline he sketched.

Gregory saw from the first that Synods regularly held by the Popes, and new codes of Church law, were the means for introducing the new system. Synods had been held, at his suggestion, by Leo IX. and his successors, and he himself carried on the work in those assembled after 1073. But only Popes and their legates were henceforth to hold Synods; in every other form the institution was to disappear. Gregory collected about him by degrees the right men for elaborating his system of Church law. Anselm of Lucca, nephew of Pope Alexander II., compiled the most important and comprehensive work, at his command, between 1080 and 1086. Anselm may be called the founder of the new Gregorian system of Church law, first, by extracting and putting into convenient working shape everything in the Isidorian forgeries serviceable for the Papal absolutism; next, by altering the law of the Church, through a tissue of fresh inventions and interpolations, in accordance with the requirements of his party and the stand-point of Gregory.[1] Then came Deusdedit, whom Gregory made a Cardinal, with some more inventions. At the same time Bonizo compiled his work, the main object of which was to exalt the Papal prerogatives. The forty propositions or titles of this part of his work correspond entirely to Gregory's *Dictatus* and the materials supplied by Anselm and Deusdedit.[2] The last great work of the Gregorians (before Gratian) was the *Polycarpus* of Cardinal Gregory of Pavia (before 1118), which almost always adheres to Anselm in its falsifications.[3]

The Preface of Deusdedit to his work is the programme of the whole school whose labours were at length crowned with such complete success.[4] The Roman Church, says the Cardinal, is the mother of all Churches, for Peter first founded the Patriarchal Sees of the East, and then gave bishops to all the cities of

[1] The contents of the Anselmian collection are known from the list of chapters in the *Spicilegium Rom.* (ed. Mai, vi.); from Antonius Augustinus, *Epitome Juris Pontif.* (Paris, 1641); and from the citations of Pithou in the Paris edition of Gratian, 1686.

[2] *Nova Patrum Biblioth.* (ed. Mai), vii. 3, 48.

[3] Ivo of Chartres, though a contemporary of Cardinal Gregory, cannot be reckoned among the Gregorian canonists. Much as he was influenced in his compilations by Isidore, and sometimes by Anselm, still in certain important articles he held to the old Church law.

[4] It is found in *Memorie del Card. Passionei* (Roma, 1762), p. 30.

the West. Councils cannot be held without the sanction of the Pope, according to the decisions of the 318 Fathers at Nice. The Roman clergy rule without the Pope, when the See is vacant, and therefore Cyprian and the Africans humbly submitted to their decisions before the election of Cornelius—a pet crotchet of the Cardinal's, which Anselm, who was not a Cardinal, did not adopt. He adds, that he writes in order to confirm the authority of Rome and the liberty of the Church against its assailants, and maintains that the testimonies he has collected disprove all objections, on the principle that the lesser must always yield to the greater—*i.e.*, the authority of Councils and Fathers to the Pope. With this one axiom—which not only opened the door wide for the Isidorian decretals, but prevented any attempt to moderate their system by an appeal to the ancient canons—the revolution in the Church was accomplished in the simplest and least troublesome manner.

Clearly and cautiously as the Gregorian party went to work, they lived in a world of dreams and illusions about the past and about remote countries. They could not escape the imperative necessity of demonstrating their new system to have been the constant practice of the Church, and it is difficult, if not impossible, to distinguish where involuntary delusion merged into conscious deceit. Whatever present exigencies required was selected from the mythical stores at their command hastily and recklessly; then fresh inventions were added, and soon every claim of Rome could be shown to have a legitimate foundation in existing records and decrees.

It is so far true to say, that without the pseudo-Isidore there would have been no Gregory VII., that the Isidorian forgeries were the broad foundation the Gregorians built upon. But the first object of Isidore was to secure the impunity of bishops, whereas the Roman party—which for a long time had a majority of the bishops against it—wanted to introduce a state of things where the Popes or their legates could summarily depose bishops, intimidate them, and reduce them to complete subjection to every Papal command. The newly invented doctrines about the deposing power contributed to this end. In a word, a new history and a new civil and canon law was required, and both had to be obtained by improving on the Isidorian principles with new forgeries. The correction of history was to some extent provided for in Germany by the monk Bernold, and in Italy by the zealous Gregorian Bonizo, Bishop of Piacenza, who tried, among other things, to get rid of the coronation of Charles the Great.[1] Their other assistants had to invent or adapt historical facts for party purposes, for their new codes of Church law innovated largely on ancient Church history. Gregory himself had his own little stock of fabricated or distorted facts to support pretensions and undertakings which seemed to his contemporaries strange and unauthorized. It was, for instance, an axiomatic fact with him that Pope Innocent I. excommunicated the Emperor Arcadius, that Pope Zachary deposed the Frankish king Childeric, and that Gregory the Great threatened to depose the kings who should rob a hospice at Autun.[2] He treated the Donation of Constantine as a valuable and important document; it gave him a right over Corsica and Sardinia.[3] His pupil Leo IX. used it against the Greeks, and his friend Peter Damiani against Germany; Anselm and Deusdedit assigned it a prominent place in their legal books.

[1] See Jaffé's Introduction to his edition of Bonitho in *Monvmenta Gregor.*, pp. 596 *seq.*

[2] He appealed to a recently forged document in Autun, which Launoi (*Opp.* v. p. ii. 445) has dissected.

[3] Döllinger is mistaken in saying (*Pabstfabeln*, p. 84) that Gregory never appealed to it.

At the same time, Gregory thought it most important, with all his legislative activity and lofty claims
and high-handed measures, not to seem too much of an
innovator and despot; he constantly affirmed that he
only wished to restore the ancient laws of the Church,
and abolish late abuses. When he drew out the whole
system of Papal omnipotence in twenty-seven theses in
his *Dictatus*, these theses were partly mere repetitions
or corollaries of the Isidorian decretals; partly he and
his friends and allies sought to give them the appearance of tradition and antiquity by new fictions.[1]

Gregory's chief work is his letter to Bishop Hermann
of Metz, designed to prove how well grounded is the
Pope's dominion over emperors and kings, and his right
to depose them in cases of necessity. In this he
showed his adherents how to manipulate facts and
texts, by twisting a passage in a letter of Pope Gelasius
to the Emperor Anastasius so skilfully, by means of
omissions and arbitrary collocations, as to make Gelasius say just the opposite of what he really said,—viz.,
that kings are absolutely and universally subject to
the Pope, whereas what he did say was, that the rulers

---

[1] As to this *Dictatus* being his own work, and an authentic part of the
Register edited by himself, see Giesebrecht, *Gesetzgeb. der Röm. Kirche.*,
Münchner hist. Jahrbuch, 1866, p. 149.

of the Church are always subject to the laws of the emperors, only disclaiming the interference of the secular power in questions of faith and the sacraments.[1]

How what was a falsification to begin with was falsified again in the interests of the new system, and accentuated to serve the cause of ecclesiastical despotism, may be seen from the eleventh canon of *Causa* 25, Q. 1, in Gratian. The Council of Toledo in 646 had excommunicated the Spanish priests who took part in the rebellion against the King, and included the King himself in the anathema if he violated this censure (*hujus canonis censuram*). Out of this Isidore made, two hundred years afterwards, the following:—The anathema applied to all kings who violated any canon binding under censure, or allowed it to be violated by others; and this he put into the mouth of Pope Hadrian.[2] In the new text-books compiled by Anselm, Deusdedit, and Gregory of Pavia, the (pretended) decrees of the Popes were put in place of the canons of Councils, and this supplied just what was wanted—a system of ancient Church law to justify the procedures of Gregory VII. and Urban II. against the princes of their own day—and a Pope would never lack some pre-

---

[1] *Registr.* (ed. Jaffé), p. 457.   [2] *Capp. Angilram.* p. 769 (ed. Hinsch.)

text for threatening excommunication, with all its consequences.[1]

Gregory borrowed one main pillar of his system from the False Decretals. Isidore had made Pope Julius (about 338) write to the Eastern bishops,—"The Church of Rome, by a singular privilege, has the right of opening and shutting the gates of heaven to whom she will."[2] On this Gregory built his scheme of dominion.[3] How should not he be able to judge on earth, on whose will hung the salvation or damnation of men? The passage was made into a special decree or chapter in the new codes.[4] The typical formula of binding and loosing had become an inexhaustible treasure-chamber of rights and claims. The Gregorians used it as a charm to put them in possession of everything worth having. If Gregory—who was notoriously the first to undertake dethroning kings—wanted to depose the German Emperor, he said, "To me is given power to bind and loose on earth and in heaven."[5] Were sub-

---

[1] The monk Bernold, in his *Apol. contr. Schismat.*, written in 1087 (Ussermann, ed. p. 361), fabricates "Apostolicæ Sedis statuta."

[2] *Decret. pseudo-Is.* (ed. Hinsch.), p. 464.

[3] *Monum. Gregor.* (ed. Jaffé), p. 445.

[4] By Deusdedit ; see *Galland. Syll.* ii. 745 ; by Anselm, *Maii Spicil. Rom.* vi. 317. 23 ; by Bonizo, *Maii Pat. Nov. Biblioth.* vii. 3, 47 ; Gregory's *Polycarpus,* i. 4, tit. 34.

[5] See the form in Mansi, xx. 467.

jects to be absolved from their oaths of allegiance?—
which he was also the first to attempt,—he did it by
virtue of his power to loose. Did he want to dispose
of other people's property? he declared, as at his Roman
Synod of 1080,—" We desire to show the world that we
can give or take away at our will kingdoms, duchies,
earldoms, in a word, the possessions of all men; for
we can bind and loose."[1] In the same way a saying
ascribed to Constantine, at the Council of Nice, in a
legend recorded by Rufinus, was amplified till it was
fashioned into a perfect mine of high-flying pretensions.
Constantine, according to this fable, when the written
accusations of the bishops against each other were laid
before him, burned them, saying, in allusion to a verse of
the Psalter, that the bishops were gods, and no man
could dare to judge them. Nicolas I. quoted this to
the Emperor Michael.[2] Anselm adopted the story into
his collection, Gratian followed, and Gregory himself
found in it clear evidence that he, the Pope, the bishop
of bishops, stood in unapproachable majesty over all
monarchs of the earth. For, as the passage stood in
Anselm and Gratian, it was the Pope whom Constan-

---

[1] Mansi, xx. 536, " Quia si potestis in cœlo ligare et solvere, potestis in
terrâ imperia . . . et omnium hominum possessiones pro meritis tollere
unicuique et concedere."   [2] Mansi, xv. 215.

tine called a god, and so it has been understood and explained ever since.[1]

A man like Gregory VII., little familiar as he was with theological questions, must have held the prerogative of Infallibility the most precious jewel of his crown. His claims to universal dominion, to the deposing power, and the right of dispensing subjects from their oaths, all rested ultimately on his own authority. All was to be believed because he, the infallible Pope, affirmed it. Accordingly, stronger proofs and testimonies than Isidore supplied had to be found for this infallibility of his.

Pope Agatho had said at a Roman Synod, in 680, that all the English bishops were to observe the ordinances made in former Roman Synods for the Anglo-Saxon Church.[2] Cardinal Deusdedit made this into a decree issued by Agatho to all bishops in the world, saying they must receive all Papal orders as though attested by the very voice of Peter, and therefore, of course, infallible.[3] One of the boldest falsifications the

---

[1] *Dist.* 96, 97. "Satis evidenter ostenditur a sæculari potestate nec ligari prorsus nec solvi posse *Pontificem, quem constat a pio Principe Constantino Deum appellatum,* nec posse Deum ab hominibus judicari manifestum est."

[2] Labbé, *Concil.* vi. 580.

[3] It occurs in the same spurious form in Gregory's *Polycarpus,* Ivo's Collection, and—which was, of course, quite conclusive—in Gratian's *Decretum,* Dist. 19, c. 2.

Gregorians allowed themselves occurs first in Anselm's,[1] and then in Cardinal Gregory's works, from whom Gratian borrowed it. St. Augustine had said that all those canonical writings (of the Bible) were pre-eminently attested, which Apostolical Churches had first received and possessed. He meant the Churches of Corinth, Ephesus, etc. The passage was corrupted into,—" Those Epistles belong to canonical writings which the Holy See has issued;" and thus it came to pass that the mediæval theologians and canonists, who generally derived their whole knowledge of the Fathers from the passages collected by Peter Lombard and Gratian, really believed that St. Augustine had put the decretal letters of Popes on a par with Scripture.[2] When Cardinal Turrecremata, about 1450, and Cardinal Cajetan, about 1516, put the Infallibility doctrine into formal shape, they too relied on the clear testimony of St. Augustine, which left no doubt that the first theologian of the ancient Church had declared every Papal utterance to be as free from error as the Apostolical Epistles.[3]

---

[1] See Pithou's ed. of Gratian. Cf. Grat. *Dist*. 19, c. 6.

[2] The title of the canon in Gratian is, " Inter canonicas Scripturas decretales epistolæ annumerantur."

[3] Turrecremata, *Summa de Eccl*. P. ii.; Cajetan, *De Primat. Rom*. c. 14. Alphonsus de Castro has exposed the whole forgery in his work *Adv. Hæres.* (Paris, 1565) i. 11.

That Papal Infallibility might be more firmly believed, personal sanctity was also ascribed to every Pope. This notion was first invented by Ennodius, deacon and secretary of Pope Symmachus, who wrote in 503 to defend him against certain charges. The Popes, he said, must be held to inherit innocence and sanctity from Peter.[1] Isidore eagerly seized on this, and invented two Roman Synods, which had unanimously approved and subscribed the work of Ennodius.[2] Gregory VII. made this holiness of all Popes, which he said he had personal experience of, the foundation of his claim to universal dominion.[3] Every sovereign, he said, however good before, becomes corrupted by the use of power, whereas every rightly appointed Pope[4] becomes a saint through the imputed merits of St. Peter. Even an exorcist[5] among the clergy, he added, is higher and more powerful than every secular monarch, for he casts out devils, whose slaves evil princes are. This doctrine of the personal sanctity of every Pope, put forward by the Gregorians, and by Gregory VII. himself, as a claim

---

[1] *Liber Apol., Opp.* (Sirmondi) i. 1621.
[2] *Decret. pseudo-Isidor.* (ed. Hinsch.), pp. 675, *seq.*
[3] *Ep.* viii. 21 (Jaffé), p. 463.
[4] This proviso was meant to cover the frequent cases of such evil Popes as, *e.g.*, John XII. and Benedict IX.
[5] [One of the lower ranks of the Catholic clergy.—Tr.]

II

made by Pope Symmachus, was adopted into the codes of canon law. But as notorious facts, and the crimes and excesses of many Popes, which no denials could get rid of, were in glaring contradiction to it, a supplementary theory had to be invented, which Cardinal Deusdedit published under the venerated name of St. Boniface, the apostle of Germany. It was to this effect:—Even if a Pope is so bad that he drags down whole nations to hell with him in troops, nobody can rebuke him; for he who judges all can be judged of no man; the only exception is in case of his swerving from the faith. That this could have been written nowhere but in Rome, and certainly not by St. Boniface, is self-evident. There were no "innumerable nations" in his day for the Pope to drag down into hell with him like slaves. The words imply past experience of many profligate Popes, and a period of enormously extended Papal power over the nations, and were clearly invented after the pontificate of Benedict IX. Gratian has, of course, adopted them from Deusdedit.[1]

The Gregorian doctrine since 1080 then is, that every Pope, lawfully appointed, and not thrust in by force, is holy and infallible. But his holiness is imputed, not

---

[1] *Dist.* 40, c. 53.

inherent, so that if he have no merits of his own, he inherits those of his predecessor St. Peter. Notwithstanding his holiness, he may drag countless troops of men down to hell, and none of them may withstand or warn him; notwithstanding his infallibility, he may become an apostate, and then he may be resisted. Probably the later distinction between his official or *ex cathedrâ* infallibility and his personal denial of the faith was implied here.

Gregory VII. seems to have sincerely believed that his infallibility was already acknowledged throughout the Christian world, even in the East. He wrote to the Emperor Henry, " The Greek Church is fallen away, and the Armenians also have lost the right faith, but," he adds, "all the Easterns await from St. Peter (viz., from me) the decision on their various opinions, and at this time will the promise of Peter's confirming his brethren be fulfilled."[1] He wanted then (in 1074) to go at the head of a great army to Constantinople, and there to hold his solemn judgment in matters of faith, for he does not seem to have counted on the voluntary submission of the Greeks; instead of which he contented himself with plunging Germany and Italy into a religious

[1] *Ep.* ii. 31, p. 45 (Jaffé).

and civil war, the end of which he did not live to see.
All history proves, he says, how clearly holiness is connected with infallibility in the Popes. While there are at
most only a few kings or emperors who have been holy,
out of 153 Popes 100 have not only been holy, but
have reached the highest grade of sanctity.[1] And the
Gregorians disseminated the fable, which even the
well-known annals of the Popes contradicted, that of
the thirty before Constantine all but one were martyrs.[2]
The Gregorians busied themselves greatly with the
rectification of Papal history, and as the apostasy of
Liberius—copied from St Jerome's Chronicle into so
many historical works—was not easy to reconcile with
Papal infallibility and sanctity, Anselm adopted into
his codex the earlier fable, that Liberius, when exiled,
had ordained Felix his successor, by advice of the
Roman clergy, and abdicated, so that his subsequent
apostasy did not matter.[3]

If every Pope is holy and infallible, then, according
to the Gregorian view, all Christendom must tremble
before him, as before an Asiatic despot whose disfavour
is death. Accordingly, Anselm and Cardinal Gregory

[1] *Ep.* viii. 21, p. 463 (Jaffé).
[2] Bonizo, *Patr. Nov. Bibl.* vii. 3, 37 (ed. Mai).
[3] Schelstrate (*Antiq. Illustr.* i. 456) quotes the passage from Anselm.

extracted passages from older forgeries, especially from
a spurious speech of St. Peter, to the effect that no one
should hold intercourse with a man under the Pope's
displeasure.[1] Like the successive strata of the earth
covering one another, so layer after layer of forgeries
and fabrications was piled up in the Church. This
shows itself most conspicuously in the great Church
question of Synods, where the two contradictory views
of the self-government and administration of the
Church by Councils, and of the absolute sovereignty of
the Pope and Court of Rome over the whole Church,
were at issue. In 342, Pope Julius had written to the
Eastern Bishops, who had confirmed the deposition of
St. Athanasius at the Synod of Antioch, that they
should not have acted for themselves in a matter affecting the whole Church, but, according to ecclesiastical
custom, in union with "all of us," *i.e.*, the bishops of
the West.[2] Socrates, who welcomed an opportunity of
pointing out the ambition of the Roman Church,[3] had
twisted this into Julius saying that nothing could be
decided without the bishop of Rome. His Latin trans-

---

[1] See Gratian, *Dist.* 93, c. i.
[2] *Ep. Rom. Pont.* (ed. Constant), p. 386.
[3] Thus he observes (vii. 11) that the Roman See, like the Alexandrian,
had for some time advanced to dominion (δυναστεία) over the priesthood.

lator, Epiphanius the Italian, about 500, went a step
further, and made the Pope say that no Council could
be held without his consent.[1] Isidore worked up these
materials, and made Pope Julius write, in two spurious epistles, that the Apostles and the Nicene Council
had said no Council could be held without the Pope's
injunction. And thus Anselm and the other Gregorian
canonists could quote a whole string of primitive decrees resting Councils and all their decisions on the
arbitrament of the Pope, and Gratian has borrowed the
whole of his seventeenth Distinction from Anselm.

Even this was not enough. Not only were Councils
to be made dependent, but the institution itself, as it
had existed for nine hundred years, was to be abolished.
As the kings who had become absolute in the sixteenth
and seventeenth centuries could no longer endure any
representative assemblies, so the Papacy, when it wished
to become absolute, found that Synods of particular
National Churches were better out of the way altogether.
For it was only in and by means of Synods of particular districts, provinces, and National Churches, that a
healthy and somewhat independent Church life could
spread and maintain itself.   These had therefore to be

[1] *Hist. Trip.* i. 4, 9.

put an end to, or at least broken up and made so difficult that they could only proceed at the beck of Rome.
The following forgery was used for the purpose :—

The opponents of Pope Symmachus, in 503, in order
to show that they could assemble in Rome without
him, had affirmed that the annual Provincial Synods
prescribed by the Church would not lose their force
merely because the Pope was not present at them.
Ennodius, in his defence of Symmachus, replied that
weighty causes (*causæ majores*) were by the canon of
Sardica reserved to the Pope. That was itself a misrepresentation, long current in Rome; the canon only
gave a right of appeal to Rome for bishops. Anselm
of Lucca, and Cardinal Gregory, and Gratian after him,
made out of this the following decree of Pope Symmachus—" The Provincial Councils ordered by the canons to be held annually, have lost their validity from
the Pope not being present at them." And the title
of the decree is, " Provincial Synods without the Pope's
presence have no force" (*pondere carent*).[1] And thus
an ecclesiastical revolution was brought about in three
lines.

But a formal prohibition of all Synods was still

[1] *Dist.* 17, c. 6.

wanted, and this was attained by Anselm, Cardinal Gregory, and Gratian after them, making Pope Gregory the Great declare that no one ever had been, or ever would be, permitted to hold a particular (not Œcumenical) Synod.[1] The fraud lay in converting what Pelagius I. had said, in the particular case of the schism of Aquileia, of a Council assembled against the Fifth Œcumenical, into a general prohibition issued by Gregory I. against all Synods, while, by changing the plural into the singular, a reference to the authority of the Apostolic Churches of Alexandria and Antioch was altered into an exaltation of Papal authority.[2] And thus the double end was attained of putting down all meetings of bishops as in itself an illegal act of presumption, and at the same time bringing out prominently the plenitude of the Papal power, which could even withdraw from all Christendom the apostolical institution of Synods at its will.

But Isidore's chief contribution to the designs of Gregory VII. was by his inventions about the effect of excommunication, for this, in the extended sense given it by Gregory, was the sharpest weapon in the

---

[1] *Decret.* Dist. 17, c. 4.
[2] Cf. on this and other falsifications, Berardi, *Gratian. Can.* ii. 489.

struggle for Papal domination. Isidore had made the
earliest Popes assert that no speech ever could be held
with an excommunicated man, whence Gregory and his
allies inferred that this applied also to kings and emperors, and that nobody could, even in matters of
business, hold any intercourse with them if excommunicated, so that they were no longer fit to reign, and
must be deposed. By this extension of the idea, wholly
unknown to the ancient Church, and destructive of the
entire original character of the institution, an enormous
instrument of power was created, which not only might
be abused, but was itself a standing abuse, a confusion of
things human and divine, and a perpetual source of civil
disturbance and division. Bossuet has admitted that
it was a false doctrine which Gregory introduced into
the Church, by altering and distorting the notion of
excommunication.[1] Gregory himself must have known
he was the first to make the claim, and that even in the
Isidorian decretals there was nothing like it, yet at
the Synod of 1078[2] he grounded it exclusively on the
statutes of his predecessors. To make their spiritual
arms irresistible, the Gregorians also borrowed from

[1] *Defens. Declar.* pars. 1. 1. 3. c. 7.
[2] Ivo and Gratian, for the misfortune of Europe, received this into their
codes (c. 15, qu. 6. 4).

Isidore an alleged rule of Pope Urban I., addressed to all bishops, that even an unjust excommunication by a bishop must be respected, and nobody could receive the condemned man.[1]

If we look at the whole Papal system of universal monarchy, as it has been gradually built up during seven centuries, and is now being energetically pushed on to its final completion, we can clearly distinguish the separate stones the building is composed of. For a long time all that was done was to interpret the canon of Sardica so as to extend the appellant jurisdiction of the Pope to whatever could be brought under the general and elastic term of " greater causes." But from the end of the fifth century the Papal pretensions had advanced to a point beyond this, in consequence of the attitude assumed by Leo and Gelasius, and from that time began a course of systematic fabrications, sometimes manufactured in Rome, sometimes originating elsewhere, but adopted and utilized there.

The conduct of the Popes since Innocent I. and Zosimus, in constantly quoting the Sardican canon on appeals as a canon of Nice, cannot be exactly ascribed to conscious fraud—the arrangement of their collection

---

[1] Thus Anselm and Card. Gregory, and then Gratian, c. 11, qu. 3. 27.

of canons misled them. There was more deliberate purpose in inserting in the Roman manuscript of the sixth Nicene canon, " The Roman Church always had the primacy," of which there is no syllable in the original,— a fraud exposed at the Council of Chalcedon, to the confusion of the Roman legates, by reading the original.[1]

Towards the end of the fifth and beginning of the sixth century, the process of forgeries and fictions in the interests of Rome was actively carried on there. Then began the compilation of spurious acts of Roman martyrs, which was continued for some centuries, and which modern criticism, even at Rome, has been obliged to give up, as, for instance, is done by Papebroch, Ruinart, Orsi, and Saccarelli. The fabulous story of the conversion and baptism of Constantine was invented to glorify the Church of Rome, and make Pope Silvester appear a worker of miracles. Then the inviolability of the Pope had to be established, and the principle that he cannot be judged by any human tribunal, but only by himself. For four years before 514 Rome was the scene of a bloody strife about this question; the adherents of Symmachus and his opponent Laurentius murdered one another in the streets, and the Arian Goth, King Theo-

---

[1] Mansi, *Concil.* vii. 444.

doric, was as little acceptable as a judge as the Emperor, who was hated in Rome. So the acts of the Council of Sinuessa and the legend of Pope Marcellinus were invented, and the "Constitution of Silvester," viz., the decision of a Synod of 284 bishops, pretended to have been held by him in 321 at Rome, evidently compiled while the bloody scenes in which clerics were murdered or executed for their crimes were fresh in men's minds. There again the principle was inculcated that no one can judge the first See.[1]

Some other records were fabricated at Rome in the same barbarous Latin, such as the *Gesta Liberii*, designed to confirm the legend of Constantine's baptism at Rome, and to represent Pope Liberius as purified from his heresy by repentance, and graced by a divine miracle. Of the same stamp were the *Gesta* of Pope Xystus III. and the History of Polychronius, where the Pope is accused, but the condemnation of his accuser follows, as also of the accuser of the fabulous Polychronius, Bishop of Jerusalem. These fabrications of the beginning of the sixth century, which all belong to the same class, had a reference also to the attitude of Rome towards the Church of Constantinople. It was the period of the long inter-

---

[1] *Append. ad Epp. Pont. Rom.* (ed. Constant), pp. 38 *seq.*

ruption of communion between East and West caused by the *Henoticon* (484-519), when Felix II. even summoned the Patriarch Acacius to Rome, and Pope Gelasius, about 495, for the first time insulted the Greeks and their twenty-eighth canon of Chalcedon, by affirming that every Council must be confirmed and every Church judged by Rome, but she can be judged by none. It was not by canons, as the Council of Chalcedon affirmed, but by the word of Christ, that she received the primacy.[1] In this he went beyond all the claims of his predecessors. Thence came the fictions manufactured at Rome after his death,—a letter of the Nicene Council praying Pope Silvester for its confirmation, and the confirmation given by Silvester and a Roman Synod; the declaration in the acts of Xystus III. that the Emperor had convoked the Council by the Pope's authority; the History of Polychronius, exhibiting the Pope, as early as 435, sitting in judgment on an Eastern Patriarch; and lastly, the fabulous history of the Synod held by Silvester, which adopted Gelasius's saying about the divine origin of the Roman primacy, and confirmed the order of precedence of the Churches of Alexandria and Antioch next after Rome, making no mention of Con-

[1] Mansi, viii. 54.

stantinople, and thus upsetting the canons of 381 and 451, which gave her the precedence.[1]

While this tendency to forging documents was so strong in Rome, it is remarkable that for a thousand years no attempt was made there to form a collection of canons of her own, such as the Easterns had as early as the fifth century, clearly because for a long time Rome took so very little part in ecclesiastical legislation. No doubt constant appeal was made to the canons of Councils, and Rome professed her resolve to secure their observance with all her might, and by her conspicuous example; but the canon she had chiefly at heart - was the third of Sardica, and the Sardican canons were never received at all in the East.[2] When Dionysius gave the Roman Church her first tolerably comprehensive collection of canons, viz., his translation of the Greek canons, with the African and Sardican, more than twenty Synods had been held in Rome since 313, but there were no records of them to be found.

[1] These documents are printed from MSS. of the eighth century in Amort's *Elementa Juris Canon.* ii. 432-486.

[2] Dionysius Exiguus observes this in the Preface to the second edition of his Collection, prepared by command of Pope Hormisdas. See Andres, *Lettera à G. Morelli* (Parma, 1802), p. 66. It will be seen that there was always a quarrel about the Nicene canons, and one party wished to replace them (probably the sixth canon) by others. This points to the decisions of Silvester and his Synod, mentioned above.

Towards the end of the sixth century a fabrication
was undertaken in Rome, the full effect of which did
not appear till long afterwards. The famous passage in
St. Cyprian's book on the Unity of the Church was
adorned, in Pope Pelagius II.'s letter to the Istrian
bishops, with such additions as the Roman pretensions
required. St. Cyprian said that all the Apostles had
received from Christ equal power and authority with
Peter, and this was too glaring a contradiction of the
theory set up since the time of Gelasius. So the following words were interpolated : " The primacy was
given to Peter to show the unity of the Church and of
the chair. How can he believe himself to be in the
Church who forsakes the chair of Peter, on which the
Church is built?"[1] The varying judgments of the
later Roman clergy on Cyprian, who had up to his
death been a decided opponent of Rome, seem to have
had an influence on this interpolation. He was at
first almost the only foreign martyr whose annual
feast was kept in Rome ; but after Gelasius had included
his writings in a list of works rejected by the Church,
it became necessary to find some way of reconciling the

[1] Cf. the notes of Rigault, Baluze, and Krabinger, to their editions of
Cyprian.

high reverence accorded to the man with the disapproval of his writings. This seems to have led to the interpolation, so that the first rank among orthodox Fathers was assigned to Cyprian in the revised edition of the catalogue of Gelasius, in direct contradiction to the passage in the same decree placing him among " apocryphal," viz., rejected authors.[1] But as Cyprian's writings had not spread from Rome, but had long been much read in the Gallican and North Italian Churches, the additions did not get into the manuscripts.

Earlier than this an interpolation of the old catalogue of Roman bishops had been undertaken for a definite purpose, and thus the foundation was laid of the *Liber Pontificalis*,[2] afterwards enlarged. It exists in Schelstrate's

---

[1] When in later times Cyprian was edited at Rome by Manutius in 1563, the Roman censors insisted on the interpolated passages being retained, though not found in the mss., as the editor, Latino Latini, complains in his Letters (Viterbii, 1667, ii. 109). The minister, Cardinal Fleury, made the same condition for the Paris edition of Baluze. See Chiniac, *Histoire des Capitul.* (Paris, 1772), p. 226. The minister named a commission to decide whether the interpolations erased by Baluze, and expunged from every critical edition, should be printed, but Fleury was Cardinal as well as minister, and " à moins que de vouloir se faire une querelle d'état avec Rome impérieuse, il falloit que le passage fût restitué, parceque en le laissant supprimé en vertu d'une décision ministérielle, il auroit semblé qu'on vouloit porter atteinte à la primauté Romaine. Le passage fut restitué par le moyen d'un carton."

[2] The *Liber Pontificalis,* or *Anastasius* (falsely so called), was usually quoted as a work of Pope Damasus in the middle ages.

edition, in its original form, of about 530.[1] The second
edition, and continuation to the time of Conon (687)
written about 730, and afterwards brought down to 724
by the same hand, is based on contemporary records for
the sixth and seventh century. It is the first edition -
of 530 which is chiefly to be reckoned as a calculated
forgery, and an important link in the chain of Roman -
inventions and interpolations. It is all composed in -
the barbarous and ungrammatical Latin common to the
Roman fabrications of the sixth century.[2] The objects
were—*first*, to attest the mass of spurious acts of Roman
martyrs, and the reiterated statements that the earliest
Popes had appointed a number of notaries to compile these
acts, and seven deacons to superintend them ; *secondly*,
to confirm the existing legends of Popes and Emperors,—
such as the Roman baptism of Constantine, the stories
about Silvester, Felix, and Liberius, Xystus III., and the
like ; *thirdly*, to assign a greater antiquity to some later
liturgical usages ; *fourthly*, to exhibit the Popes as legislators for the whole Church, although, apart from the -
liturgical directions ascribed to them, and the constantly -

---

1 He has collated the two editions in his *Antiq. Eccl. Rom.* 1693,
i. 402-495 ; in parallel columns.

2 See the careful analysis of the whole work in Piper's *Einleitung in
die Monum. Theol.* (Gotha, 1867), pp. 315-349.

recurring assertion that they had marked out the parishes
and the hierarchical grades of the clergy in Rome, no
particular ordinances of theirs could be quoted, and people
had to be content with stating generally that Damasus
or Gelasius or Hilary had made a law binding the whole
Church.[1]   In the later and more historical portion (from
440 to 530) the Pope is specially represented as teacher
of doctrine and supreme judge, with a view to the Greeks.
In the first edition every historical notice, except about
buildings, sacred offerings, and cemeteries, is false : the
author's statements about the fortunes and acts of particular Popes never agree with what is known of their
history, but rather contradict it, sometimes glaringly ;
and thus we must regard as fabulous even what cannot
be proved such from sources now accessible to us, for
there is almost always an obvious design.[2]

The fictions of the *Liber Pontificalis* had a far-reaching influence after they became known, and were used—

---

[1] The phrase " fecit Constitutum de omni Ecclesiâ" is repeated on nearly
every page, but what the ordinance was is never specified, while the pretended liturgical appointments are always precisely expressed.

[2] The *Liber Pontificalis* has been critically examined by Tillemont, and
more fully by Coustant, and its gross anachronisms proved, so that there
can be no doubt about its fabulous character, and it gives one the impression throughout of deliberate fraud. Clearly the compilers had no historical
or documentary evidence. The first enlargement of the Liberian catalogue
reached almost to Damasus, and must have been composed early in the

first by Bede about 710—in the rest of the West. They
supplied the basis for the notion of the Popes having
constantly acted from the first as legislators of the whole
Church, and they greatly helped on the later fabrication
of Isidore, who incorporated these records of Papal
enactments into his decretals, and thereby gave them
an appearance of being genuine. This agreement of
the forged decretals with the annals of the Popes is
what gave the former so long a hold on public belief.

After the middle of the eighth century, the famous
Donation of Constantine was concocted at Rome. It is
based on the earlier fifth-century legend of his cure from
leprosy, and baptism by Pope Silvester, which is repeated at length, and the Emperor is said, out of grati-
tude, to have bestowed Italy and the western provinces
on the Pope, and also to have made many regulations
about the honorary prerogatives and dress of the Roman
clergy.[1] The Pope is, moreover, represented as lord

sixth century. The two letters of Damasus and Jerome were invented for
it, according to which Damasus collected and sent to St. Jerome what could
be found of the biographies of the Popes. In a second and altered edition,
some twenty years later, about 536, was added the list of Popes from Damasus to Felix IV. This last part, from 440, is historical, but strongly
coloured, and garnished with fables devised in the interest of Rome.

[1] The "western provinces" must not be understood of Gaul, Spain, etc.
The phrase is used for the northern parts of the Peninsula—Lombardy,
Venetia, and Istria,—which do not properly belong to Roman Italy.

and master of all bishops, and having authority over the four great thrones of Antioch, Alexandria, Constantinople, and Jerusalem.

The forgery betrayed its Roman authorship in every line; it is self-evident that a cleric of the Lateran Church was the composer. The document was obviously intended to be shown to the Frankish king, Pepin, and must have been compiled just before 754. Constantine relates in it how he served the Pope as his groom, and led his horse some distance. This induced Pepin to offer the Pope a homage, so foreign to Frankish ideas, and the Pope told him from the first that he expected, not a gift, but restitution from him and his Franks.[1] The first reference to this gift of Constantine occurs in Hadrian's letter to Charles the Great in 777, where he tells him that, as the new Constantine, he has

[1] There can be no doubt as to the Roman origin of the "Donation." The Jesuit Cantel has rightly recognised this in his *Hist. Metrop. Urb.* p. 195. He thinks a Roman subdeacon, John, was the author. The document had a threefold object,—against the Longobards, who were threatening Rome, against the Greeks, who would acknowledge no supremacy of the Roman See over their Church, and with a view to the Franks. The attempt of the Jesuits in the *Civiltà* to make a Frank the author, simply because Æneas of Paris and Ado of Vienne mention the gift in the ninth century, is not worth serious notice; it refutes itself. There is the closest agreement in style and idea between the "Donation" and contemporary Roman documents, especially the *Constitutum Pauli I.* (Harduin, *Concil.* iii. 1999 *seq.*) and the *Epistola S. Petri,* compiled in 753 or 754. The phrase "Concinnatio

indeed given the Church what is her own, but that he has more of the old Imperial endowments to restore to her. The Popes had already been accustomed, for several years, since 752, to speak, not of gifts, but restitutions, in their letters; the Italian towns and provinces were . to be restored, sometimes to St. Peter, sometimes to the . Roman republic.[1] Such language first became intelli- · gible when the Donation of Constantine was brought · forward to show that the Pope was the rightful pos- · sessor as heir of the Roman Cæsars in Italy; for, he · being at once the successor of Peter and of Constantine, · what was given to the Roman Republic was given to · Peter, and *vice versâ.* In this way it was made clear to · Pepin that he had simply to reject the demands of the Greek Imperial Court about the restoration of its terri- tory as unauthorized.

It would indeed be incomprehensible how Pepin

luminarium," used only in Papal letters of that date, and in the *Consti- tutum* and *Donatio,* betrays a Roman hand. So does the form of impreca- tion and threat of hell-torments, found also in the *Constitutum* and *Epis- tola S. Petri,* and the term "Satrapæ," wholly foreign to the West, and found only in the "Donation," and in contemporary Papal letters. See Cenni, *Monum. Dominat. Pontif.* i. 154.

1 "Exarchatum Ravennæ et rei-publicæ jura seu loca *reddere*" is the phrase in the *Liber Pontif.* See Le Cointe, *Annal. Eccl. Franc.* v. 424. Again, in the letter of Pope Stephen we read, "per Donationis paginam civitates et loca . . . *restituenda* confirmâstis." And so constantly when the Exarchate and Pentapolis are spoken of.

could have been induced to give the Exarchate, with
twenty towns, to the Pope, who never possessed it,
and thereby to draw on himself the enmity of the still
powerful Imperial Court, merely that the lamps in the
Roman churches might be furnished with oil,[1] had he
not been shown that the Pope had a right to it by the
gift of Constantine, and terrified by the threat of ven-
geance from the Prince of the Apostles, if his property
should be withheld. There was no fear of such documents as the Epistle of Peter and the Donation of Constantine being critically examined at the warlike Court
of Pepin. Men who might be written to that their
bodies and souls would be eternally lacerated and tormented in hell if they did not fight against the enemies
of the Church, believed readily enough that Constantine
had given Italy to Pope Silvester. Those were days of
darkness in France, and, in the complete extinction of
all learning, there was not a single man about Pepin
whose sharpsightedness the Roman agents had reason
to dread.[2]

One is tempted to ascribe to the same hand the
Epistle of St. Peter to his " adopted son" the King of

[1] This was always given in the covetous begging-letters of the Popes as
their main ground for demanding the gifts of land they wished for.

[2] See the Benedictine *Hist. Lit. de la France,* iv. 3.

the Franks, which appeared also at this moment of great danger and distress, as well as of lofty hopes and pretensions,—a fabrication which for strangeness and audacity has never been exceeded. Entreating and promising victory, and then again threatening the pains of hell, the Prince of the Apostles adjures the Franks to deliver Rome and the Roman Church. The Epistle really went from Rome to the Frankish kingdom, and seems to have produced its effect there.[1]

Twenty years later the need was felt at Rome of a more extensive invention or interpolation. Pepin had given the Pope the Exarchate, taken away from the Longobards, with Ravenna for its capital, and twenty other towns of the Emilia, Flaminia, and Pentapolis, or the triangle of coast between Bologna, Comacchio, and Ancona.[2] More he had been unable to give, for this was all the territory the Longobards had shortly before acquired, and were now obliged to give up. In 774 Pepin's son, Charles the Great, after taking Pavia, became king of the Longobardic territory, stretching far southwards. No more could be said about the gift of

---

[1] It was incorporated in the official collection of the *Codex Carolinus.* Cf. Cenni, *op. cit.* 150.

[2] This is clear from the enumerations in the *Liber Pontif.* and the notice in Leo of Ostia. See Le Cointe, v. 484, and Mock, *De Donat. à Car. M. oblatâ,* pp. 8 *seq.*

Constantine ; Charles would have had at once to abdicate. Moreover, a strong Italian sovereign was wanted
at Rome, who from his own part of the peninsula could
also keep the Papal dominions in subjection ; at the
same time, the Roman lust for land and subjects and
revenues was not long satisfied with the Exarchate
and its belongings. So a document was laid before the
King in Rome, professing to be his father's gift or
promise (*promissio*) of Kiersy. He renewed it, as it
was shown him, and gave away thereby the greater part
of Italy, including a good deal that did not belong to
him ; for the document, as quoted in Adrian's Biography, specifies as territories to be assigned to the
Popes all Corsica, Venetia, and Istria, Luni, Monselice,
Parma, Reggio, Mantua, the duchies of Spoleto and
Benevento, and the Exarchate.[1]

It has seemed to every one mysterious and inexplicable
that Charlemagne should have made so comprehensive
a gift, leaving himself but little of his Italian kingdom
Accordingly Muratori, Sugenheim, Hegel, Gregorovius,
and Niehues have either declared the passage spurious,
or accused the Papal biographer of falsehood ; else, observes Niehues, we must accuse Charles of consciously

[1] *Lib. Pontif.* (ed Vignol.) ii. 193.

indorsing a perjury, and Adrian of a cowardly negligence.[1] Abel thinks the suspicions against the genuineness of the passage are strong, but not conclusive, and contents himself with assuming that the gift was really equal to Pepin's, but was very limited.[2] Lastly, Mock accepts the extent of the gift, but rejects its equality to Pepin's, and therefore the truth of Adrian's Biography; and Baxmann, the latest authority, leaves all uncertain.[3] In short, no one has succeeded in unravelling the secret.

But the thing explains itself when we compare the twice printed and wholly fabulous document,[4] professing to be the pact or bond of Pepin, and which really describes the geographical extent of the gift as it is stated in Adrian's Biography, only with the addition of more names of towns. This document is closely related to the Donation of Constantine. Like Constantine, Pepin gives an express account of his relations to the Pope as an explanation to the Greeks and Lombards of his gifts, and disclaims for himself and his successors all interest in the alienated territories, except the right

---

[1] *Geschichte des Verhältn. zwischen Kaiserthum und Pabsthum.* i. 565.

[2] *Forschungen zur deutschen Geschichte,* i. 469 seq. *Jahrbüch,* i. 131.

[3] *Politik der Päbste.* 1. 277.

[4] Fantuzzi, *Monum. Ravennati.* vi. 264; Troya, *Codice diplom. Longobard.* (Napoli, 1854), iv. 533 seq. Troya thinks the document genuine, which is unintelligible in a man of his information.

of having prayers offered for the rest of their souls, and the title of a Roman patrician ; for those territories were become the lawful property of the Pope through so many imperial deeds of gift. For this document, obviously composed in the style of the Donation of Constantine and the Roman biographies of Popes, it is difficult to assign any other origin or object than the purpose of having it laid before Charlemagne ;[1] and it shows how he was induced to make a promise he found it impossible to keep; for he henceforth vigorously withstood the perpetually renewed demands of the Popes, and made the counter requisition that Rome should prove its title to each particular domain separately.

There have unquestionably been some falsifications in the privileges granted to the Roman See by Emperors later than Charles the Great, though they do not go so far as has often been maintained. The pact or gift of Louis the Pious in 817 bears internal signs of genuineness, but has evidently been interpolated.[2]

[1] It must else have been meant for the eye of one of the later Carlovingians. Clearly it was designed for the eye of a Frankish king, and after the establishment of the empire Pepin's disclaimer of reserving any power in the alienated dominions would have no further object. We must therefore hold to Charles the Great, and the date of 774, and attribute the wrong name of the Pope to the ignorance of a later copyist.

[2] It has been held as a pure invention by most scholars, as Pagi, Muratori, Beretto, Le Bret, Pertz, Gregorovius, Baxmann, and lastly, that great

It makes the Emperor give the islands of Corsica, Sardinia, and Sicily, with the opposite coasts, and all Tuscany and Spoleto, to Pope Pascal. It is needless to observe that if Louis had really partly given and partly confirmed to the Pope the greater part of Italy in this elastic and unlimited fashion, the whole subsequent history of the Papacy to Gregory VII. would be an insoluble riddle ; for the Popes neither possessed nor once claimed those territories, which together make up a large kingdom. Innocent III. was the first to maintain that all Tuscany belonged to the Popes ; no one did so before him. Gregory VII. first claimed the duchy of Spoleto. The falsification certainly took place towards the end of the eleventh century, when matters were managed so actively and astutely at Rome ; for Gregory VII. was also the first to claim Sardinia, but he takes occasion to observe that the Sardinians have hitherto had no relations with the Roman See, or rather, as he thinks, have become as much strangers to it, through the negligence of his predecessors, as the people at the ends of the earth.[1] Urban II., indeed, in 1091, proved that Corsica was a Papal fief, not merely from

master in the criticism of the Caroline documents, Sickel, while Marini (*Nuovo Esame*, etc., Roma, 1822) and Gfrörer defend it as genuine.

[1] *Epist.* i. 29.

the gift of Louis or Charlemagne, but from the Donation of Constantine, which, as then interpreted, assigned
to Pope Silvester all islands of the West, including the
Balearic Isles, and even Ireland. So again with the
privileges of the Emperors Otho I. in 962, and Henry II.
in 1020. The documents are in both cases genuine, or
copies of genuine ones, in the main, but the statement
of the *Liber Pontificalis* about Charlemagne's Donation
was manifestly interpolated wholesale afterwards.[1]

It is well known that the Countess Matilda, who
was entirely under the influence of Gregory VII. and
Anselm of Lucca, gave Liguria and Tuscany to the
Roman See in 1077.[2] When we remember that Gregory VII., in 1081, required of the pretender Rudolph an
oath that he would restore the lands and revenues
which Constantine and Charlemagne had given to St.
Peter,[3] that Leo IX. had already solemnly appealed to
the Donation of Constantine, and that Matilda's adviser, Anselm, had inserted this Donation in his Codex,
we may easily judge what document was used to con-

---

[1] Cf. Watterich, *Vitæ Pont.* i. 45; Hefele, *Concil. Geschichte*, iv. 580;
Beiträge, i. 255.

[2] Leo Cassinensis in Pertz, *Monum. Germ.* ix. 733. Liguria means the
Lombardic duchies belonging to Matilda.

[3] *Ep.* viii. 8. 26.

vince her that she was obliged in conscience to make
so extensive an abdication or restitution.

We cannot suppose that such a man as Gregory VII.
would consciously take part in these fabrications, but,
in his unlimited credulity and eager desire for territory
and dominion, he appealed to the first forged document
that came to hand as a solid proof. Thus, in 1081,
he affirmed that, according to the documents preserved
in the archives of St. Peter's, Charles the Great had
made the whole of Gaul tributary to the Roman Church,
and given to her all Saxony.[1] A document forged at
Rome in the tenth or eleventh century is undoubtedly
referred to, which may be found in Torrigio.[2] Charles
there calls himself Emperor in the year 797, and his
kingdoms are Francia, Aquitania, and Gaul; Alcuin is
his Chancellor, and each of his kingdoms is to pay an
annual tribute of 400 pounds to Rome.

We have put forward these facts about the deeds of
gift, because they set in a clear light the line habitually
followed at Rome from the sixth to the twelfth century,

---

[1] *Ep.* viii. 23.

[2] *Le Grotte Vaticane* (Roma, 1639), pp. 505-510. As Acts of the Martyrs
had been fabricated there earlier, so, from the tenth century, false documents were fabricated wholesale at Rome, as the monographs about particular Roman churches prove. So the first document of 570 Marini quotes
(*Papiri Diplom.*, Roma, 1805) is an invention. See Jaffé, *Regesta*, p. 933.

and because their authors are undoubtedly the very persons chargeable with the fictions undertaken in the interests of ecclesiastical supremacy. We shall now continue our enumeration and examination of the forgeries by which the whole constitution of the Church was gradually changed.

The pseudo-Isidorian forgery of the middle of the ninth century has been already mentioned. Rome, as we have seen, had no part in that, though she afterwards took full advantage of it for extending her power, the substance of these forgeries being incorporated into the canonical collections of the Gregorian party.

The most potent instrument of the new Papal system was Gratian's *Decretum*, which issued about the middle of the twelfth century from the first school of Law in Europe, the juristic teacher of the whole of Western Christendom, Bologna. In this work the Isidorian forgeries were combined with those of the Gregorian writers, Deusdedit, Anselm, Gregory of Pavia, and with Gratian's own additions. His work displaced all the older collections of canon law, and became the manual and repertory, not for canonists only, but for the scholastic theologians, who, for the most part, derived all their knowledge of Fathers and Councils from it.

No book has ever come near it in its influence in the Church, although there is scarcely another so chokefull of gross errors, both intentional and unintentional. Not only Anselm, Deusdedit, and Cardinal Gregory, whose works had little circulation, but also the German Burkard (or his assistant, the Abbot Olbert) had pioneered the way for Gratian. Burkard had not only made copious use of the Isidorian fictions in his Collection, compiled between 1012 and 1024, but had also ascribed the ecclesiastical decisions in the capitularies to various Popes, so that from the middle of the eleventh century the erroneous notion took rise that the free determinations of Frankish Synods in the ninth century were the autocratic commands of Popes. All these fabrications —the rich harvest of three centuries—Gratian inserted in good faith into his collection, but he also added, knowingly and deliberately, a number of fresh corruptions, all in the spirit and interest of the Papal system.

It may be shown by certain examples, going deep into the development of the new Church system, how Gratian the Italian forwarded by his own interpolations the grand national scheme of making the whole Christian world, in a certain sense, the domain of the Italian clergy, through the Papacy. The German and

West Frankish bishops had already bowed to the Isidorian decretals. Their influence is shown in the decisions of the German National Synod at Tribur in 895. We may see here how deeply the pseudo-Isidore, with the imperial dignity of his Popes, and their dictatorial commands, had penetrated into the very lifeblood of the German hierarchy. It came to this, that the bishops had bound themselves most closely to King Arnulf, who was present, and took a prominent part in the Synod, and that he, desiring the imperial crown, which had already once allured him into Italy, could only obtain it by the favour of Pope Formosus. So they decided that, though the yoke of Rome should become intolerable, it ought to be borne with pious resignation.

How often has this saying been repeated since! It was ascribed to Charles the Great, just as Constantine is affirmed to have called the Pope a God. And since Gratian adopted it as a capitulary of Charles, and stamped it as a universal canon,[1] it became the current view up to the time of the Council of Constance, albeit sometimes contradicted in act, that it is a duty to endure the unendurable if Rome imposes it.

The corruption of the thirty-sixth canon of the

---

[1] *Dist.* 19. c. 3.

Œcumenical Council of 692 is Gratian's own doing.[1] It renewed the canon of Chalcedon (451), which gave the Patriarch of New Rome, or Constantinople, equal rights with the Roman Patriarch. Gratian, by a change of two words, gives it a precisely opposite sense, and suppresses the reference to the canon of Chalcedon. He also reduces the five Patriarchs to four; for the ancient equality of position of the Roman bishop and the four chief bishops of the East was now to disappear, though even the Gregorians, as, *e.g.*, Anselm, had treated him as one of the Patriarchs.[2] There was no longer any room for the patriarchal dignity of the Roman See; he who had drawn to himself every conceivable right in the Church could hardly exercise a particular patriarchal power in one portion of it. The plenary powers of the Pope were become a *mare magnum*, within which there could be no sea or lake of special privileges.[3] This showed itself conspicuously in reference to the provinces of Eastern Illyricum,—Macedonia, Thessaly, Epirus,

---

[1] *Dist.* 22. 6. The Roman correctors have substituted "nec non" for Gratian's fabrication of "non tamen," which was left for 400 years.

[2] Anselm and Deusdedit set aside the famous decree of Nicolas II., giving the German Emperor the right of confirming Papal elections, on the ground that one patriarch, the Roman, could not annul the decision of five patriarchs at Constantinople.

[3] The numberless privileges accorded by Popes to the Mendicant Orders were afterwards called a "mare magnum."

K

Dardania,—which were before under the patriarchal
jurisdiction of the Roman bishop, so that the metropolitan of Thessalonica was appointed his vicar over them.
The Emperor Leo, the Isaurian, separated those provinces
from Rome about 730, and they now belonged to the
patriarchate of Constantinople. There was a long dispute about it; the perpetually renewed demands of the
Popes gained no attention at Constantinople till the
establishment of the Latin Empire there in 1204 gave
them power for the moment in these Eastern lands
also. And it is significant that Innocent III., far from
attempting to resume his ancient patriarchal rights there,
made the Bishop of Tornobus Patriarch,—an ephemeral
creation, soon to be again extinguished.[1]

The canon of the African Synod,—that immoveable
stumblingblock of all Papalists,—which forbids any
appeal beyond the seas, *i.e.*, to Rome, Gratian adapted
to the service of the new system by an addition which
made the Synod affirm precisely what it denies. If
Isidore undertook by his fabrications to annul the old
law forbidding bishops being moved from one see to
another, Gratian, following Anselm and Cardinal Gregory, improved on this by a fresh forgery, appropriating

[1] Le Quien, *Oriens Christ.* i. 96-98 ; ii. 24, 25.

to the Pope alone the right of translation.[1]   One of the -
most important of his additions, and also an evidence of
the wide divergence between the old and new Church
law, is the chapter—also based on Anselm, Deusdedit,
and Cardinal Gregory—which elaborated a system of -
religious persecution.[2]   While, on the one hand, by falsifying a canon quoted by Ivo and Burkard, he makes
Gregory the Great order that the Church should protect
homicides and murderers ;[3] on the other hand, he takes
great pains to inculcate, in a long series of canons, that -
it is lawful, nay, a duty, to constrain men to goodness, -
and therefore to faith, and to what was then reckoned -
matter of faith, by all means of physical compulsion, -
and particularly to torture and execute heretics, and -
confiscate their property.   In this he went beyond the -
Gregorian canonists.   He does not fail to urge that -
Urban ii. had declared any one who should kill an excommunicated person, out of zeal to the Church, to be
by no means a murderer, and hence draws the general
conclusion that it is clear the " bad "—all who are declared " bad " by the Church authorities—are not only
to be scourged, but executed.

Still worse things may be found in the work of the

[1] *Caus.* 7. Q. i. 34.   [2] *Caus.* 23. Q. iv. 4, 5.   [3] *Caus.* 23. Q. v. 7.

Bolognese monk, which, through the instrumentality of the *Curia*, became the manual and canonical code of the West, to the scandal of religion and the Church, and this medley, not of simple, but complicated and multiplied forgeries, was rich in materials containing the germ of future developments, and cutting deep in their consequences into both the civil and ecclesiastical life of the West. So was it with the idea of heresy, which even then was fashioned into a two-edged sword, and veritable instrument of ecclesiastical domination. Pope Nicolas I. had affirmed, in his letter to the Greek Emperor Michael, that by the sixth canon of the Œcumenical Council of 381 (the first of Constantinople), which he grossly distorted, schismatics and excommunicated men were to be treated as heretics. Anselm and Gratian embodied this statement in their new codes ;[1] so that at the very time when heresy was stamped as a capital offence, the term received a terrible and unlimited extension, as indeed everything had been done by earlier fabrications to make heretics of all who dared to disobey a Papal command, or speak against a Papal decision on doctrine.

The earlier Gregorians had not laid down so clearly and nakedly as Gratian, that in his unlimited superi-

[1] *Caus.* 4. Q. i. c. 2.

ority to all law, the Pope stands on an equality with the Son of God. Gratian says that, as Christ submitted to the law on earth, though in truth he was its Lord, so the Pope is high above all laws of the Church, and can dispose of them as he will, since they derive all their force from him alone.[1] This became, and chiefly through Gratian's influence, the prevalent doctrine of the *Curia*, so that even after the great reforming Councils, Eugenius IV., in 1439, answered King Charles VII., when he appealed to the laws of the Church, that it was simply ludicrous to come with such an appeal to the Pope, who remits, suspends, changes, or annuls these laws at his good pleasure.[2]

In the fifty years between the appearance of Gratian's *Decretum* and the pontificate of the most powerful of the Popes, Innocent III., the Papal system, such as it had become in its three stages of development, through the pseudo-Isidore, the Gregorian school, and Gratian, worked its way to complete dominion. In the Roman courts Gratian's Code was acted upon—at Bologna it was taught; even the Emperor Frederick I. had his son Henry VI. instructed in the *Decretum* and Roman law.[3] The whole decretal legislation from 1159 to 1320 -

[1] *Caus.* 25. Q. i. c. 11, 13, 16.   [2] Raynald, anno 1439, 37.
[3] Cf. Böhmer, *Diss. de Decr. Grat.* in Pref. to his *Corp. Jur. Can.* p. xvii.

is built upon the foundation of Gratian. The same is true of Aquinas's dogmatic theology on all kindred points, as, indeed, the whole scholastic system in questions of Church constitution was modelled on the favourite science of the clergy of the period, Jurisprudence, as interpreted by Gratian, Raymund, and the other compilers of decretals. The theologians borrowed theory, texts, and proofs, alike from these compilations. As early as the twelfth century, in quoting a passage from Gratian, the Popes used to say, it was "*in sacris canonibus*," or "*in decretis.*"[1] And about 1570, the Roman correctors of the *Decretum*, appointed by three Popes, said the work was intrusted to them, that the authority of this most useful and weighty Codex might not be weakened.[2] So high stood the character of this work, saturated through and through as it is with deceit and error and forgeries, which, like a great wedge driven into the fabric of the Church, gradually loosened, disjointed, and disintegrated the whole of its ancient order, not, indeed, without putting another, and, in its way, very strong constitution in its place.

---

[1] Thus Alex. III. (*Decr. c. 6 de Despons. inpub.*), Clem. III. (*De Jure Patron. c. 25*), and Innoc. III., cite Gratian with the words, "in corpore decretorum."

[2] "Ne hujusce utilissimi et gravissimi Codicis vacillaret auctoritas."

§ VIII. *Progress of the Papal Power.*

Alexander III. (1159-81) and Innocent III. (1198-1216) were the chief authors of the development of the new system, and creators of the decretal canon law, through the number of their edicts, and the unity and coherence of their policy, based on one fundamental idea. The notion is more prominent with Innocent than even with Gregory VII., that the Pope is God's *locum tenens* on earth, set to watch over the social, political, and religious condition of mankind, like a Divine Providence, as chief overseer and lord, who must put down all opposition. The radical principle with him, as with Gregory, is that all rank and authority not held by priests is an incongruity in the Divine plan of the world, introduced through human folly and sinfulness, while the priesthood is, properly speaking, the sole ordinance and institution of God.[1] Gregory had declared, of course in direct contradiction to the Gospel teaching about the Divine institution of government, that the royal power was set up at the instigation of Satan, by persons ignorant of God, and full of crimes, out of mere lust of dominion, whereas before men had been equal.[2]

---

[1] See *Ep. ad Joan. Angl. Reg.* in Rymer's *Fœdera Reg. Angl.* i. 1, 119, "Institutum fuit sacerdotium per ordinationem Divinam, regnum autem per extortionem humanam," etc.

[2] *Epist.* lib. viii. Ep 21 : "Quis nesciat, reges et duces ab iis habuisse

New means of influence accrued to the Roman See
through the Crusades, and the consequent change in
the system of penance and indulgences, the privileges
awarded to Crusaders, and the leadership in these holy
wars, which, as a matter of course, devolved on the
Popes. The same end was served by the military
Orders, which acknowledged the Pope as their only
superior; the constant union with France, clergy as
well as kings (before 1300); and still more by the
intellectual power the Papal monarchy derived from the
two great Universities—Bologna, the school of Papal
canon law, and Paris, the home of scholasticism, which
was more and more lending itself to the Papal system.
But, above all, from the beginning of the thirteenth
century, the new Religious Orders of Mendicants, which
swarmed over the whole Christian world—Franciscans,
Dominicans, Augustinians, and Carmelites, especially
the two first—were the strongest pillars and supports
of this monarchy. After the Isidorian decretals and
Gratian, the introduction of these Orders, with their
rigid monarchical organization, was the third great lever
whereby the old Church system, resting on the grada-

principium, qui Deum ignorantes, superbiâ, rapinis, perfidiâ, homicidiis
postremo universis pene sceleribus, mundi principe diabolo videlicet agi-
tante, dominari cæcâ cupiditate et intolerabili præsumtione affectaverunt !"

tion of bishops, presbyteries, and parish priests, was undermined and destroyed. Completely under Roman control, and acting everywhere as Papal delegates, wholly independent of bishops, with plenary power to encroach on the rights of parish priests, these monks set up their own churches in the Church, laboured for the honour and greatness of their Order, and for the Papal authority on which their prerogatives rested. We may say that that authority was literally doubled through their means. They became masters of literature, of the pulpits, and of the university chairs ; they travelled about as Papal tax-gatherers and preachers of indulgences, with plenary power, even of inflicting excommunication. And thus the spiritual campaign organized at Rome was carried into every village, and the parish clergy generally succumbed to the Mendicants, armed as they were with privileges from head to heel. For they possessed and used the effective expedients of easy absolution, and new devotions and methods of salvation, invented by themselves, to which the parish priests had nothing to oppose, while their isolation made every attempt at open resistance on their part useless. They could compel both priest and people, by excommunication, to hear them preach the Papal indulgences, and could absolve from reserved sins in the confessional. Bishops and priests felt their impotence against the new power of these monks, strengthened by the Inquisition, and had, however indignantly, to bend under the yoke laid on their necks by two powers irresistible in their union.

If Gregory VII. supported his new claims, his political lordship and subjugation of the monarchy, on falsehoods, not indeed of his own coining, Innocent III. went further in this direction, and dealt with history as with the Bible, according to the exigencies of the case. He invented the story that the Empire had been transferred from the Greeks to the Franks by a Papal sentence;[1] and thence inferred that the German princes derived their right of electing the Emperor from the Pope only, and asserted that he had the right of rejecting their nominee. Later Papal authors have transformed these assertions into historical facts invented by themselves.

One of Gregory VII.'s maxims, ascribing personal holiness to every rightly elected Pope, was suffered to drop. There was danger of the want of holiness suggesting the invalidity of the election, and therefore the decretal books, while upholding the rest of Gregory's postulates, were silent about this. Moreover, every

[1] *De Elect.* c. 34.

one knew and said that simony, which was generally treated as heresy, was rampant in the Roman Court, and that taking bribes for benefices and legal proceedings was a daily occurrence with the Popes and Cardinals. The charge of heresy going on under the very eyes of the Pope, and with his express or tacit consent could not be answered, and was constantly urged, till the canonists hit upon the resource of maintaining that what was simony in others was not simony in the Pope, because he is superior to law, and everything in the Church is his property, which he can deal with as he will.[1]

The Gregorian system required the most complete immunity of the whole clergy from the secular power and civil courts. It served to create an immense army, exclusively belonging to the Pope, and widely separated by common caste feeling and caste interests from the lay world. Every clergyman was to recognise but one lord and ruler, the Pope, who disposed of him indirectly, through the bishops, who were bound by oath to himself, or directly, in cases of exemption, and used him as a

---

[1] Thus the canonist John of God, about 1245, quotes and repudiates the statement, "Lex Julia dicit quod apud Romam simonia non committitur" (*De Pœn. D. Papœ*). See excerpts in *Theodori Pœnitent.* (ed. Petit.) Paris, 1677. There was a long controversy about it.

tool for the execution of his commands. Gratian has adapted his Codex to these views, partly by means of the pseudo-Isidorian fabrications, partly by later corruptions of his own and the Gregorians.[1] The Papal prescriptions in the code of decretals, completely establish the principle that clerics are exempt from secular courts, and that by Divine ordinance.[2] The Popes added that no cleric could renounce this privilege, as it belonged to the whole Church.

One would have supposed there would be no further need for so perilous an instrument as falsification of texts, when all that was required for the development of Papal domination in Church and State could easily be built on the strong and broad foundation of Gratian's *Decretum.* And yet the same method was still pursued, and that too with texts of Scripture. Innocent III. wished to make Deuteronomy a code for Christians, that he might get Bible authority for his doctrine of Papal power over life and death; but for that the words had to be altered. It is there said that an Israelite may

---

[1] Thus (*Caus.* ii. Q. i. c. 5) he has expunged the words of a law of Theodosius confining the exemption to spiritual matters, and thereby wholly altered it. So (*ib.* c. 5) he changed the words "sine scientiâ Pontificis" into "sine licentiâ," to make the civil authority over clerics dependent on delegation from the bishops.

[2] *Decr. de Judic.* c. 4, 8, 10; *De Foro Compct.* c. i. 2. Q. 12, 13.

appeal to the high priest and chief judge, and if he does not abide by their sentence shall be put to death.[1] Innocent, by a slight interpolation in the text of the Vulgate, made this into a statement that whoever does not submit to the decision of the high priest (whose place the Pope occupies under the New Covenant) is to be sentenced by the judge to execution.[2] And Leo x. quoted the passage with the same corruption, in a Bull of his, giving a false reference to the Book of Kings instead of Deuteronomy, to prove that whoever disobeyed the Pope must be put to death.[3]

Innocent went beyond Gratian, above all, in fixing the relations of the Church to the State and secular princes. He taught that the Papal power is to the imperial and royal as the sun to the moon, which last has only a borrowed light, or the soul to the body, which exists not for itself, but only to be the slave of the soul, and the two swords (Luke xxii. 38) are a symbol of the ecclesiastical and secular power, both of which belong to the Pope, but he wields one himself and intrusts the other to princes to use at his behest, and

---

[1] Deut. xvii. 12.
[2] *Decr. Per Venerabilem,* "Qui filii sint legitimi," 4. 17.
[3] *Pastor Æternus,* Harduin, *Concil.* ix. 1826.

for the service of the Church.[1] In his famous decretal
Novit, Innocent was the first to lay down the theory,
often repeated by later Popes, that wherever a serious
sin has been committed, or is charged by one party on
the other, it behoves the Pope to interpose with his
judgment, to punish, and to annul the decisions of the
civil tribunal.[2] The principle this newly devised claim
is based upon must apply to every clergyman, parish
priest, or bishop, within his own sphere, and a general
domination of clergy over laity would follow, as in
Thibet; the Popes, however, claimed the right for
themselves alone.   Moreover there accrued to the Popes
new and unlimited powers, exalting them over princes,
peoples, and courts of justice, beyond what any mortal
had yet enjoyed, from the so-called "Evangelical
denunciation." It means that by asserting that it is
a sin on the part of the defendant not to admit the
right of the plaintiff, any cause can be brought before
the Pope, if he chooses to meddle with it,—before a
judge, that is, who is reponsible to God alone.[3]

[1] Innoc. III. in c. 6, *De Majorit. et Obed.*, D. i. 33.   Gregory VII. had
before used the symbol of the two heavenly luminaries, *Ep. ad Guil.
Regem.*
[2] C. 13 *de Judic.* D. 2. 1.   It belongs to the Pope " de quocunque peccato
corripere quemlibet Christianum."
[3] The chief authority is *Decret.* c. 13, De Judic. ii. i.

All roads at that time led to Rome. Whichever of the Isidorio-Gregorian maxims one started from, the result was the same. Either it was said the right of the Church is alone Divine, and therefore takes precedence of all other rights, but in the Church the Pope is the fountain and possessor of all rights, and thus every one is absolutely subject to him ; or, the Pope is the ruler of souls, but the body is the mere vassal and instrument of the soul,—therefore the Pope is also supreme over bodies, with power of life and death. And again, whoever disobeys a Papal command shows thereby that he holds wrong notions about the extent of Papal power, and the irresistible force of Papal commands and pro hibitions, and thus he incurs at least vehement suspicion of heresy, and must answer for his orthodoxy before the Holy Office.

The very names the Popes assumed or accepted mark the broad division between the earlier and new Gregorian Papacy. To the end of the twelfth century they had called themselves Vicars of Peter, but since Innocent III. this title was superseded by Vicar of Christ.[1] In fact the gulf between the position and rights of a Gregory I. and the pretensions and plenary power of a

---

[1] Beugnot. *Scriptor. Rerum Gallic.* x. Prof. 47.

Gregory IX., or between 600 and 1230, is as wide as from Peter to Christ. All bishops had formerly been styled representatives of Christ, but when the Pope laid claim to this title, it meant—"I am the representative on earth of the Almighty, and my power stands high above all earthly power and limitations, in me and through me is the Church free,"—according to the mediæval clerical view of Church freedom, which regarded the Church as free only if omnipotent, and the Church in the last resort as simply meaning the Pope.

Gregory IX. went still further in his assertion of an absolute domination over the State, when he declared, on the strength of the forged Donation of Constantine, that the Pope is properly lord and master of the whole world, things as well as persons, so that his predecessors had only in some sense delegated their power to emperors and kings, but had relinquished nothing of the substance of their jurisdiction.[1] Innocent IV. claimed, as self-evident, the same direct dominion over the world, and all that is in it, only that he proclaimed in yet stronger terms the absolute universal supremacy of the Popes, and the union of the two supreme powers

---

[1] See Huillard Bréholles, *Codex dipl. Frieder.* ii. iv. 921. "Ut in universo mundo rerum obtineret et corporum principatum."

in one hand. He thought it false to say that Constantine had given secular power to the Papal Chair, for this it possessed from the nature of the case and directly from Christ, who founded a kingdom, and gave to Peter the keys both of earthly and heavenly sovereignty. Secular power was only so far legitimate as secular princes used it by commission from the Pope. Constantine had in truth only given back to the Church part of what was hers from the beginning, and what he had no right to hold. If possible, he spoke even more disparagingly than Gregory VII. of the origin of secular princedoms and their possessors. Innocent IV. supplemented the hierarchical organization by adding a link hitherto wanting to the papal chain, when he established the principle that every cleric must obey the Pope, even if he commands what is wrong, for no one can judge him. The only exception was if the command involved heresy or tended to the destruction of the whole Church.[1] Boniface VIII. gave a dogmatic and

[1] *Comment. in Decretal.* Francof. 1570, 555. Innocent wrote this commentary as Pope. He has openly told us what amount of Christian culture and knowledge, both for clergy and laity, suits the Papal system. It is enough, he says, for the laity to know that there is a God who rewards the good, and, for the rest, to believe implicitly what the Church believes. Bishops and pastors must distinctly know the articles of the Apostles' Creed; the other clergy need not know more than the laity, and also that the body of Christ is made in the sacrament of the altar.—*Com-*

biblical foundation to the doctrine of the universality of papal dominion in his Bull, *Unam Sanctam*, where he condemns the independence of the civil power in its own sphere as Manicheism. He affirms that the Pope is judge over all secular matters where sin is involved, and holds the two swords, one to be used by himself, the other by kings and warriors, but at his beck and by his permission ; that he judges all, but is judged by none, being responsible to God only ; and that whoever denies this subjection of every human being to the Pope cannot be saved. His violent perversion of the clearest texts of Scripture in support of these claims was matter of astonishment and mockery even at the time.[1]

After the removal of the Papal See to Avignon, when the *Curia* had become French both in its *personnel* and its political line, the juristic dogmatism of the Popes was applied principally to the empire, and for centuries the steady aim of their policy was to break the imperial power in Germany and Italy and dissolve

ment. in Decr. 2. Naturally, therefore, the laity were forbidden to read the Bible in their own tongue, and, if they conversed publicly or privately on matters of faith, incurred excommunication by a Bull of Alexander IV., and after a year became amenable to the Inquisition.—*Sext. Dec.* 5, 2.

[1] See the writings of contemporary French jurists and theologians in Dupuy's collection.

its unity. Clement v. declared "by apostolical authority" that every emperor must take an actual oath of obedience to the Pope, so that he might form no alliance with any sovereign suspected by him.[1]

The Popes even insisted to the Greek emperors and patriarchs on the undoubted truth of faith that all fulness of spiritual and secular power, at least in Christendom, belonged to them. Thus Gregory IX. and Gregory X. "We know this," said the latter, "from reading the Gospel." Innocent III. wrote to the Patriarch of Constantinople that "Christ has committed the whole world to the government of the Popes." And he gives, as conclusive evidence of this, that Peter once walked on the sea, —the sea signifying the nations,—whence it is clear that his successors are entitled to rule the nations.[2]

One of the most far-reaching principles gradually developed from the Gregorian system was, that every baptized man becomes thereby a subject of the Pope, and must remain such all his life, whether he will or no. Every Christian, even though baptized outside the papal communion, is not only therefore subject to all papal laws (though invincible ignorance may be a

---

[1] *Clementin. de Jurej.* Tit. 9, p. 1058 (ed. Böhmer).
[2] Innoc. III. lib. ii. 209, *ad Patr. Constantin.* "Dominus Petro non solum universam Ecclesiam, sed totum reliquit sæculum gubernandum."

conceivable excuse in particular cases), but the Pope can call him to account and punish him for every grave sin, and this may extend to the penalty of death. For, in the first place, all disobedience to a papal command is either heresy or proximate heresy; and, moreover, the Pope can excommunicate him for his offences, and if he does not submit and receive absolution within a year, he is declared a heretic, and incurs death and confiscation of his goods.

§ IX.—*Papal Encroachments on Episcopal Rights.*

In order completely to subvert the old constitution of the Church and the regular administration of dioceses by bishops, the institution of Legates was brought in from Hildebrand's time. Sometimes with a general commission to visit Churches, sometimes for a special emergency, but always invested with unlimited powers, and determined to bring back considerable sums of money over the Alps, the legates traversed different countries surrounded by a troop of greedy Italians, and armed against opposition by ban and interdict, and held forced synods, the decrees of which they themselves dictated. Contemporaries in their alarm compared the appearance of these legates to physical calamities, hailstrokes or pestilence.[1] Complaints and appeals to Rome availed nothing, for it was a fixed principle with the Popes to uphold the authority of their legate.

The Pope in the new system is not only the chief, but is in fact the sole legislator of the Church. He, as Boniface VIII. expressed it, carries all rights in the shrine of his breast, and draws out thence from time to time what he thinks the needs of the world and Church require. And so it comes to pass that a single Pope of the thirteenth or fourteenth century, an Innocent III., Gregory IX., or John XXII., has made more laws than fifty Popes of an earlier period put together. The notions about the plenary powers of the Cæsars prevalent in the latter days of the Roman empire had their influence here, and the Popes called their acts by the same name as the Cæsarean laws, Rescripts and Decrees. And as the Pope makes laws by his supreme authority, so too he can wholly or temporarily suspend them ; thus he, and he alone, can dispense with Church laws, whether canons of Councils

---

[1] Cf. *e.g.*, Johann. Sarisb. *Opp.* (ed. Giles), iii. 331. *Polycrat.* 5, 16: "Ita debacchantur ac si ad Ecclesiam flagellandam egressus sit Satan a facie Domini."—*Petri Blesensis epist. ap. Baron. a.* 1193, 2 ff.

or decrees of Popes. The customary limitation—that he cannot dispense with the law of God—was frequently superseded by the canonists, especially since Innocent III., by his declaration about marriage, and the yet holier bond between a bishop and his diocese, which the Pope can dissolve at his good pleasure, prepared the way for the belief that it is not beyond papal power to dispense with some at least of the laws of God.

Whenever the Pope issued a new law the *Curia* reckoned what the necessary dispensations would bring in, and many laws were unmistakably framed with a view to the purchase of dispensations. So too with exemptions from episcopal jurisdiction; every exempted corporation or monastery had to pay a yearly tribute to the See of Rome, whose interest it was to thwart and restrain episcopal authority whenever it tried to act. And thus a bishop who took in hand the administration of his diocese in good earnest found himself cramped at every step, surrounded, as it were, in his own country by hostile fortresses closed against him, and in perpetual danger of incurring suspension or excommunication, or being cited to Rome for violating some papal privilege ; for every college and convent watched jealously over its own privileges and exemptions, and regarded the bishops as its natural enemies. And as bishops and corporations were in mutual hostility, so the parochial clergy found opponents and dangerous rivals in the richly privileged Mendicant Orders, who were indefatigable in their attempts to appropriate the lucrative functions of the priesthood, and to decoy the people from the parish churches into their own. The members of the *Curia*, as John of Salisbury remarks, had one common view : whoever did not agree to their doctrines was either a heretic or a schismatic.[1] The *Curia* wanted to be infallible even before the Popes made that claim. They thought this shield indispensable for carrying on their business.

The Popes made their first experience with the Pallium of the irresistible charm, which signs of honour, decorations, titles, distinctions in the colour and cut of a garment, have for ordinary men, and especially clerics, and thus learnt what effective instruments of power they might become. From the fifth century the Popes had bestowed the pall on archbishops named as vicars of their patriarchal rights, and in the eighth it began also to be given to metropolitans, although

---

[1] *Polycrat.* 6, 24. *Opp.* (ed. Giles), iv. 61. "Qui a doctrinâ vestrâ dissentit, aut haereticus aut schismaticus est."

these last hesitated to receive it on the conditions offered by Rome, as was proved by the attitude of the Frankish archbishops towards the thoroughly Romanizing Boniface.[1] On the strength of the pseudo-Isidorian fabrications, which exercised a most destructive influence on metropolitan rights, the Popes who became founders of the new system—Nicolas I., John VIII., Gregory VII.—insisted that a metropolitan could perform no ecclesiastical function before receiving this ornament. The next step was to ascribe a secret and mystical power to it, and when Paschal II., and all the Popes after him, and the Decretals maintained that the fulness of high priestly office was attached to it, it inevitably followed that this office is an outflow of the papal plenary power, so far as it extends. Meanwhile this notion of metropolitan jurisdiction being delegated from the Pope was developed in contradiction to facts; for the Popes had appropriated to themselves the weightiest and most valuable rights of metropolitans, and did this still more after the beginning of the thirteenth century; and next they began to give the pall to some bishops avowedly as a mere ornament, and without any single right being attached to it. But as a means

[1] Bonif. *Epist.* (ed. Serarius); Ep. 141, 142, pp. 211, 212.

for reducing metropolitans to complete dependence on Rome, sealed moreover by an oath of obedience, it quite answered its end. Gregory VII. altered the previous form into a regular oath of vassalage, so that the relation was one of personal loyalty, and the terms of the oath were borrowed from oaths of civil fealty.[1]

The next thing was to mould the bishops by a vow of obedience into pliant tools of the Roman sovereignty, and guard against any danger of opposition on their part to the expanding schemes and claims of the *Curia*. For a long time bishops were much better off than metropolitans, for in the thirteenth century they still received their confirmation—which in the ancient Church was not separated from ordination—from the metropolitan, while the latter had to buy the pall and the accompanying license to exercise this office at a high price from Rome.[2]

Innocent III. grounded on a misrepresentation of a passage of Leo I.'s letter to the Bishop of Thessalonica, whom he had made his vicar, saying, that he had committed to him part of his responsibility, and on one

---

[1] The "Regulæ Patrum," which the metropolitan previously swore to observe, was changed into "Regalia S. Petri."

[2] In the fifteenth century, German archbishops had to pay 20,000 florins [£1600], equivalent to ten times that sum now, for the pallium.

of the Isidorian fabrications, the principle that the
Pope alone has plenary jurisdiction in the Church,
while all bishops are merely his assistants for such
portions of his duty as he pleases to intrust to them.
This may be said to be the completion of the papal
system. It reduces all bishops to mere helpers, to
whom the Pope assigns such share of his rights as
he finds good, whence he can also assume to himself
at his arbitrary will such of their ancient rights as he
pleases.[1]

And now the term "Universal Bishop," used by the
Pope, gained its true significance. Though rejected even
by Leo. IX., it described quite correctly the Pope's position as understood at Rome since the beginning of the
thirteenth century. In the ancient sense of the word
there were no more any bishops, but only delegates and
vicars of the Pope.

A number of rights never thought of by the ancient
Popes followed as a matter of course. There was no
need of particular laws or papal reservations in many
cases ; it was enough to draw the necessary consequences
from the Isidorian or Gregorian fabrications and interpolations. It seemed self-evident that the Pope alone

---

[1] *Innoc.* III. *Ep.* i. 350 ; *Decret. Greg.* 3. 8.

could appoint and depose bishops, could interfere always and directly in their dioceses by the exercise of a concurrent jurisdiction, and bring any cases before his own Court. Innocent III., as we have seen, claimed a special Divine revelation for the Pope's right of deposing bishops. It has been charged against him as a wicked error and capricious invention; but we must remember that, when he had persuaded himself and others that every Pope possesses the fulness of jurisdiction, and is absolute ruler of the whole Church, not by concession of the Church, but by Divine appointment, he might fairly assume a Divine right to dispose of his bishops as an absolute monarch disposes of his officials. And, in fact, some bishops soon began to subscribe themselves as such "by the favour of the Papal See."

Whatever relics of freedom had hitherto been preserved . from the ancient Church were now trampled and rooted · out. No one had doubted before that a bishop could resign his office when he felt unequal to its duties. This was usually done at Provincial Synods. But from the time of Gratian and Innocent III., the new principle, that only the Pope can dissolve the bond between a bishop and his Church, was extended to the case of resignation also.[1] And then came the further requirement, made into a rule by John XXII., that sees vacated by resignation lapsed to the Pope.

Again, the appeals encouraged in every way by the Popes, and the ready grants of dispensations, paved the way for their acquiring one of the most important rights, in the appointment of bishops.   As the pseudo-Isidore had given an unprecedented extension and impetus to appeals to Rome, the new Decretal legislation since Alexander III. was specially adapted for multiplying and encouraging appeals to the *Curia.*   Alexander knew well what he was about when he declared appeals, which hung like a Damocles' sword over the head of every bishop, to be the most important of his rights. Some thirteen new articles in the Decretals[2] provided for the *Curia* being occupied annually with thousands of processes, which often extended over many years, bringing in a rich harvest to the officials, and filling the streets and also the churchyards of Rome. And a further point was secured by this, for the bishops and arch-deacons, impeded and disabled by the endless number of Papal exemptions and privileges, lost all desire to

[1] *D. de Translat.* c. 2 (1, 7).
[2] They are quoted in *Die Geschichte der Appel. von Geistl. Gerichtshof.* Frankfort, 1788, p. 127 *sqq.*

take Church discipline in hand, and thereby involve themselves in tedious and costly processes at Rome. And thus the anarchy in dioceses and wild demoraliza- tion of the clergy reached a point one cannot read of without horror in contemporary writers. When appeals came to Rome on disputed presentations to benefices or episcopal elections, the Popes often took occasion to oust both the rival claimants, and appoint a third person. Abbot Conrad of Lichtenau says,—"There is no bishopric or spiritual dignity or parish that is not made the subject of a process at Rome, and woe to him who comes empty-handed! Rejoice, mother Rome, at the crimes of thy sons, for they are thy gain; to thee flows all the gold and silver; thou art become mistress of the world through the badness, not the piety, of mankind."[1]

No people suffered more from these appeals and processes than the Germans. After the Concordat of Worms (1122), the Popes had gradually managed to exclude the German emperors from all share in episcopal appointments, and practically to nullify the Concordat. And then, partly from the circumstances of the German dioceses, partly from the new Papal enactments, most

[1] *Chron.* p. 221.

elections came to be disputed, and a handle was given to one party or the other for an appeal to Rome, which was taken full advantage of. The candidates or their proctors had to waste years in Rome, and either died there or carried home with them nothing but debts, disease, and a vivid impression of the dominant corruption there. The Popes could now dispose as they liked of the German archbishops and their votes for the empire; for besides the pallium, the heavy tax, and the oath of obedience, they had the Roman debts and censures to fear, in case of insolvency, and this constrained them to follow the Pope's guidance even in secular matters, supposing the oath they had sworn was not sufficient to make them into mere machines of the will of the *Curia.* These facts alone explain the elections of Henry Raspo in 1246, William of Holland in 1247, Richard and Alphonsus in 1257, and the miserable interregnum from 1256 to 1273. Only in this way could the ruin of the Hohenstaufen House have been accomplished, and Germany have been kept in the state of weakness and division required for the French and Angiovine interest, and the policy of the French Popes, Urban IV., Clement IV., and Martin IV.

During the thirteenth and fourteenth centuries the

Popes made gigantic strides in the acquisition of new rights and the suppression of other peoples'. Innocent III. had recognised the right of archbishops to confirm and ordain their suffragans,[1] but Nicolas III. (1280) reserved their confirmation to the Pope. In the ancient Church it was held uncanonical for a Pope or Patriarch to make appointments or bestow benefices out of his own district. The Popes began their meddling in the matter only by begging recommendations of favourites of their own, and without specifying any particular benefice. So was it still in the twelfth century. But soon these recommendations took the form of mandates. Italians, nephews and favourites of the Popes, persons who had aided them in the controversies of the day, or suffered in their interest, were to be provided for, enriched, and indemnified in foreign countries. Rights of patronage were not respected if they stood in the way; the Papal lawyer knew how to manage that, often through means of Papal executors appointed for the purpose. This caused loud discontent in national Churches; protests were made even at the Synod of Lyons in 1245. Meanwhile the Popes had another gate open for attaining rights of patronage. A great number of bishops and

[1] *D. De Elect.* c. 11, 20, 23 (1, 6).

prelates were drawn to Rome and detained there by
processes spun out interminably. They died off by
shoals in that unhealthy city, the home of fevers, as
Peter Damiani calls it, and now suddenly a new Papal
right was devised, of giving away all benefices vacated
by the death or resignation of their occupants at Rome.
Clement IV. announced it to the world in 1266, while at
the same time broadly affirming the right of the Pope
to give away all Church offices without distinction.[1]

Then came the reservations of the French Popes at
Avignon. They reserved to themselves a certain number of bishoprics, which, however, in France they often
had to bestow according to the pleasure of the king. At
the same time commendams were introduced, whereby
they sometimes gave abbacies to secular priests, and
other Church dignities to laymen.

The oath of obedience or vassalage the bishops had
now to take to the Pope was understood as binding
them to unconditional subjection in political as well
as ecclesiastical matters, whence Innocent III. declared the German bishops perjured who acknowledged
any other emperor than Otho whom he had chosen.[2]
It was by means of this oath that the Popes carried the

---

[1] *Sext. Decr.* 3, 4. 2.   [2] *Registr. de Neg. Imp.* Ep. 68.

exclusion of the Hohenstaufen from the throne.[1] According to Pius II., a bishop broke his oath who uttered any
truth inconvenient for the Pope, and he required the
Archbishop of Mayence by virtue of it to convoke no
imperial parliament without the Pope's consent.[2]

Thus the Roman Court became the universal heir of
all former authorities and institutions in the Church.
It had appropriated the rights of metropolitans, synods,
bishops, national Churches, and besides that, the powers
formerly exercised by the emperors and Frankish kings,
in ecclesiastical matters. The inevitable consequence
was to cripple the pastoral, whether parochial or diocesan
administration throughout the Church, and introduce a
general state of religious disease and decay, bishops and
parish priests withdrawing more and more from their
pastoral charges. This gave an immense lift to monas-
ticism, with its strongly organized centralization, and
the great religious communities became the centres of
all active Church life. The exemptions and other privileges, only to be obtained at Rome, bound them closely
to the Papacy, whose great support they were well
known to be against the bishops. Leo X. assembled
a commission, composed of members of the Religious

[1] Raynald. *Annal.* a. 1206, 13 ; Leibnit. *Prodr. Cod. Jur. Gent.* i. 11, 12.
[2] Gobellin, *Comm. Pii II.*, 65, 143.

M

Orders in Rome, to consult on the means for forwarding papal interests and their own against their common enemies, the bishops.[1] " For," says Pallavicini, " every monarchical Government must have a select body of subalterns in every province of the kingdom not subject to the immediate local authorities ; hence exemptions."[2] The monks were the willing and devoted servants and agents of the Roman Court against the bishops,[3] who were looked upon and treated as its born enemies.

At no time or place has the contradiction been so glaring between theory and practice, principles and proceedings, as during those centuries at Rome and Avignon. The Popes condemned all taking of interest, but the most elaborate banking business was carried on under their very eyes, and in close connexion with the *Curia,* who would have lost the breath of life, if the Florentine and Siennese capitalists and brokers had not advanced the required sums at usurious interest to the prelates, place-hunters, and numberless litigants. The papal bankers were a protected and privileged class, while everywhere else their fellows were under the ban,

[1] Bzovius, *Annal. Eccl.* xix. a. 1516.

[2] *Storia del Concil. di Trento,* 12, 13. 8.

[3] Bossuet says, " La cour de Rome regardant les évêques comme ses ennemis, n'a plus mis sa confiance et ses espérances que dans cette multitude d'exempts."—*Œuvres,* xxi. 461. Ed. de Liége, 1768.

and collected their debts and interest without mercy - under shelter of Papal censures.[1] As early as the twelfth century the *Curia* had made the discovery, which they were already reaping the fruits of in the thirteenth, that it was greatly for their interest to have a number of bishops, dioceses, and beneficiaries in their debt all over Europe, who were all the more pliant the more easily they could be held to payment by excommunication, and by putting on the screw of interest, at a time when ready money could generally be procured with difficulty only, and at an enormous interest. Thus Cardinal Nicolas Tudeschi, the first canonist of his day, observes that the Church dignities were so loaded with excessive imposts and extortions that they were always subject to debts, and nothing of their revenues was available for religious purposes.[2] Cardinal Zabarella saw clearly enough that the root of the ecclesiastical corruption was the doctrine of legal sycophants about the papal omnipotence, whereby they had persuaded the Popes that they could do whatever they liked. " So

---

[1] Cf. *Biblioth. de l'Ecole de Chartres*, 19e *année* (Paris 1858), p. 118, and Peter Dubois' account, about 1306 ("De Recup. Terræ Sanctæ," Bongars, *Gesta Dei per Francos*, ii. 315), of how one had to borrow many thousands " sub gravibus usuris ab illis qui publicé Papæ mercatores vocantur " to spend on the Pope and Cardinals.

[2] *Tract de Concil. Basil.* in *Pragmatica Sanctio* (ed. Paris, 1666), p. 913.

completely has the Pope destroyed all rights of all lesser
Churches that their bishops are as good as non-exist-
ent."[1]   Chancellor Gerson says, still more emphatically,
" In consequence of clerical avarice, simony, and the
greed and lust of power of the Popes, the authority of
bishops and inferior Church officers is completely done
away with, so that they look like mere pictures in the
Church, and are almost superfluous."[2]   The Bishop of
Lisieux observes later how the whole constitution of the
Church is in a state of dissolution, and everything has
long been full of quarrels and divisions through the
conduct of the Popes.[3]   And the Church, torn to pieces
with discontents and dissensions, made the impression
on thinking men like Gerson, Pelayo, d'Ailly, Zabarella,
and others, of having become " brutal," a hard prison-
house, where only dungeon-air could be breathed, and
therefore full of hypocrisy and pretence.   The Venetian Sanuto, in 1327, reckoned that half the Christian
world was under excommunication, including the most
devoted servants of the Popes, so lavish had they
been in the use of ban and interdict since 1071.[4]   Epis-

[1] *De Schismatibus* (ed. Schardius), pp. 560, 561.
[2] *Opp.* (ed. Dupin), ii. p. 1, 174.
[3] In a letter to Louis XI.   See Durand de Maillane, *Libertés de l'Eglise Gallicane*, iii. 6, 61, *sqq.*
[4] *Epist. ap. Bongars. Gesta Dei per Francos*, ii. 310.

copal officials, archdeacons, and all who could then excommunicate, followed the papal example in this respect. They considered the Roman Church their model, and inferred that they should not be niggardly in the use of such weapons. And if, as often happened, bishops themselves were suspended or excommunicated, simply for being unwilling or unable to pay the legates their journey money, why should laymen fare better? Thus it came to pass, as Dubois said in 1300, that at every sitting of the episcopal officials in France more than 10,000 souls were thrust out of the way of salvation into the hands of Satan;[1] and in every parish, thirty, forty, or even seventy persons were excommunicated on the slenderest pretexts. Absolution from censures could indeed be purchased, but an exorbitant price was often demanded.[2]

§ X.—*The Personal Attitude of the Popes.*

The means used by the Popes to secure obedience, and break the force of opposition among people, princes, or clergy, were always violent. The interdict which ⁻ suddenly robbed millions, the whole population of a

---

[1] *Mémoires de l'Acad. des Inscript.* (1855), xviii. 458.

[2] See the episcopal memorial drawn up for the General Council of 1311, Bzovius, *Annal. Eccl.* ann. 1311, p. 163 (ed. Colon.)

country,—often for trifling causes which they had no-thing to do with themselves,—of Divine worship and sacraments, was no longer sufficient. The Popes de-clared families, cities, and states outlawed, and gave them up to plunder and slavery, as, for instance, Cle-ment v. did with Venice, or excommunicated them, like Gregory XI., to the seventh generation, or they had whole cities destroyed from the face of the earth, and the in-habitants transported,—the fate Boniface VIII. deter-mined on for Palestrina.

It is a psychological marvel how this unnatural theory of a priestly domination, embracing the whole world, controlling and subjugating the whole of life, could ever have become established. It would have required superhuman capacities and Divine attributes to wield such a power even in the most imperfect way with some regard to equity and justice, and conscientious and really religious men would have been tormented, nay, utterly crushed, under the sense of its rightfulness and the corresponding obligations it involved. There was indeed no want of modest phraseology; every Pope asserts in the customary language that his merit and

---

[1] Verci, *Storia della Marca Trivig.* iii. 87.

[s] *Opere di S. Cat. de Siena,* ii. 160.

capacities are unequal to the dignity and burden, but for all that, their constant endeavour for centuries to increase their already excessive power is a proof that no need for restricting themselves was usually realized. There have been kings who said they would not be absolute rulers if they could. So the Popes of the first centuries could say, We desire not to rule over canons and councils, but to be ruled by them. But since Nicolas I., and especially since Gregory VII., the principle was avowed that the Pope is lord of canons and councils ; the law is not his will, but his will is law. In numberless cases, of course, his will was simply the custom and practical tradition of the *Curia*, and the Pope, the mightiest ruler in the world, was in one sense the most limited since the eleventh century, for he could only act as the temporary depositary of this capital of power, a steward who ought to increase, but must never suffer it to be diminished. The strongest will must succumb before the quiet, passive, but energetic resistance of a corporation bound together by common interests, working by a common rule, and striving for a common end ; how much more the good intentions of individual Popes, generally of great age when elected, who saw but a few years of work before them, and knew by long experience the firmness of that serried phalanx of officials surrounding them, whose opposition soon reduced them to a mere trunk without arms or feet. And thus it came to pass that, while those at a distance felt and said that the proverbial shortness of Popes' lives was a providential dispensation to save the Church from utter ruin,[1] the Popes admitted that they felt themselves the most unfortunate of men. Thus Adrian IV. was driven to the melancholy avowal that no condition is so pitiable as a Pope's, whose throne is planted thick with thorns, and his destiny only bitterness, with a heavy weight pressing on his shoulders.

It was this consciousness of supreme power in theory, and of lamentable slavery and dependence on a purely selfish Court in practice, combined with a feeling of the curse that must rest on such an administrative machine, composed of clerical parasites and vampires, which extorted the complaint uttered by Nicolas V. before two Carthusian monks, that no man in the world was more wretched and unhappy than he was, that nobody who came near him told him the truth, and that his Italians were insatiable,[2] etc. Still later, Marcellus II. exclaimed,

---

[1] Joh. Sarisb. *Polyc.* 6. 24 ; *Opp.* iv. 60 (ed. Giles).
[2] Vespas, *Vita Nicol.* v. in Muratori, *Script. Rer. Ital.* xxv. 286.

under a similar feeling of anguish, that he did not see how a Pope could be saved.[1]

One may say without exaggeration, that the individual Popes did not know the whole extent of their power, it was so immense. More than a century's legislation, steadily directed to the one end of self-aggrandizement, from the *Dictatus* of Gregory to the latest articles of the *Extravagantes*, had so well provided for every contingency, that a Pope could never be at a loss for some legitimate plea for interference, however purely secular the point at issue might be. By the formula, "non obstante," etc., the Pope's right was secured of suspending for that particular case any papal law which chanced to conflict with the interests of the *Curia.* The whole legislation of the ancient Church was gradually abrogated, or sometimes changed into the precise opposite. The papal decretals had devoured the decisions of councils, like Pharaoh's seven lean kine. What had become of the Nicene, Chalcedonian, and African canons? Like half-buried tombstones in a deserted churchyard, scattered fragments of this older order cropped up here and there. "It is clear as the noonday sun," said Chancellor Gerson, the

[1] Pollidor. *Vit. Marc. II.*, 132 (Roma, 1744).

most learned theologian and warmest friend of the Church in that age, " that the ordinances of the four first and subsequent General Councils have been metamorphosed and exposed to mockery and oblivion through the ever-increasing avarice of Popes, Cardinals, and Prelates, through the unjust constitutions of the papal Court, the rules of the Chancery, and the dispensations, absolutions, and indulgences granted from lust of domination." [1]

To the Popes, not to the German emperors, belongs the title "semper Augustus" as formerly understood. They are "always aggrandizers of the kingdom," *i.e.*, of their own. They became such under the sincere conviction, cherished from earliest youth, that the welfare of the whole Church and Christian world depended on their power being great and irresistible ; that their right and power, and theirs alone, was truly divine, and therefore unlimited, because no mere earthly right could limit an authority given from heaven. And we must recognise the sincerity of this conviction, by which the Popes were thoroughly possessed, even when it drove them to the use of crooked means, to falsification, forgery, and misrepresentation.

Everything which Popes had formerly shrunk from or

---

[1] *Tract. de Ref. Eccl. in Conc. Univ.* c. 17.

avoided, or been cautioned against, they now eagerly
seized upon. Gregory the Great had complained that,
under the pressure of business, his mind could not rise
to higher things.[1] Even Alexander II., in 1066, when
the great centralization movement was just beginning,
said that for five years he had scarcely been able to pay
any attention to the internal affairs of his own special
flock, the Church of the city of Rome, still less of
foreign Churches.[2] Early Church history was one long
warning for the Popes not to mix themselves up with
the affairs of foreign Churches, and want to decide
from a distance on one-sided and partial information.
Every one in the ancient Church, the Popes included,
was persuaded that nothing is more injurious in Church
matters than decisions made at a distance, in ignorance
of local circumstances. As a rule they made mistakes,
and involved themselves in humiliations and contradictory judgments. So it was with Basilides in Spain,
Hilary of Arles in Gaul, Marcellus of Ancyra, Eusta-
thius of Sebaste, Meletius at Antioch, with Eros and
Lazarus, and with Apiarius in Africa; constantly the
Popes made rash mistakes, and were deceived, imposed

[1] Greg. M. *Ep.* i. 1; vii. 25. 5.
[2] Bouquet, *Script. Rer. Gall.* xiv. 543.

upon, and misled through their hurried or importunate action. And constantly had the wisdom of the Nicene decision been commended, that everything should be examined and decided on the spot. The Popes and Gregorians were ready enough, indeed, to appeal to the Nicene canon, but they appealed to the spurious one. And if, in the fourth and fifth centuries, the Popes only interfered with the concerns of foreign Churches now and then at long intervals, and in the same way as the bishops of other apostolical sees, such cases occurred now by thousands in one year, and every new reservation was a copious source of emolument, so that Bishop Alvaro Pelayo tells us that whenever he entered the apartments of the Roman Court clergy, he found them occupied in counting up the gold coin which lay there in heaps.[1]

Every opportunity of extending the jurisdiction of the *Curia* was welcome. Nothing was too insignificant. Exemptions and privileges were so managed that fresh grants became constantly necessary. Thus, *e.g.*, the immunity from episcopal censures granted beforehand to individuals and whole colleges was an inexhaustible source of revenue. And the bishops on their side were

[1] *De Planctu Eccl.* ii. 29.

compelled to procure papal privileges, at least to enable
them to guard their property with censures against
holders of Roman privileges; the Bishop of Laon
obtained such a privilege from Urban IV.[1] So far was
the principle, "divide et impera," carried at Rome, that
even cathedral chapters, who are supposed to be the
immediate counsellors and presbytery of the bishop,
were armed with privileges and exemptions against him,
and he against them. If we look at the huge number
of Papal privileges conferred in the thirteenth century
on one national Church only, the French, we cannot
but marvel at the slavish spirit of the bishops, who
dared not move an inch without sanction from Rome,
as well as at the utter insignificance of the objects for
which special authorization or dispensation from Rome
was thought necessary. If a monastery wanted leave
for the sick to eat meat, or the inmates to talk at dinner,
a permission from the Pope was required. Above all,
bishops, convents, and individuals needed to protect
themselves by Papal privileges against the censures and
spiritual methods of extortion employed so prodigally
by the Legates.[2]

[1] *Gallia Christ.* vi. instr. 308.

[2] A clear idea of these may be formed from inspecting Brequigny's and
Pardessus' *Tables Chronologiques*, 1230-1300, A.D.

§ XI.—*The Relation of Popes to Councils.*

Hitherto the Church had known but one means of protection against internal corruption, that of Councils. But the attitude towards Councils taken up by the Popes since Gregory VII. made this too unavailing. Councils were perverted, as we shall see, into mere tools of Papal domination, and reduced to a condition of undignified servitude, which made them mere shadows of the Councils of the ancient Church.

All synods counted as œcumenical, and whose decrees had force throughout the universal Church, were held during the first nine centuries in the East,—at Nicæa, Ephesus, Chalcedon, and Constantinople. During that period the Popes had never once made the attempt to gather about them a great synod of bishops from differ-ent countries. Two centuries followed, the tenth and eleventh, without any great synod. In 1123, immedi-ately after the close of the Investiture controversy, and to confirm and seal the great victory won through the Gregorian system, Calixtus II. assembled a numerous synod, afterwards called Œcumenical (the first Lateran) at which, very significantly, twice as many abbots as bishops (600 to 300) were present. No contemporary

tells us anything of this first general assembly of the
West; it passed unnoticed, and left no trace behind.
The Pope promulgated at it certain laws on subordinate
points—simony, clerical marriages, and the Truce of
God. There is no sign of any action on the part of the
bishops; they seem to have been summoned merely as
a foil to the Papacy, for this was the first example of a
council professing to be œcumenical, where not the
Council, as for a thousand years, but the Pope published
the decrees in his own name.[1]

Sixteen years later, in 1139, Innocent II. assembled a
second Œcumenical Synod, again at Rome (the second
Lateran). Once more the bishops appeared as mere
passive witnesses to hear the Pope's lofty commands,
and to see him tear, with words of abuse, the pastoral
staff from the hand and the pallium from the shoulders
of prelates ordained by his rival, Pierleone.[2]

More serious and eventful was the third of these
Roman Church assemblies, held in 1179 by Alexander III.
(the third Lateran). There were but three sessions, and
the Pope published the twenty-seven canons he had put

---

[1] "Auctoritate sedis apostolicæ prohibemus" in first canon. Harduin,
Concil. vi. ii. 111.
[2] Harduin, i. 2. 1214. [Pierleone was the anti-pope Anacletus II.—
Tr.]

before them as enacted "with the consent of the Synod."
So completely did the world regard these assemblies as
mere arrangements for the solemn promulgation of papal
commands, that the Emperor described the third Lateran
Synod in a document as "the Council of the Supreme
Pontiff."[1]

Any free deliberation in presence of an Innocent III.,
when in 1215 he summoned 453 bishops to the fourth
Lateran Council, was not to be thought of. From the
standpoint of the Popes at that time, the only business of
bishops at a Council must be to inform the Pope of the
condition of their dioceses, to give him their advice, and
form a picturesque background for the solemn promulgation of his decrees. Perhaps the greatest number of
bishops ever seen at a Western Council were present,
- besides ambassadors of sovereigns. Innocent had his
- decrees read to them,[2] and after listening in silence they
- were allowed to give their assent.[3] When they wished
to return home, the Pope forbade them until they had
paid him large sums of money, which they had to

[1] See Trouillart, *Docum. de Bâle*, i. 389,—"In generali Concilio summi
Pontificis . . . judicatum est."

[2] See Matt. Paris, *Hist. Angl.* ann. 1215. "Recitata sunt in pleno Concilio, capitula 70."

[3] We know the decisions only from their appearing in different parts of
Gregory IX.'s decretal book under the heading, "Innocentius III. in Concil.
Lat."

borrow at high interest from the brokers of the papal Court.[1]

The one act of the first Council of Lyons in 1245 worthy of record, was the deposition of Frederick II. by Innocent IV. with 144 bishops, chiefly Spanish and French.[2] In this affair of such high importance to Italy and Germany, these two nations were either not at all, or very inadequately, represented ; it was an assembly chiefly composed of prelates from foreign nations which supported the Pope in his procedure, and allowed itself thus to help him in meddling with the concerns of Italy and Germany. The right of deposing the Emperor, and thereby plunging Germany and Italy into confusion and a long civil war, was again proved by the fables to which Gregory VII. had before ap-

[1] Matt. Paris, *Hist. Minor*, Lond. 1866, ii. 176.

[2] We learn from from Raynaldus (*Annal.* ann. 1245, i.) that Innocent only summoned the Archbishop of Sens with his suffragans, the King of France, and a number of English bishops. Raynaldus, who had the papal Register, with all the documents before him, could not disclose more. The German prelates, who had come to Lyons, departed shortly before the opening of the Council. Innocent therefore avoided calling it a General Council ; and it is a proof of the unhistorical and unscientific character of so many theological manuals, that they usually cite this as an Œcumenical Council, though it has no claim on the conditions they themselves give to being such. Still more glaringly is this true of the Council of Vienne in 1311, to which Clement V. himself said, that he had only summoned certain selected bishops.—See his Letter to the Emperor Henry III. in Raynald. *Annal.* ann. 1311.

N

pealed, viz., that Pope Innocent had excommunicated
the Emperor Arcadius, and Pope Anastasius had not
only excommunicated the Emperor Anastasius, but
deprived him of his empire.[1] The natural inference
was, that the Popes could do to a German Emperor
what they had done to the Greek Emperor at Constantinople. This time again the bishops and abbots had
to pay or promise the Pope large sums for carrying on
his war against the Emperor, and thus to burden their
churches and convents with heavy debts.[2]

The second Synod of Lyons, counted as the sixth
Œcumenical Council of the West, at which 500 bishops
and twice as many abbots assembled in 1274, was convoked by the best Pope of that age, who, had it only
been possible, would gladly have repaired the mischief
done by the policy of his predecessors—Gregory x.
But even he did not venture to restore the old forms of
Councils, necessary and helpful as they would have
been for effecting a reformation of the desolated and
disjointed Church. The union with the Greek Church
was a mere formal act concluded without any deliberation, and broke up again in a few years. For the rest,

---

[1] See the official historian of the *Curia*, Nicolas of Curbio, *Vita Innoc.*
IV. in Baluze, *Miscell.* i. 198, ed. Mansi.
[2] For fuller particulars, cf. Tillemont, *Vie de S. Louis*, iii. 83.

it is impossible to say what decrees the Pope had published at the Council, for the thirty-one articles found in the papal Decretals, under the title, "Gregory x. at the Synod of Lyons,"[1] were partly promulgated during the Council, and partly afterwards, as the Pope himself declares.[2] Of the intended reform of the Church nothing was effected.

As the deposition of the Emperor Frederick was the one event of the first Synod of Lyons, so the suppression of the Templars was the one result of the Synod of Vienne in 1311. When at that Synod, to which he only admitted bishops previously selected by himself, Clement v. observed that a majority was favourably disposed towards the Order of Templars, he ordered a cleric to proclaim, that any bishop who spoke a word without being first asked for his opinion by the Pope, would incur the greater excommunication. And thereupon he announced that, " by the plenitude of his power," he annihilated the Order, although he could not abolish it on the strength of the criminal charges brought against it. But Clement himself was a mere tool of the French King ; to accommodate him he had ordered his inquisitors everywhere to extort confessions

---

[1] *Sextus Decretal.*   [2] Harduin, *Concil.* vii. 705.

from the ill-fated Knights-Templars by torture. And
yet he must have known before the Council met, that
the result of the investigation did not justify the penal
abolition of the Order. All he gained by it was, that
the King allowed him to put a stop to the process
against his predecessor Boniface VIII., which was a
source of pain, anxiety, shame, and humiliation for
Clement and the Papacy generally ; for if Boniface had
been condemned on the charge of heresy and unbelief
brought against him by King Philip, all his acts would
have become null and void, and a terrible confusion in
the Church must have followed. "This assemblage,"
says the contemporary writer, Walter of Hemingburgh,
" cannot be called a Council, for the Pope did everything out of his own head, so that the Council neither
answered nor assented."[1] The servitude of bishops
and degradation of Councils could go no further. And
now came a change for which the Great Schism prepared the way.

After the deposition of the last German Emperor
who deserved the name, July 17, 1245, the Papacy became the prey for French and Italians to quarrel over.
In the long contest of Popes and anti-popes, the old

---

[1] *Chron.* Walt. de Hemingb.   Lond. 1849, ii. 293.

weapons by which the Papacy had acquired its gigantic power became somewhat blunted ; the nations rebelled. A different spirit and different principles prevailed at the fifteenth century Councils of Pisa, Constance, and Basle, and the preponderance of Italian bishops was broken by new regulations. Even at the Synod of Florence in 1439, the forms of the ancient Councils and free discussion had to be allowed on account of the Greeks, and the mere dictation and promulgation of decrees previously prepared in the papal *Curia* had to be abandoned.

Soon, however, better days for the *Curia* returned. Julius II. inaugurated, and Leo X. concluded, the fifth Lateran Synod with about fifty-three Italian bishops and a number of cardinals (1512-17). That such an assemblage is no representation of the whole Church, that it sounds like a mockery to put it on a par with the Synods of Nicæa, Chalcedon, and Constantinople at a time when, by the admission of a bishop who was present, there were not four capable men among the 200 bishops of Italy, is evident to the blindest eye. Julius showed his appreciation of it, when he had a decree laid before it at the third session forbidding the annual market hitherto held at Lyons, and transferring it to

Geneva.[1] Prior Kilian Leib of Rebdorf expresses wonder in his annals at this being called a General Council, at which hardly any one was present besides the
usual attendants of the Court, and nothing of importance was done.[2] The papal decrees published there were,
however, far from unimportant. On the contrary, a decree was issued exceeding in weight and significance any
published in former Roman Councils, viz., Leo X.'s Bull,
Pastor Æternus, in which, while abolishing the Pragmatic Sanction in France, he declares as a dogma that
" the Pope has full and unlimited authority over Councils; he can at his good pleasure summon, remove, or
dissolve them." The proofs for this cited in the Bull
are all spurious or irrelevant. Earlier and later fictions,
partly borrowed from the pseudo-Isidore, are quoted to
show that the ancient Councils were under the absolute
authority of the Pope, that even the Nicene Council
supplicated him for the confirmation of its decrees, etc.
The long deduction, in which every statement would be
a lie, if the compiler could be credited with any knowledge of Church history, closes with the renewal of
Boniface VIII.'s Bull, *Unam Sanctam.*

---

[1] *Concil.* ed. Labbé, xiv. 82.   [2] See Aretin's *Beiträge,* vii. 624.

§ XII.—*Theological Study at Rome.*

It may seem strange that since the new system of
Church government centralized at Rome had come into
vogue, and the Councils had pretty well lost their
importance, the Popes should not have thought of
establishing a theological school in Rome at the seat
of the *Curia.* The profound ignorance of the Roman
clergy, and their incapacity for judging theological questions, was proverbial. As early as the end of the
seventh century, Pope Agatho had to make the humi-
liating confession to the Greeks, that the right interpretation of Holy Scripture could not be found with the
Roman clergy, who had to work with their hands for
their support. They could do no more than preserve
the traditions handed down from the ancient Councils
and Popes.[1] The Greeks, who were better versed in
Biblical studies, might well ascribe to this ignorance,
admitted by the Popes, the interpreting the prayer of
Christ for St. Peter (Luke xxii. 32) in a sense which
had never occurred to any one before, and which clearly
had but one object, viz., to secure authority in doctrinal
matters to the Roman Church, in spite of the undeni-

[1] Harduin, *Concil.* iii. 1078.

able rudeness and ignorance of its clergy. Their defects in learning and knowledge had to be supplied by special Divine inspiration. Gregory II. speaks, fifty years later, as modestly as Pope Agatho. Otho of Vercelli, in the tenth century, and Gerbert in the eleventh, expressed themselves strongly about this theological ignorance of the Roman clergy.[2] But since Gratian's time jurisprudence became the queen of sciences; exegesis of Holy Scripture, and study of tradition and the Fathers were dropped, for they would have led to suspicious results and dangerous disclosures, and would eventually have exposed the evil contradictions between the old and new law of the Church. The new codes of canon law, Gratian, the decretals, and the Roman imperial law, were studied; and, accordingly, Innocent IV. established a school of law in Rome, leaving theology to the distant Paris. Theology was never extensively prosecuted at Rome, or with any result, nor did those who wished to study it go there during the Middle Ages. Among the cardinals there were always at least twenty jurists to one theologian; and herein the *Curia* was genuinely Italian, or Italy genuinely Roman; for though from the beginning of the thirteenth

---

[1] Pertz, *Monum.* iii. 675.

[2] Maii, *Nova Coll.* vi. ii. 60. "In tantâ Ecclesiâ vix unus posset reperiri, quin vel illiteratus, vel simoniacus, vel esset concubinarius."

century there had been an emulation in establishing universities, it was never theology, but jurisprudence and medicine, that was thought of. Although they had some great theologians to show, as Aquinas, Bonaventure, Ægidius Colonna, the Italians gladly left the care of theology to the French, English, and Germans, and such of them as desired to become theologians, like those just named, had to seek their education and sphere of work abroad. Dante says of his countrymen that they only study the Decretals, and neglect the Gospels and the Fathers. And among Italians the Roman clergy did least for the cultivation of theological science.[1]

The Popes were the more ready to abdicate all influence through the cultivation of science, since so many other means of action were open to them, and such as could not in the long-run bear scientific examination. Moreover, they had the new Religious Orders of Dominicans and Minorites for that work, who, acting under the most stringent censure and discipline of Rome, exercised through their own Generals, and being accustomed to identify the interests of their own Order with those of the

[1] Reumont observes (*Geschichte der Stadt Rom*, ii. 678) that the intellectual productiveness of Rome was at best very slight.

Curia, had given every guarantee that they would repudiate whatever did not subserve the new Roman system. It was from the bosom of these Orders, especially the Dominicans, that the *Curia* selected its official court theologian—for one at least it was obliged to have—the Master of the Sacred Palace.

And thus, as Roger Bacon and contemporary writers generally state, juristic science, and not theology, was the sure road to Church dignities and preferment. For theology, as conducted by the school of St. Anselm of Canterbury, Abailard, Bernard, Robert Pullus, Hugh and Richard of St. Victor, and the other scholastics before Aquinas, had done nothing directly for strengthening the papal dominion over the world and establishing the Gregorian system. Nowhere in the writings of these theologians is there any exposition of the doctrine of Church authority on the basis of the papal system. The dealings with the Greeks, before and after the Synod of Lyons in 1274, and the newly discovered spurious testimonies of Greek Fathers and Councils, as well as Gregory IX.'s collection of Decretals, first introduced it into theology. The jurists were the first to prostitute their science to an instrument of flattery, and it was not till after the end of the thirteenth century that the theolo-

gians followed them in the same path. Those who took
that line belonged mostly to the great Mendicant Orders,
who had the most urgent reasons for advancing rather
than depreciating the plenary papal jurisdiction, to
which they owed the privileges and exemptions so
lavishly bestowed on them; and if any of their members
had written in an opposite sense, they would have been
sure soon to find themselves in the convent prison.
Only men in so extraordinary and abnormal a position
as Occam and other "Spirituals," could be influenced
in a contrary direction; and such writers, as we see in
the case of the acute Marsilio of Padua, could find no
certain track in the maze of forgeries and fictions, though
they saw through some of them.[1]

To this jurisprudence, viz., the corrupt system of
canon law perverted into an instrument of despotism,
and to the Papacy, the wretched state of moral and religious degradation throughout Western Christendom was
generally ascribed. By the united streams flowing from

---

[1] [Marsilio of Padua, a famous jurist, wrote a book called "Defence of
the Faith against the Usurped Jurisdiction of the Roman Pontiff," which
had the distinction of being the first work condemned in a papal Bull,
issued by John XXII. in 1327. It was answered in the *Summa* of Agostino
Trionfo of Ancona (dedicated to John XXII.), an Augustinian friar, who
maintained the Pope's absolute jurisdiction over the whole world, Christian or Pagan, and over Purgatory.—TR.]

these two fountains—both, up to 1305, Italian—the Bolognese School of Law and the *Curia*—men said the whole world was poisoned. " It is the jurists," according to Roger Bacon, "who now rule the Church, and torment and perplex Christians with processes endlessly spun out."[1]   And, in fact, the most powerful Popes, such as Innocent III. and Innocent IV., Clement IV. and Boniface VIII., attained as jurists the highest dignity and sovereignty over the world.   Bacon thought the only remedy was for canon law to become more theological or Biblical.   He saw a source of corruption, just as Dante did, in the papal Decretals, and the precedence over Holy Scripture assigned to them.[2]

We see how deep that remarkable man, Roger Bacon, saw into the causes of corruption which were hidden from most of his contemporaries, although he, like all the rest, could only form conjectures, and could not gain that clear insight which was impossible without historical and critical information unattainable in his day.   But he believed, and many for forty years (since 1225) had been hoping with him, that a purification of the Church was approaching, through the means of a God-fearing Pope, and, perhaps, with the co-operation

---

[1] *Opus Tert.* ed. Brewer, 1859, p. 84.   [2] Paradiso ix. 136-8.

of a good emperor, consisting essentially in a thorough reform of the system of Church law.[1]

§ XIII.—*The College of Cardinals.*

The two main pillars of the new Papacy, and, at the same time, the two institutions which knew how to fetter the Popes themselves, and make them subservient to their own interests, were the College of Cardinals and the *Curia.* In proportion as the rupture, partly conscious, partly unconscious, between the Papacy and the old Church order and legislation was consummated, the College or Senate of Cardinals took shape, and in 1059, when the right of papal election was transferred to it, became a body of electors.[2] Through the Legations, and their share in the administration of what had become

[1] Rog. Bacon, *Compend. Stud.* ed. Brewer, pp. 399-403. " Totus clerus vacat superbiæ, luxuriæ, avaritiæ," etc. Here, too, he dwells on the decay of all learning for forty years past, attributing it principally to the corruption of Church law.

[2] [Before 1059, the right of election resided in the whole body of Roman clergy, down to the acolytes, with the concurrence of the magistrates and the citizens. Nicolas II., acting under Hildebrand's advice, issued a Bull conferring the elective franchise exclusively on the College of Cardinals, reserving, however, to the German Emperor the right of confirmation. By a Bull of Alexander III., in the third Lateran Council (1179), two-thirds of the votes were required for a valid election, and this regulation is still in force. See Cartwright's *Papal Conclaves,* pp. 11-16, and cf. Hemans's *Mediæval Christianity,* pp. 73, 101, where the Bull of Nicolas is quoted at length. The forms to be observed in Conclave, still in force, were fixed by a constitution of Gregory X. in the Second Council of Lyons, 1272. —Cartwright, pp. 20 *seq.;* Hemans, pp. 362-3.—Tr.]

an unlimited sovereignty, the cardinals rapidly rose to a height from which they looked down on the bishops, who, as late as the eleventh century, took precedence of them in Councils. While the new system of Papalism was yet in its birth-throes, in 1054, the cardinal-bishops claimed precedence of archbishops; but in 1196 the archbishops still always took precedence of them. At the Synod of Lyons, in 1245, the precedence of all cardinals, even presbyters and deacons, to all the bishops of the Christian world was first fixed, and never afterwards disputed. By degrees it came to this, that bishops could only venture to speak to cardinals on their knees, and were treated by them as servants.[1]

It was not without set purpose that the Gregorians, Anselm and Gregory of Padua, and Gratian after them, had incorporated into their codes those passages of St. Jerome which affirm the original equality of bishops and presbyters, and reduce the superiority of bishops to mere customary law. These short-sighted architects of the papal system did not perceive that they were thereby laying the axe to the root of the Roman Primacy; all they wanted was to pave the way for

[1] See an anonymous French writing of the end of the fourteenth century, given in Paulin Paris, *Manuscr. Franc.* vi. 265.

the superiority of cardinals, and with it the domination of the *Curia*, and to build up the papal system on the ruins of the ancient episcopal system. As their views of the Church and the hierarchy were drawn exclusively from Gratian, bishops towards the end of the thirteenth century were brought to allow themselves to be made cardinal-presbyters, and even to regard as a promotion this degradation of the Episcopate to the Presbyterate, which in the first centuries of the Church would have been thought a monstrosity. In the palmy days of exemptions, of the overthrow of all ancient Church laws, and the loosening of the diocesan tie, at a time when the parochial system was torn to pieces by the strolling mendicant monks, this too became part of the system.

The rival principles of a cardinal oligarchy and of papal absolutism were long trembling in the balance in the Roman Church. There were Popes like Martin iv. and Clement v. who carried out their French policy against the resistance of the Italian cardinals; Popes before whom the cardinals scarcely dared to lift their eyes or utter a word, like Boniface viii. and Paul iv.; Popes who put to death their cardinals, like Urban vi., Alexander vi., and Leo x. But, as a rule, the College of Cardinals, to which the Pope owed his election, and which preserved the interests and traditions of the papal system, took the lead. They took care that the Popes should give up nothing of the accepted principles or let drop any particle of the plenary authority Rome had gained, and took in fact, as well as in theory, their full part in the government of the Church. They contrived to make the Popes in many cases the mere executive of their will. The later and still prevalent device, of carrying out plans the majority are opposed to with the aid of two or three cardinals like-minded with the Pope, and without consulting the College, was hardly adopted in the thirteenth century, or only under Martin IV. But Boniface VIII., Clement V., and John XXII., and the Popes after the middle of the fifteenth century, nearly all understood and adopted it energetically, and the more securely as they held the greater part of the body in their hands, through the dispensation of benefices and emoluments.

The struggle between absolute monarchy and oligarchy lasted really for two centuries. The cardinals wanted the Pope to be absolute and omnipotent in his external rule over national Churches, but they sought to bind him by conditions at the time of

election, and by a recognised share in the government
in the name of the *Curia*. Innocent VI., in 1353, had
repudiated any such conditions, on the ground that the
papal power bestowed by God in all its plenitude
could not be limited. But the attempt was constantly
renewed. A series of articles was put forward in conclave, which the new Pope, immediately after his election, and before consecration, swore to observe, partly
drawn up in the interests of the cardinals, as, *e.g.*, for
a participation of revenues between the Pope and cardinals, and their being irremoveable, partly with a view
of restricting the worst acts of extravagance and arbitrary power on the part of the Popes, by requiring the
assent of the cardinals. Eugenius IV. confirmed these
articles without thereby really binding himself.[1] Pius
II. took a similar oath, and swore to reform the Roman
Curia. It was an urgent necessity to keep secret these
capitulations, which in themselves presented a gloomy
picture of the misgovernment of the Church, as the Popes
of that age, in addition to all the other bitter complaints
against them, would have been charged on all sides with
perjury. Pius II., in spite of the articles he had sworn to,
acted just as arbitrarily as his predecessors. Nevertheless

[1] Raynald. *Annal.* ann. 1431.

the oath imposed on Paul II. in conclave in 1464 included still more articles. He was to have them read in public once a month, and to allow the cardinals to assemble twice a year to discuss how the Pope had kept his oath. Paul soon discovered, and was told by his flatterers, that his papal freedom was too much limited, and accordingly broke his oath, and compelled or induced the cardinals to subscribe a new and entirely changed capitulation, without reading it. He dragged back Bessarion, who was escaping from the room, and enforced his signature by the threat of excommunication. He rewarded the cardinals with a new head-dress, a silk cap, besides a scarlet cape, hitherto only worn by the Popes.[1] This occurrence did not prevent them from again devising a capitulation, on the death of Sixtus IV. (1484), for the new Pope to swear to; it provided afresh for the advantage and enrichment of the cardinals at the expense of Church discipline and order. Innocent VIII. took—and broke it.[2]

The same farce was enacted with Julius II. in 1503. The Popes swore to summon an Œcumenical Council at the earliest opportunity, and so the controversy went

[1] Card. Jacobi Papiens. *Comment. Francof.* 1614, p. 372.
[2] Raynald. *Annal.* ann. 1484. 23.

on repeating itself for nearly a century, the cardinals wanting a larger share in Church government and emoluments, the Popes refusing to stint themselves in the full enjoyment of their despotic power. The victory at last, as was inevitable, remained with the Popes, and in the course of the sixteenth century the cardinals lost again the rights they had hitherto maintained, and were reduced simply to advisers, whom the Pope might consult or not as he pleased, but whose opinions could not bind him.

It seemed like a Nemesis, that the Popes, who since Gregory VII.'s time were so ingenious in inventing oaths to entangle men's consciences and bring everything under their own power, now themselves took oaths, which they regularly broke. On the other hand, it is a riddle how the very cardinals who elected a Sixtus IV., an Innocent VIII., and an Alexander VI., one after the other, and thereby broke their own oaths, could suppose a Pope would be really withheld, by swearing to certain conditions at his election, from the seductions of absolute power. It was perhaps the lesser evil that the Popes eventually triumphed, for the despotism of an oligarchy is apt to be more oppressive than that of a single individual.

Unquestionably the influence over Church life exercised by the cardinals was mainly an injurious one. The institution was a later artificial creation, a foreign and disturbing element newly interpolated, a thousand years after the foundation of the Church, into the original hierarchy based on the ordinance of Christ and the Apostles. The cardinals wanted to excel the wealthiest bishops in expenditure, pomp, and number of servants, and Rome and the environs did not supply means for this. They wanted to provide their nephews and friends with benefices, and to enrich their families. In their interest, and to satisfy their wants, the order of the Church had to be disintegrated, heaping incompatible offices on one person to be allowed,[1] and the system of increasing the revenues of the *Curia* by simony to be constantly extended. It was they who lived and battened on the grasping corruption of the Church.[2] Before the thirteenth century there were only two examples of the union of the cardinalate with foreign bishoprics, but under Innocent IV.(1250) it became common, and thus the Roman Church supplied the precedent of the contempt

---

[1] This was carried so far in the fourteenth century that one cardinal held five hundred benefices. Cf. "De corrupto Eccles. statu," Lydius' edition of *Werke Clemang.* 1614, p. 15.

[2] Alv. Pelag. *De Planct. Eccl.* ii. 16, f. 52.

and neglect of official duties. Jacob of Vitry thought, even in his day, the revenues of the whole of France were insufficient for the expenditure of the cardinals.[1] The great Schism, from 1378 to 1429, was ascribed by Western Christendom solely to their greed and lust of power.

In the thirteenth and fourteenth centuries the cardinals sometimes elected Popes not of their own body, but this never occurred after the middle of the fifteenth. During all the twelfth and the first half of the thirteenth century papal elections took place within a few days of the decease of the last Pope, but after the Papacy had reached the summit of its power, and the Pope was regarded as the spouse of the Church, widowed by his death, long vacancies, sometimes of years, became common. It seemed as if the cardinals wanted to show the world by a rare irony how easily the Church could get on without him from whom, in the new theory, all her authority was derived. Thus Celestine IV. was elected after a vacancy of two years, Gregory X. after three, Nicolas IV. after one. Two years and three months elapsed between his death and the election of Celestine V. There was a vacancy of eleven months after the death of Benedict XI., and of

[1] *Acta Sanct.* Bolland. 23 Jun. p. 675.

two years and four months after Clement V., and the
Christian world had to get accustomed to every conclave
being the theatre of intrigues and quarrels between the
French and Italian nations, which fought for the possession of the Papacy, till at last the French acquired
exclusive possession of it.

The German nation was practically excluded from
the College of Cardinals at that time. The German
Popes, from 1046 to 1059, made no German cardinals.
During the contest of the Papacy against the Salic and
Hohenstaufen emperors, some Germans who declared
themselves against the Emperor were made cardinals;
as Cuno, Cardinal-bishop of Præneste in 1114, who, more
papal than the Popes, filled all Germany with excommunications in his office of Legate. After him there
is the Cluniac, Gerhard, and Ditwein in 1134. Then
Conrad of Wittelsbach, and Siegfried of Eppenstein, were
appointed on account of their hostility to the Hohenstaufen, and Conrad of Urach by Honorius III. After
him, the only German cardinal in the thirteenth
century is Oliverius of Paderborn, and then, for above
a century and a half, no German enjoyed the dignity.
We must remember that every German would lean to
the imperial side, and this, especially after French

policy became dominant in the *Curia*, would secure their exclusion. Urban VI., in 1379, when repudiated by the French and in the extremest distress, was the next to name some German cardinals.

§ XIV.—*The Curia.*

If we describe the great change which took place between the end of the eleventh century and about 1130, in the space of some forty years, by saying that *the Roman Church became the Roman Court*, this indicates a phenomenon of world-wide historical interest in its enormous consequences. The distinction between a Church and a Court is in truth a very great one. By the Church of Jerusalem, or Alexandria, or Ephesus, or Rome, or Carthage, had always been understood a Christian people united with their bishop and presbyters, a community of clergy and laity bound together by the ties of brotherhood.[1] Ordinary matters were settled in the permanent synod of the bishop and his clergy; weightier and extraordinary matters in a council composed of the neighbouring bishops. In such a Church there were laymen bishops and priests teaching and dispensing

---

[1] Thus in the well-known definition of St. Cyprian (*Ep.* 69), "Ecclesia est sacerdoti plebs adunata et pastori grex adhaerens."

sacraments, but no legal functionaries. Such a Church
could never become a court as long as the ecclesiastical spirit and usage prevailed. But now what used
to be called the Roman Church had become a Court,
that is to say, an arena of rival litigants ; a chancery
of writers, notaries, and tax-gatherers, where transactions about privileges, dispensations, exemptions, etc.,
were carried on, and suitors went with petitions from
door to door; a rallying-point for clerical place-hunters
from every nation of Europe. In earlier days those who
were ordained for the divine service in Rome and the
Roman Church had managed the business which its superior rank rendered necessary. Weightier matters were
settled at synods comprising the bishops of the province,
and a few persons sufficed for so limited a circle of affairs
as is indicated by the official collection of formularies,
the *Liber Diurnus*, so late as the beginning of the eighth
century. What a complete difference after the Worms
Concordat of 1122, and still more after Gratian! In comparison with the enormous mass of business, processes,
graces, indulgences, absolutions, commands, and decisions addressed to the remotest countries of Europe,
and even to Asia, the functions of the local Church
service sunk into insignificance, and a troop of some

hundreds of persons was required whose home was the *Curia*, and their ambition to rise in it, and whose constant aim was to contrive fresh financial transactions, to multiply taxes, and enlarge the profits that accrued to them and the papal treasury, which was always in want. Secure and unassailable in the service of such a power, the officials of the *Curia* did not trouble themselves about the hatred and contempt of the world which had been made tributary to them. " Oderint, dum metuant."[1] The warnings of the most enlightened men were vain. Early in the twelfth century, the great danger this change of the Roman Church into a Court must bring upon the Christian world had been seen through by men like Gerhoch of Reigersberg, St. Bernard, John of Salisbury, Peter of Blois, and almost all in that age whose mind we are still acquainted with.[2]

[1] What giant strides centralization had made, and the consequent increase of the business of the *Curia*, may be illustrated from the case of a single official. About the middle of the thirteenth century there was but one " Auditor Cameræ." About 1370, twenty auditors were hardly enough for the Pope alone, and every cardinal had several besides. Cf. Baluze and Mansi, *Miscel.* i. 479. It is mentioned here that under Gregory XI. seven bishops were at one time under excommunication, simply for not having paid the " servitia " for the decree of provisions.

[2] Gerhoch observes in his letter to Eugenius III., about 1150, " De corrupto Ecclesie statu " [Baluz. *Miscel.* v. 63), as something new and deplorable, " quod nunc dicitur Curia Romana quod antea dicebatur Ecclesia Romana." In his work, written some fifteen years later, *De Investigatione Antichristi,* he painted in darker colours the disintegration of the

Jacob of Vitry, who subsequently became a cardinal, after making some stay at the Court, perceived, as he writes to his friend (1216), that it had lost every vestige of real Church spirit, and its members busied themselves solely with politics, litigation, and processes, and never breathed a syllable about spiritual concerns.[1]

Among the bishops of Innocent IV.'s time there was not one more highly honoured and admired than Grostête, Bishop of Lincoln, nor one for a long time more devoted to the Pope. Dominated by Gratian and the Gregorian system, he supposed his episcopal jurisdiction was simply intrusted to him as a derivation from the papal. But the corruptions, which like a poisonous miasma penetrated from the *Curia* into every portion of the Church, the gross hypocrisy exhibited in declaring the taking of interest a mortal sin, while the papal usurers and brokers exhausted the churches and corporations in all countries with usurious imposts, and, beginning from London, had made every English bishopric

Church through exemptions bought at Rome, and the greed of the Romans. Cf. *Archiv. für österreich. Geschichtsquellen*, xx. 140 *seq.* He variously supplements and confirms St. Bernard's complaints about the disorder at Rome.

[1] Saint Genois, *Sur les Lettres inédites de Jacques de Vitry*, Bruxelles, 1846, p. 31.—"Cum autem aliquanto tempore fuissem in curiâ, multa inveni spiritui meo contraria, adeo enim circa sæcularia et temporalia, circa reges et regna, circa lites et jurgia occupati erant, quod vix de spiritualibus aliquid loqui permittebant."

tributary to them ; this and a great deal more led him shortly before his death to reproach the Pope with his tyrannical conduct in a letter sharply warning him to repent ; and he still prophesied, when on his deathbed, that the Egyptian bondage, to which the whole Church had been degraded by the Roman *Curia*, would become yet worse.[1]

Somewhat later, when Pope Nicolas III. wanted to make John of Parma, General of the Minorites, whom Pius IV. beatified in 1777, a cardinal, he declined, saying :—"The Roman Church hardly concerns itself with anything but wars and juggleries ('*truffæ*') ; for the salvation of souls it takes no care." The Pope answered, sighing, "We are so accustomed to these things

[1] *Epist. Roberti G.*, ed. Luard, p. 432, Lond. 1861 ; Matt. Par., *Hist. Angl.* p. 586, Paris 1644.—[There is a curious story told in the *Liber Monasterii de Melsâ* (ed. E. A. Bond, vol. ii. London, 1867, in the Master of the Rolls' Series) which illustrates the contemporary view of the subject in England, as to why "St. Robert Grostête," as the monastic chronicler calls him, was not canonized. It is said that, being summoned to Rome by Innocent IV. and excommunicated, he appealed from the judgment of the Pope to the tribunal of Christ, and two years after his death appeared by night to Innocent, in full pontificals, saying, " Arise, wretched man, and come to judgment," and struck him with his pastoral staff. In the morning the bed was found covered with blood and the Pope dead. "And therefore," adds the chronicler, "the *Curia* would not let him be canonized, although he was honoured by illustrious miracles." Cf. for another version of the story, Milman's *Lat. Christ.* vi. 293. It is true that Grostête excited the Pope's anger by refusing to confer a rich canonry at Lincoln on his nephew, a young boy (*puerulus*), but not true that he was excommunicated.—Tr.]

that we think everything we say and do is really beneficial." [1]

From the middle of the twelfth century the whole secular and religious literature of Europe grew more and more hostile to the Papacy and the *Curia.* German as well as Provençal poetry, historians as well as theologians— none of them as a rule attack the authority or rights of the Pope, but they all abound in sharp denunciations and bitter complaints of the decay of the Church occasioned by Rome, the demoralization of the clergy corrupted by the *Curia,* the simony of an ecclesiastical court where every stroke of a pen, and every transaction, has its price, where benefices, dispensations, licenses, absolutions, indulgences, and privileges are bought like so much merchandise. St. Hildegard, that famous prophetess on the Rhine, highly honoured by Popes and Emperors, predicted of the Popes, as early as 1170,—" They seize upon us, like ravening beasts, with their power of binding and loosing, and through them the whole Church is withered. They desire to subjugate the kingdoms of the world, but the nations will rise against them and the too rich and haughty clergy, whose property they will reduce to its right limits. The pride of the Popes,

---

[1] Salimbene, in Affo's *Vit. del B. Giov. di Parma,* 1777, p. 169.

who no longer observe any religion, will be brought
low ; Rome and its immediate neighbourhood will alone
be left to them, partly in consequence of wars, partly
by the common agreement of the States."[1]

More cutting and more terrible sound the words of
the northern prophetess, St. Bridget, who lived in Rome
some two centuries later. It has not prejudiced the
high reverence felt for her visions, universally regarded
as inspired, and defended in an express treatise by
Cardinal Torquemada, that they contain the most vivid
pictures of the corruption of the Papal See and its
Court, and their mischievous influence on the Church.
She calls the Pope worse than Lucifer, a murderer of
the souls intrusted to him, who condemns the innocent
and sells the elect for filthy lucre.[2]

Every one told the same tale. Bishops and abbots
had to exhaust and denude their churches and establishments to satisfy the greed of the court officials and
get their causes settled.[3] They bid against each other
in bribery. Every one, from doorkeeper to Pope, had

---

[1] This remarkable prophecy, with many more of St. Hildegard's, is in the
collections of Baluze and Mansi, *Miscel.* ii. 444-447.

[2] *Revel.* i. c. 41, p. 49, cf. iv. c. 49, p. 211.

[3] Bishop Stephen of Tournay, in 1192, said, "Romano plumbo nudantur
cclesiæ."—*Ep.* 16.

to be paid and fee'd, or the case was lost. It may be seen from the accounts of ambassadors, *e.g.*, of the deputies sent in 1292 from the Commune of Bruges, that giving once was not enough, but the fee had to be constantly repeated as long as the process lasted.[1] The cardinals' and Popes' nephews were quite inordinately insatiable. The jurist, Peter Dubois, thought it a misfortune for the whole of Christendom that the cardinals found themselves compelled to live by robbery, as their benefices were not productive enough. The upshot was, that poor men could neither hope to gain preferment nor could keep it, and bishops entered on their office already loaded with heavy debts, which were further augmented by the annates introduced in the fourteenth century.

In the eleventh century there was an energetic movement throughout the whole Church with a view to putting an end to the sale of benefices at royal courts, but now the Roman Court had made simony the supreme power everywhere. The little finger of the *Curia* pressed more heavily on the churches than ever

---

[1] They may be found in Kervyn of Lettenhove, *Hist. de Flandre*, ii. 589. Again Herculano (*Hist. de Portugal*) cites from the *Codex Vatican.* 3457, a bill of the Archbishop of Bruges, showing that he paid through the Roman bankers the sum of 3000 florins to nineteen cardinals in 1226.

the arm of kings. No one knew what remedy to suggest ; complaints and reproaches were disregarded, and synods were powerless and condemned to silence in the absence of the Pope or his legates. Every cleric excused his simonaical conduct by the example of the Roman Church. It was the common saying, that every one was taught from youth upwards to look on the Roman Church as the mistress of doctrine and the bright example for all other Churches; that what she approved and openly practised others must also approve and copy, and that they might on their side make their profits out of spiritual minis- tries and sacraments who had dearly bought the right to do so at Rome with their benefices, and who, indeed, could in no other way pay off the debts incurred there.

§ XV.—*The Judgments of Contemporaries.*

Bishop Durandus of Mende contemplates the Church of his age from many points of view, especially its con- dition in 1310 in Italy and the south of France, but he is always brought back to the one crying evil, and source of so many corruptions, the papal Court. "It is that Court," he says, "which has drawn all things to itself, and is in danger of losing all. It is always sending out into the various dioceses immoral clerks, provided with

benefices, whom the bishops are obliged obediently to
receive, while they have no persons fit for the work
of the Church.   It is continually extorting large sums
from prelates, to be shared between the Pope and his
· cardinals, and by this simony is corrupting the Universal Church to the utmost of its power.   While the
Curia goes on in this way, all remedies for the Church
are vain."[1]   He then enumerates the most necessary
reforms, without which the Church must sink deeper
and deeper in corruption, but they cut, in fact, at the
roots of the whole papal system as it had existed for
200 years, and therefore his book produced no effect
worth mentioning, though the Pope asked for it, and
it was laid before the Council of Vienne.

---

[1] Durandus says the Roman Church is reviled in every country.
Every one is ashamed of her, and charges her with corrupting the whole
clergy, whose immorality has exposed them to universal hatred.   It is the
fault of the *Curia*, he says, " ut . . . inde tota Ecclesia vilipendatur et quasi
contemptui habeatur."—*Tract. de modo Gen. Concil. celeb.* (Paris, 1761),
p. 300.   He, at the same time, differs widely in his devotion to the Pope
from his contemporaries Pelayo and Trionfo.   He maintains the Pope's
absolute dominion over monarchs, and insists on the Donation of Constan-
stine, and the rights that flow from it.   But he desiderates a certain decen-
tralization.   He wants the *Curia*, which has absorbed all Church rights
and jurisdiction, to give back some of them, and restore to national Churches
and bishops some freedom of action.   See *Tract. (ut sup.)*, p. 294, where
he says the Roman Court understands " omnia traham ad Me Ipsum " as
authorizing its appropriating the rights of all others exclusively to itself.
One would like to know whether this book, which holds up to the Pope
and cardinals, as in a mirror, so terrible a reflection of their misdeeds and
iniquitous acts against the Church, was ever read in Avignon.

One of the French Popes, Urban v., who had some good instincts, acknowledged the misery and corruption of the Church, and thought (in 1368) the cessation of Councils was the main cause of the mischief.[1] But he did not perceive, or at least did not say, that this was the fault of his predecessors, whose systematic policy had brought matters to such a pass that it was partly impossible and partly useless to hold Councils. This state of things led theologians, who wished to use Biblical language, to appropriate involuntarily the sayings of Old Testament prophets on the corruptions of their people, and to describe the Church of the day as the venal harlot whose shame God would shortly uncover in sight of all men. Nicolas Oresme, Bishop of Lisieux, for instance, does so in an address before Urban v. and the cardinals at Avignon in 1363.[2] Great, indeed, must have been the evil, when even bishops applied such expressions and metaphors to the Church and the Papal See; which coincided with those used by the sectaries of the time, and bordered closely on suspicious inferences as to their right of separating from so terribly corrupt an institution.

When we read all these accusations and these descrip-

---

[1] *Concil.* (ed. Labbé), xi. 1958.   [2] Brown, *Fasc. Rer. Expet.* ii. 487.

tions, agreeing in the main, of the *Curia* and the Papal administration—and the strongest things are invariably said by eye-witnesses,—and observe how the impressions and experiences of all classes are the same, we can understand how the Apocalyptic images and their fulfilment in Rome and in the *Curia* occurred to every mind. The transference of power from Italians to Frenchmen, through the removal of the *Curia* to Avignon, and the succession of French Popes who appointed for the most part cardinals of their own nation only, led to no important change. Only the Italians then became as keen-sighted as others in detecting the corruption of the Church, for the Papacy, with all its endless resources for the enrichment of so many Italian families, had slipped out of their grasp. They felt what Italy, or rather what "the Latin race," had thereby lost, for as yet there was no Italian but only a Latin national sentiment. Lombardy was half German. The inhabitants of Tuscany and the States of the Church believed themselves the genuine and only rightful descendants of the old Romans, and entitled, as such, to rule the world through the Papacy, which was their appanage; and thus Dante urges them in his letters not to endure any longer that the fame and honour of the Latin name should be disgraced by the avarice of the Gascons[1] (Clement v. and John xxii.) Even a man like St. Bonaventure, whom the Popes had loaded with honours, and who was bound by the closest ties to Rome as a cardinal and General of his Order, did not hesitate in his Commentary on the Apocalypse to declare Rome to be the harlot who makes kings and nations drunk with the wine of her whoredoms. For in Rome, he said, Church dignities were bought and sold, there did the princes and rulers of the Church assemble, dishonouring God by their incontinence, adherents of Satan, and plunderers of the flock of Christ. He adds that the prelates, corrupted by Rome, infect the clergy with their vices; and the clergy, by their evil example of avarice and profligacy, poison and lead to perdition the whole Christian people.[2] If the General of the Order spoke thus of the Roman Court, we may easily comprehend how its stricter members, the "Spirituals," went further still, and called the *Curia* the utterly corrupt "carnal Church," and predicted a great renewal and purification through a holy Pope, the *Papa Angelicus*, long looked for, but never willing to appear.

---

[1] *Epist.* ed. Torsi, Livorno, 1843, p. 90.

[2] *Oper. Omn. Supplem. sub ausp. Clem.* xiv. Trid. 1773, ii. 729, 755, 815. Cf. *Apol. contra eos qui Ord. Min. aversantur*, Q. 1.

It was not, therefore, as was commonly said, from the blindness of Ghibelline party spirit that Dante too applied to the Popes the Apocalyptic prophecy of the harlot on the seven hills who is drunk with the blood of men, and seduces princes and peoples; he had read St. Bonaventure, and puts directly into his mouth in Paradise the denunciation on the covetous policy of the Court of Rome.[1] It had occurred to him, as to others, that the Papacy was in fact the hostile power which weakened and unsettled the Empire, and was promoting its fall, and was thus furthering and hastening the appearance of Antichrist, who was held in check by the continuance of the Empire. And why should Dante scruple to speak out, when almost at the same time a bishop and official of the Papal Court, Alvaro Pelayo, pointed, from long personal experience and observation, to the very details which showed the fulfilment of St. John's prophecy of the harlot in the then condition of the Papacy?[2] Yet the whole of his great work is devoted to proving that the Papacy

---

[1] *Parad.* xii. 91-94.

[2] Pelayo says (*De Planct. Eccl.* ii. 28) "Ecclesia," but the context shows that the Court of Avignon is meant; and he says afterwards (37), "Considering the Papal Court has filled the whole Church with simony, and the consequent corruption of religion, it is natural enough the heretics should call the Church the whore."

is the power ordained by God to rule absolutely the world and the Church. It is very instructive to observe how this man, while examining the condition of the Church from every side, and painting it in lively colours, is obliged again and again to confess that it is the Papal See itself, and that alone, which has infected the whole Church with the poison of its avarice, its ambition, and its pride; that the clergy had become bitterly hated for their vices by the whole lay world, and that the Roman Court was mainly responsible for their corruption. All this is conspicuous on almost every page of his work. He observes that the bad example given by the Popes is universally followed, and the prelates say, " The Pope does so, and why not we?" Thus the whole Church is turned, as it were, into blood, and there is an universal darkening of head and members.[1] But if the reader expects Pelayo to come to the conclusion that the old order in the Church should be restored as far as possible, and a limit be set to this unlimited despotism, he will find himself greatly mistaken. He holds to the principle that the Pope is God's representative on earth, and that one can no

---

[1] *De Planct. Eccl.* ii. 48, 49. The work was written in 1329. The author says that even right-minded people no longer dare to utter the truth because of the persecution it would entail. Yet he became Bishop of Silva.

more dream of setting limits to his power, than any-
body, or the whole Christian world, would undertake
to limit the omnipotence of God.

His contemporary, Agostino Trionfo of Ancona, an
Augustinian monk, who wrote his *Summa* on the
Church by command of John XXII., had already discovered a new kingdom for the Pope to rule over. It
had been said before that the power of God's vicar extended over two realms, the earthly and the heavenly,
meaning by the latter that the Pope could open or close
heaven at his pleasure. From the end of the thirteenth
century a third realm was added, the empire over
which was assigned to the Pope by the theologians of
the *Curia*—Purgatory. Trionfo, commissioned by John
XXII. to expound the rights of the Pope, showed that, as
the dispenser of the merits of Christ, he could empty
Purgatory at one stroke, by his Indulgences, of all the
souls detained there, on the sole condition that some-
body fulfilled the rules laid down for gaining those
indulgences ; he advises the Pope, however, not to
do this.[1] Only those of the unbaptized, whom God
by His extraordinary mercy placed in purgatory, were
not amenable there to the Pope's jurisdiction. Trionfo

---

[1] *Summa de Pot. Eccl.*, Romæ, 1584, p. 193.

observes rightly enough that he believes the Pope's power is so immeasurably great, that no Pope can ever know the full extent of it.[1]

Petrarch, who for years had closely observed the *Curia*, saw and felt, somewhat later (1350), like St. Bonaventure, Dante, and Pelayo. In his eyes, too, it is the Apocalyptic woman drunken with blood, the seducer of Christians, and plague of the human race. His descriptions are so frightful, that one would suppose them the exaggerations of hatred, were they not confirmed by all his contemporaries.[2] The letter of the Augustinian monk of Florence, Luigi Marsigli, Petrarch's friend and pupil, is quite as outspoken about the Papal Court, which no longer ruled through hypocrisy—so openly did it flaunt its vices—but only through the dread inspired by its interdicts and excommunications.[3]

For four centuries, from all nations and in all tongues,

---

[1] "Nec credo quod Papa possit scire totum quod potest facere per potentiam suam." Such things were written in 1320 at the Pope's command, and in 1584, when this work, which exhibits the Church as a dwarf with a giant's head, was republished by the Papal sacristan Fivizani, Gregory XIII. accepted the dedication.

[2] Epist. sine Titulo. *Opp.* ii. 719.

[3] *Lettera del Ven. Maestro L. M. contro i vizi della Corte del Papa,* Genova, 1859. He calls the cardinals "avari, dissoluti, importuni, e sfacciati Limogini," most of them being of the province of Limousin, and the *Curia* at this time entirely in their hands.

were thousandfold accusations raised against the ambition, tyranny, and greed of the Popes, their profanation of holy things, and their making all the nations of Christendom the prey of their rapacity ; and, what is still more surprising, in all this long period no one attempted to refute these charges, or to represent them as calumnies or even exaggerations. The Roman Court, indeed, always found champions of its rights, knowing, as it did so well, how to reward them for their services. The later scholasticism moulded on St. Thomas, the copious literature of canon law, and the host of decretalists on the side of the *Curia*,—Italians first, and then from 1305 to 1375 from the south of France,—who fought and wrote for the Papacy as their special and eminently profitable subject, never yielded an inch of the enormous jurisdiction it had already acquired, but were always spinning out fresh corollaries of its previously acknowledged rights. During the long period from 1230 to 1520 the parasites of the Roman Court ruled and cultivated the domain of canon law as interpreters of the new codes; or, in the scriptural language of the cardinals who composed the Opinion of 1538, the Popes heaped up for themselves teachers after their lusts, having itching ears, to invent cunning devices for building up a system which made it lawful for the Pope to do exactly what he pleased.[1]

Nevertheless, not one of all this multitude undertook the defence of the Popes and their government against the flood of reproaches and accusations which rolled up from all sides upon them, nor one of the theologians and practical Church writers; all confined themselves to the question of legitimate right. They insist continually that the first See can be judged by no man, that none may dare say to the most reprobate and mischievous of Popes, " Why dost thou do so?" One must endure anything silently and patiently, bending humbly beneath the rod. That is all they have to say; only now and then the indignation of the secular and married jurists, who could not hold benefices, broke out against the clergy, who reserved all the good things of this world to themselves. Or they intimated the ground of their silence and connivance, like Bartolo, who said, " As we live in the territory of the (Roman) Church, we affirm the Donation of Constantine to be valid."

---

[1] *Consil. Delect. Card.* p. 106, in Durandus, *Tract. de Modo Concil.* Paris, 1671 ; " ut eorum studio et calliditate inveniretur ratio, quâ liceret id quod liberet." The Opinion was drawn up by Cardinal Caraffa, with the assistance of the most respected men in Italy, but when he became Pope Paul IV. he had the *Consilium* put on the Index. There have not been wanting persons who regarded it as an act of heroism for a Pope to put himself on the Index.

But the strength of a power like the papal must rest ultimately on public opinion ; only while contemporaries are convinced of its legitimacy, and believe that its use really rests on a higher will, can it maintain itself. In the thirteenth and fourteenth centuries, no one in Europe knew or even suspected the true state of the case ; no one was able to distinguish between the original germ of the primacy in the apostolic age and that colossal monarchy which presented itself before the deluded eyes of men as a work that came ready-made from the hand of God. The notion that manifold forgeries and inventions had co-operated with favourable circumstances to foster its growth, would have been generally rejected as blasphemy. They grumbled at the use the Popes made of their power, but did not question their right to it, and the obedience paid was more willing than enforced. At the beginning of the fifteenth century, and after the commencement of the Great Schism, a few men, like Gerson, D'Ailly, and Zabarella, began to open their eyes gradually to the truth, as they compared the existing state of the law with the ancient canons. They saw there must have been a portentous revolution somewhere, but how or when it happened they were still ignorant.

§ XVI.—*The Inquisition.*

A wholly new institution and mighty organization had been introduced to make the papal system irresistible, to impede any disclosure of its rotten foundations, and to bring the infallibility theory into full possession : it was the Inquisition.

Through the influence of Gratian, who chiefly followed Ivo of Chartres, and through the legislation and unwearied activity of the Popes and their legates since 1183, the view of the ancient Church on the treatment of the heterodox had been for a long period completely superseded, and the principle made dominant that every departure from the teaching of the Church, and every important opposition to any ecclesiastical ordinances, must be punished with death, and the most cruel of deaths, by fire.

The earlier laws of the Roman Emperors had distinguished between heresies, and only imposed severe penalties on some on account of their moral enormity, but this distinction was given up after the time of Lucius III., in 1184. Complete apostasy from the Christian faith, or a difference on some minor point, was all the same. Either was heresy, and to be punished with death.

The Waldenses, the Poor Men of Lyons, who at first did but claim the right of preaching, although laymen, and who with more gentle treatment would never have formed themselves into a hostile sect, were dealt with just like the Cathari, who were separated by a broad gulf from Catholics. Innocent III. declared the mere refusal to swear, and the opinion that oaths were unlawful, a heresy worthy of death,[1] and directed that whoever differed in any respect from the common way of life of the multitude, should be treated as a heretic.

Both the initiation and carrying out of this new principle must be ascribed to the Popes alone. There was nothing in the literature of the time to pave the way for it. It was not till the practice had been systematized and carried out in many places, that scholastic theology undertook its justification.[2] In the ancient Church, when a bishop had become implicated in the capital punishment of a heretic, only as accuser, he was sepa-

---

[1] *Concil.* (ed. Labbé) xi. 152.

[2] Thus St. Thomas (*Summa.* ii. 9, 11, art. 3, 4) tries to prove from the symbolic names given them in Scripture, that heretics should be put to death. Thus, *e.g.*, heretics are called "thieves" and "wolves," but we hang thieves and kill wolves. Again, he calls heretics sons of Satan, and thinks they should share even on earth the fate of their father, *i.e.*, be burnt. He observes, on the apostle's saying that a heretic is to be avoided after two admonitions, that this avoidance is best accomplished by executing him. For the Relapsed he thinks all instruction is useless, and they should be at once burnt.

rated from the communion of his brethren, as Idacius and Ithacius were by St. Martin and St. Ambrose in 385. It was the Popes who compelled bishops and priests to condemn the heterodox to torture, confiscation of their goods, imprisonment, and death, and to enforce the execution of this sentence on the civil authorities, under pain of excommunication. From 1200 to 1500 the long series of Papal ordinances on the Inquisition, ever increasing in severity and cruelty, and their whole policy towards heresy, runs on without a break. It is a rigidly consistent system of legislation; every Pope confirms and improves upon the devices of his predecessor. All is directed to the one end, of completely uprooting every difference of belief, and very soon the principle came to be openly asserted that the mere thought, without having betrayed itself by outward sign, was penal. It was only the absolute dictation of the Popes, and the notion of their infallibility in all questions of Evangelical morality, that made the Christian world, silently and without reclamation, admit the code of the Inquisition, which contradicted the simplest principles of Christian justice and love to our neighbour, and would have been rejected with universal horror in the ancient Church. As late as the eleventh, and first half of the twelfth century, the most influential voices in the Church were raised to protest against the execution of heretics. Men, like Bishop Wazo of Liege,[1] Bishop Hildebert of Le Mans, Rupert of Deutz, and St. Bernard, pointed out that Christ had expressly forbidden the line of conduct afterwards prescribed by the Popes, and that it could only multiply hypocrites and confirm and increase the hatred of mankind against a bloodthirsty and persecuting Church and clergy.

It is only the resolve to foster and develop the Infallibility theory at any cost that can explain the fact of not one Pope in the long line from Lucius III. downwards having swerved from this policy. Men of gentler views and milder character, like Honorius III., Gregory X., and Celestine V., would else certainly have mitigated the severity of the maxims of their predecessors, and put some restraint on the unlimited and arbitrary power the Popes had placed in the hands of fanatical and greedy inquisitors; for there was no want of complaints against the inquisitors, who often used their office for extorting money, and made the tribunal of the faith into a finance establishment. The Popes were overwhelmed with complaints and petitions for redress

---

[1] See Martene and Durandus, *Ampliss. Coll.* iv. 898, *sqq.*

—Clement V. mentions them;[1] but neither he nor a single Pope before or after him substantially diminished the power of the Inquisition, or in any way softened its Draconian code; on the contrary, the *Curia* was always requiring greater strictness and energy, and the Popes suffered the inquisitors, without a word of opposition, to formulize their cunning in bringing their victims to the stake, into the regular system of deceit and treacherous outwitting of the accused, that may be seen in the work of Eymerich the Dominican, adopted and disseminated by the *Curia*.[2]

It was Papal legates who induced Louis IX., when barely fourteen years old, to make the cruel law which punished all heterodoxy with death.[3] The Emperor Frederick II., busied in crushing the Guelphs in Italy, had, during the period when everything depended on his securing the goodwill or the neutrality of the Popes, who

[1] *Constit. Clementin.* Tit. 3. De Hæret.; " Multorum querela Sedis Apostolicæ probavit auditum," etc. Yet all previous and subsequent Bulls of the Popes only urged the inquisitors to a " justa severitas."

[2] *Direct. Inquis.* (composed at Avignon in 1376) Venet. 1607. [Several extracts from Eymerich may be found in the Appendix to Dr. Harris Rule's *History of the Inquisition.*]

[3] On April 12, 1229, the treaty was concluded at Paris, with the concurrence of two Papal legates, which robbed Count Raymond of Toulouse of the greater part of his possessions; and on April 14 appeared the law, enacted immediately for these territories of Languedoc and Provence, which Papal policy had torn from their possessor, and given to the Crown of France.—Vaissette, *Hist. Gen. de Langued.* (Paris, 1737), iii. 374 *seq.*

were threatening and pressing on him, issued those barbarous laws against heretics in 1224, 1238, and 1239, punishing them with burning and confiscation of goods, depriving them of every legal remedy, and imposing severe penalties even on their friends and patrons. Innocent IV. repeatedly confirmed these laws also, and herein the later Popes followed him, who constantly referred to them, and inculcated their fulfilment, pointing out that Frederick II., that great enemy of the Church, was under her obedience when he issued them. A Papal vice-legate, Peter of Collemedio, was the first to promulgate Louis's law in Languedoc; and it was again the Papal legate, the Cardinal of St. Angelo, who, on entering Toulouse that year, at the head of an army, introduced the Inquisition there.[1] In 1231, and the following years, inquisitors, delegated by the Pope, Conrad of Marburg and the Dominican Dorso, were raging in Germany, Robert, surnamed le Bougre, in France. And now Gregory IX., in 1233, handed over the office in permanence to the Dominicans, but always to be exercised in the name, and by authority of, the Pope.[2]

The binding force of the laws against heretics lay not

[1] Vaissette, iii. 382.
[2] No bishop, observes the Jesuit Salelles, has named even one inquisitor, only the Pope does that.—*De Mat. Tribunal. S. Inquis.* (Romæ, 1651), i. 81.

in the authority of secular princes, but in the sovereign dominion of life and death over all Christians, claimed by the Popes as God's representatives on earth.[1] Every prince or civil magistrate, according to the constant doctrine of the Court of Rome, was to be compelled simply to carry out the sentence of the inquisitors, by the following process : first, the magistrates were themselves excommunicated on their refusal, and then all who held intercourse with them. If this was not enough, the city was laid under interdict. If resistance was still prolonged, the officials were deprived of their posts, and, when all these means were exhausted, the city was deprived of intercourse with other cities, and its bishop's see removed. Thus Eymerich in the fourteenth, and Cardinal Albizzi in the seventeenth century, describe the process as drawn out by the Popes for the judges in questions of faith. Only the latter measure, Eymerich thinks, ought to be left to the Pope himself.[2]

The practice of the Inquisition, as time went on,

---

[1] As Innocent III. expressly states it, "non puri hominis sed veri Dei vicemgerens."

[2] *Director.* p 432; *Rispost. all' Hist. del Inquis.* Romæ, p. 104. In this one case the Papal legislation was really softened, for Boniface VIII. had ordered that magistrates who refused to execute the condemned should, if they remained a year under excommunication, then be themselves treated as heretics, and burnt.

became further and further removed from all principles
of justice and equity.   Innocent IV. especially occupied
himself (1243-1254) in increasing its power and severity; he directed the application of the torture, which
Alexander IV., Clement IV., and Calixtus III. approved.
The tribunal, as carried on in all important points
down to the fourteenth century, and described in
Eymerich's classical work, presents a phenomenon singular in human history.   Here mere suspicion sufficed for the application of torture; it was by an act
of grace that you were imprisoned for life between
four narrow walls, and fed on bread and water, and it
was a conscientious obligation for a son to give up his
own father to torture, perpetual imprisonment, or the
stake.   Here the accused was not allowed to know the
names of his accusers, and all means of legal protection
were withheld from him ; there was no right of appeal,
and no aid of legal adviser allowed him.   Any
lawyer who undertook his cause would have incurred
excommunication.   Two witnesses were enough to secure
conviction, and even the depositions of those refused a
hearing in all other trials, either from personal enmity
to the accused, or on account of public infamy, such as
perjurers, panders, and malefactors, were admitted.   The

inquisitor was forbidden to show any pity; torture in
its severest form was the usual means of extorting confessions. No recantation or assurance of orthodoxy could
save the accused; he was allowed confession, absolution,
and communion, and his profession of repentance and
change of mind was accepted *in foro sacramenti*, but he
was told at the same time that it would not be accepted
judicially, and he must die if he were a relapsed heretic.
Lastly, to fill up the measure, his innocent family was
deprived of its property by legal confiscation, half of it
passing into the Papal treasury, the other half into the
hands of the inquisitors.[1] Life only, said Innocent III.,
was to be left to the sons of misbelievers, and that as
an act of mercy. They were therefore made incapable
of civil offices and dignities.

The civil authorities had to build and keep up the
prisons, to provide wood for the burnings, and to carry
out the sentences of the Holy Office. If they refused

---

[1] Calderini (*De Hæret.*, Venet. 1571, p. 98), writing in 1330, appeals to
the directions of Benedict XI. that all the confiscated property should go
into the Papal treasury. The manual of the Inquisition, composed later,
at the beginning of the sixteenth century (ed. Venet. 1588, p. 270), says,
"Inquisitores . . . dicunt quod Romana Ecclesia vult, quod dimidia dic-
torum bonorum assignetur suæ cameræ." And the famous jurist, Felino
Sandei, bishop of Lucca in 1499, says, in his *Commentar. in Decret.* (De
Off. Ord. in cap. irref.), "Per Extravagantes pontificios bona hæreticorum
dividuntur inter Romanam Ecclesiam, episcopum et inquisitorem."

these menial services, or wanted to take cognizance first of the grounds of the sentence, they incurred excommunication, and if they did not repent and submit within a year, they fell themselves under the jurisdiction of the Inquisition on suspicion of heresy. But the inquisitors derived their whole power from the Pope;[1] they were his delegates, and no one was ever condemned to torture or the stake but in his name and by his general or special order. This began in 1183 with Lucius III. directing a number of heretics to be burnt in Flanders by his legate, the Archbishop of Rheims, and was continued for centuries afterwards with terrible consistency.[2] And thus it came to pass that perhaps more executions took place in the name and by command of the Popes of that period than in the name of any civil ruler.

In the thirteenth and fourteenth centuries the number of decisions on points of faith received throughout the Church was small as compared with the period after the Council of Trent, and the inquisitors had therefore full scope for the exercise of their own judgment as to

---

[1] The constitution of Benedict XI., quoted by Calderini, assures the inquisitors they are " absoluti a pœnâ et a culpâ" by Papal favour, through the privilege of Clement IV., and enjoy all the same rights as the Crusaders.

[2] Pagi, *Critic. in Baron.* a. 1183.

what was heretical, and used the frightful power left to them over the life and death of men simply according to their pleasure, for from their sentence there was no appeal. And as they almost always belonged to one or other of the two Mendicant Orders, whose great object was the furthering of the Papal system, they took the teaching of the Pope, so far as they knew it, as the safest and simplest criterion of the true faith. And as the great majority of the inquisitors were Dominicans, it is self-evident that, as Thomists, they would adopt this convenient and easy test. Whoever contradicted a Papal decision, or knowingly disobeyed a Papal command, thereby incurred the guilt of heresy, and was handed over to the secular power to be put to death. The Popes themselves had long since laid down this principle. " Whoever does not agree with the Apostolic See," says Paschal II., making a (spurious) citation from St. Ambrose, " is without any doubt a heretic."[1] And when the Archbishop of Mayence complained of the Concordat being violated by the Pope, Calixtus III. answered him, in 1457, that he must know this was an attack on the authority of the Pope, and that he thereby committed a flagrant crime of heresy, and incurred

---

[1] Martene, *Thesaur. Anecdot.* i. 333.

the penalties prescribed for it by divine and human laws.[1]

That contradicting the Pope was treated and punished as heresy was shown in the most pointed way, when the Minorites, who, as genuine disciples of St. Francis, wished to observe the rule of poverty in all its strictness, were condemned. John of Belna, the inquisitor at Carcassonne, appealed to the most famous canonist of that time, Henry of Segusio, who had declared that he is a heretic who does not receive Papal decrees, and that he lapses into heathenism who refuses to obey the Papal See.[2] As we said before, a number of the " Spirituals " paid with their lives for disputing the right of John XXII. to upset their rule and the Bull of his predecessor, Nicolas III.[3] No Council had condemned their opinion; it was only Papal authority, and in this case the authority of the reigning Pope, on the strength of which they were sentenced to the stake, and it went against all natural feeling to ascribe possibility of error to an authority which it was a capital offence to reject. Jurists and theologians who were building up the rights of the Inquisition went further still. Ambrose of Vignate

---

[1] Raynald. *Annal.* ann. 1457, p. 49.
[2] " Peccatum Paganitatis incurrit."—Baluze and Mansi, *Miscell.* ii. 275.
[3] *Tract. de Har.* (Roma, 1581), f. 11.

(who wrote about 1460) declares him to be a heretic who thinks of the sacraments otherwise than the Roman Church, so that if a theologian had then raised his voice against the recent decree of Eugenius IV. to the Armenians, and the errors contained in it, he would have incurred sentence of death.

As in the thirteenth century, so it was still in the sixteenth. Cornelius Agrippa describes the conduct of the inquisitors in his time, about 1530, as follows : " The inquisitors act entirely by the rule of the canon law and the Papal decretals, as if it was impossible for a Pope to err. They neither go by Scripture nor the tradition of the Fathers. The Fathers, they say, can err and mislead, but the Roman Church, whose head the Pope is, cannot err. They accept as a rule of faith the teaching of the *Curia,* and the only question they ask the accused is, whether he believes in the Roman Church. If he says Yes, they say, ' The Church condemns this proposition—recant it.' If he refuses, he is handed over to the secular power to be burnt."[1]

In the long strife of Guelphs and Ghibellines, inquisitors and trials for heresy were among the means constantly employed by the Popes to crush the opponents of

---

[1] *De Vanit. Scient.* c. 96.-- *Hagæcomit.* 1662, p. 444.

their policy and of the Angiovine preponderance. The Bolognese jurist, Calderini, maintains that whoever despises Papal decretals is a heretic, for he thereby seems to contemn the power of the keys. That might be applied to every Ghibelline.[1] Thus Innocent IV., in 1248, declared his great Guelphic enemy, Ezzelino, a heretic. In vain did he give assurance, through an ambassador, of the purity of his faith, and offer to swear to it ; Innocent stuck to his point, that Ezzelino was one of the Paterines (a new Gnostic sect), without being able to bring forward even any plausible ground for the charge.[2] John XXII. made still more copious use of the same means, partly for carrying out his own territorial claims, partly in support of the rule of King Robert in Italy. On this ground the Margraves Rinaldo and Obizzo of Este, zealous Catholics, and never Ghibellines, but Guelphs, found themselves suddenly declared heretics by the Pope in 1320, and subjected to a process of the Inquisition.[3] Two years afterwards the same thing happened to the whole of the stanchly Ghibelline house of the Visconti at Milan ; a Papal Bull announced to them that they were heretics,

---

[1] *Tractat. Novus Aureus et Solemn. de Hæret.* (Venet. 1571), f. 5. Calderini, adopted son of the famous Giovanni d'Andrea, wrote about 1330.

[2] Verci, *Storia degli Ecelini*, ii. 258.

[3] Muratori, *Annali*, xii. 138 (Milano, 1819).

and condemned all their adherents and subjects to slavery.[1] Similar cases occurred repeatedly.

When the Popes themselves made such a use of their judicial power in matters of faith, when Nicolas III. is reproached by his contemporaries with enriching his family through the plunder extorted by means of the Inquisition, one cannot be much surprised to find the inquisitors so habitually using their office for purposes of extortion, as Alvaro Pelayo complains. Clement V., however, declared that an inquisitor, "simply following his conscience," has full power to imprison, and even put into irons, any one he pleases.[2]

§ XVII.—*Trials for Witchcraft.*

When we affirm that the whole treatment of witchcraft, as it existed from the thirteenth to the sixteenth century, was partly the direct, partly the indirect, result of the belief in the irrefragable authority of the Pope, this will perhaps sound like a paradox, and yet it is not difficult to show that such is certainly the case.

For many centuries the relics of heathen misbelief, and the popular notions about diabolical agency, nocturnal meetings with demons, enchantments, and witch-

[1] Muratori, *op. cit.* 150.   [2] *Clement de Hæret.* c. " Multorum."

craft, were viewed and treated as a folly inconsistent with Christian belief. Many Councils directed that penance should be imposed on women addicted to this delusion. A canon, adopted into the collections of Regino, Burkard, Ivo, and Gratian, and always appealed to, ordered the people to be instructed on the nonentity of witchcraft, and its incompatibility with the Christian faith.[1] It was long looked upon as a wicked and unchristian error, as something heretical, to attribute superhuman powers and effects to the aid of demons. In the eleventh century it was still considered a heinous sin merely to believe in enchantments and the tricks of professors of witchcraft, as may be seen from Burkard and the penitentiaries. No one could then anticipate a time when the Popes would acknowledge this belief in their Bulls, and direct their subordinates to condemn thousands of men to death on the strength of it.

There is no trace of any belief in diabolical sorcery to be found throughout the liturgical literature of the

[1] This canon got into Gratian's *Decretum* as a canon of Ancyra, through a mistake of Burkard's, who took it from Regino, but misinterpreted the reference, as though this passage also came from the Ancyran canon. See Berardi, *Gratian. Can.* i. 40; *Regino* (ed. Wassersahleben), p. 354. Regino has compiled his chapter 371 from passages in the pseudo-Augustinian writing, *De Spiritu et Animâ*, with some additions.

ancient Roman Church. Even in the twelfth century John of Salisbury reckons the various kinds of belief in magic among fables and illusions. But at that time the writings of the Cistercians and Dominicans, filled with visions, legends, and miracles, began to spread in the Church,—writings such as the compilations of Cæsarius of Heisterbach, Thomas of Cantimpré, Stephen of Bourbon, and the like. At the same time, the principle became more and more definitely laid down that there were miracles among the numerous heretical sects, which could only be Satanic. And to this was added a notion wholly unknown in earlier times. As the legend of Theophilus spread in the West, the notion got into vogue that men could make a compact with Satan, securing them many enjoyments and the possession of preternatural powers.[1] Cæsarius and Vincent of Beauvais brought the first reports of such compacts being actually made, and soon the official Papal historians themselves, Martin the Pole and others, related that a Pope, Silvester II., had really attained the high-

[1] The story of the sorcerer Theophilus, " qui diabolo homagium fecit et per diabolum ad quod volebat promotus erat," appeared so important, that Martin the Pole and Leo of Orvieto embodied it in their abridgments of Papal and Imperial history. And from the end of the thirteenth century there are constant charges of persons, as, *e.g.*, the Bishop of Coventry in 1301, doing homage to the devil.

est dignity in the Church through a compact with Satan.

Hardly was the Inquisition established by the Popes, and the first inquisitors, acting under Papal commission, in full work in Germany and France, than heresy came to be mixed up with sorcery or Satan-worship. The Dominican theologians seized on an incidental expression of St. Augustine, used in mere blind credulity, in order to spin out a theory of impure commerce between human beings and demons, and children born of the *incubus.*[1] Aquinas became the master and oracle of this new doctrine ;[2] and soon it was not safe even to dispute the dark delusion.

In a Bull of 1231 Gregory IX. ordered the secular sword to be unsheathed in Germany against the newly discovered heretical abomination of which his inquisitors had informed him.[3] He related with full belief nocturnal meetings, where the devil appeared in the form of a toad, a pale spectre, and a black tom-cat, and

---

[1] *De Civ. Dei*, xv. 23.   He afterwards confessed himself, in reference to a similar statement (*Retract.* ii. 30), " se rem dixisse occultissimam audaciori asseveratione quam debuerit."

[2] *Summa*, Pars. i. Q. 51, art. 3, 6.

[3] Cf. Mansi, *Concil.* xxiii. 323 ; Ripoll. *Bullar. Ord. Prœd.* i. 52.   The Bull was wrongly referred to the Stedinger, as Schumacher shows, *Die Stedinger*, pp. 225 *sqq.*

wicked abominations were practised. The Pope owed this information principally to Conrad of Marburg, who had every one burnt who did not admit that he had touched the toad, and kissed the lean white man and the tom-cat.[1] In the south of France, the inquisitors, somewhat later, made similar discoveries; in 1275 a woman of sixty was burnt there for sexual intercourse with Satan.

It was chiefly the introduction of torture by Innocent IV. into trials for heresy, which helped to establish this idea by procuring all the requisite confessions. When Clement V. named inquisitors for the trial of the Knights-Templars, they soon extorted confessions at Nîmes by torture, that the devil had appeared as a black tom-cat in their nightly meetings, and demons in the form of women had committed fornication with them after the lights were extinguished.[2] About 1330, John XXII. ordered in a Bull, couched in general terms, that all who meddled with sorcery (the enumeration of such acts is

---

[1] So says Archbishop Siegfried of Mayence, in his letter to the Pope (*Albericus*, ann. 1233, p. 544, ed. Leibnit.) The Jesuit Spee, in his well-known *Cautio Crimin.* dub. 23, n. 5, has rightly observed that it was the Papal inquisitors who naturalized the notion in Germany:—" Vereri incipio, imo saepe ante sum veritus, ne praedicti inquisitores omnem hanc sagarum multitudinem primum in Germaniam importârint torturis suis tam indiscretis, imo, inquam verissime, discretis et divisis."

[2] Ménard, *Hist. de Nîmes*, Preuves (Paris, 1750), i. 211.

very comprehensive) should be punished, like heretics, with the exception of confiscation of their goods.[1]

From the middle of the fifteenth century, and particularly after Innocent VIII. had issued his Bull on witchcraft, the trials, which had before been comparatively few, began to be much more numerous. At first the inquisitors, who had had their hands quite free since the Bull of Pope John, took the opinion of jurists. The most renowned jurist of his age, Bartolo, about 1350, decided for death by fire.[2] This decision, which inaugurated the regular burning of witches, is very remarkable. Here we plainly see the mischief done by the crude, materialistic, hierarchical interpretation of the Bible by the Popes and their juristic and theological parasites. It lay in applying what Christ and the Apostles had spoken, in Oriental imagery, describing the spiritual by sensible figures, to worldly dominion and compulsory power over the lives and property of men. St. Paul's statement that "the spiritual man judges all things," was understood, and explained in the Bull *Unam Sanctam*, to mean that the Pope is the supreme judge of nations and kings. When Jeremiah describes his prophetic

---

[1] Cf. Binsfield, *Tract. de Confess. Malef.* (Trevir. 1596), p. 760.
[2] Ziletti, *Consil. Select.* 1577, i. 8.

office of denouncing the judgments of God, in Oriental language, as a commission to destroy and lay waste, the Pope interprets this of the power conferred on him by God to destroy and uproot what and whom he will. When it is said in the Psalms, of the future Messianic King, that he shall rule the heathen with a rod of iron, this was taken to prove the right and duty of the Popes to introduce the Inquisition with its capital penalties. Thus the Papal jurists corrupted theology, and the Papal theologians jurisprudence. And in the same spirit altogether the jurists declared, like Bartolo in his decision, that a witch must be burnt, because Christ says that he that abideth not in communion with Him is cast out as a rotten branch to be burnt.

In the work of Eymerich sorcery and witchcraft is treated as an undoubted reality, coming under the jurisdiction of the Inquisition. The limits between the lawful use of pretended magical powers, and the magic forbidden under penalty of death, long remained mutable and uncertain. In a Bull of 1471, Sixtus IV. reserved to himself as an exclusive prerogative of the Pope, the fabrication and engraving of the waxen lambs used as a preservative against enchantments. According to him, their touch bestowed, besides remission of sin, security against fire, shipwreck, lightning, and hail-stones. And soon after the Pope had thus himself encouraged the crude superstition of the people, Innocent VIII. in 1484 issued his Bull on witchcraft, in consequence of the laity and clergy in some German dioceses having opposed and endeavoured to thwart the inquisitors appointed for the prosecution of sorcerers. In this Bull the Pope repeatedly expresses his belief in the possibility of sexual intercourse with demons as "incubi" and "succubi," of women and animals when pregnant, fruits, vineyards, storehouses, and fields being injured through sorcery, of men and beasts being tormented, and men and women rendered impotent. He then complains of the hindrances thrown in the way of the inquisitors he had sent to put down such wickedness, by these prying clerics and laymen, who want to know more than is necessary,[1] and arms them with fresh powers. The inquisitors were Sprenger, the author of the notorious Witches' Hammer, and Institoris. In like manner, Alexander VI., Leo X., Julius II., Adrian VI., and other Popes, for more than a century after Innocent VIII., gave an ecclesiastical sanction to this delusion by their directions for the prosecution of magic.

---

[1] "Quærentes plura sapere quam oporteat."

Theology held itself bound to follow the precedent of its great master, St. Thomas, by indorsing the greatest absurdities of this belief in witchcraft. The main difficulty was only how to evade the force of the canon Gratian had cited from Regino, which every one took for an ordinance of the Council of Ancyra, whereby the Church had, as early as 314, declared the new doctrine about the works of Satan and his worshippers to be an error and denial of Christian truth, and had thus by anticipation described Popes and inquisitors as heretics. Most persons consoled themselves with the consideration that anyhow the Pope's authority stood higher, or that a different kind of witches was intended. "So many have been executed already," says the Dominican inquisitor, Bernard Rategno, about 1510, "and the Popes have allowed it." [1] Some Minorites, however, maintained belief in the reality of witchcraft to be a folly and a heresy, as, for instance, did Samuel Cassini and Alfonso Spina, and the latter thought the inquisitors had witches burnt simply on account of that belief. [2] But the Popes and the Dominicans maintained the reality of the diabolical

---

[1] Bern. Comensis, *Lucern. Inquis.* (Romæ, 1584), p. 144.
[2] *Fortalit. Fidei* (Paris, 1511), f. 365.

agency, and thus the two views stood out in sharp contrast in the fourteenth and fifteenth centuries. A man
might at the same time be condemned as a heretic in
Spain for affirming, and in Italy for denying, the reality
of the witches' nightly rides. But by degrees the threefold authority of the Popes, of Aquinas, and of the
powerful Dominican Order, prevailed, and all contradiction was put to silence. The teaching of the Domini
cans, Nider, Jacquier, Dodo, and the two leading Papal
theologians, Bartholomew Spina and Silvester Mazzo-
lini (Prierias), on sorcery and witchcraft, had all the
weight of Papal approbation. Spina expressly stated
that the truth and reality of the Witches' Sabbath, with
its horrors and wonders, rested on the authority of the
infallible Pope, in whose name and by whose commission the inquisitors tried the accused. And as some
jurists appealed to the pretended canon of the Council
of Ancyra, in Gratian's *Decretum*, on behalf of the victims sacrificed in shoals to this fanatical folly in Italy,
Spina did not hesitate to declare that the authority of
the Council, which had pronounced all this to be a
pure delusion, must succumb to the authority of the
Pope.[1]   So, too, the Jesuit Delrio appealed, in vindication

---

[1] *Malleus Malefic.* Apol. Prima (Francof. 1588), ii. 652-653.

of this whole system of superstition, to the sentences of the Popes on sorcerers and witches, which proved that they did not regard their wild vagaries as illusions, but as sober realities. "This," he continues, "is the opinion of all ecclesiastical tribunals in Italy, Spain, Germany, and France, and all inquisitors have followed it in practice. This therefore is the opinion and sentence of the Church, and to dissent from it is a sign of a heart not sincerely Catholic, and savours of heresy."[1]

Every literary attempt of physicians, jurists, naturalists, and theologians, to throw any light on the matter, and explain the natural causes of the supposed diabolical phenomena, was put down by the Roman censure, so far as its power reached. For a century, all works written in this sense were placed on the Index, as happened in the case of the works of Weier, Godelmann, Wolfhart or Lycosthenes, Agrippa, Servin, Della Porta, and others. On the other hand, all attempts were vain to get the Jesuit Delrio's most pernicious handbook of sorcery, which served as a guide for the judges, censured. Whoever dared to express doubts on the subject, or to expose the delusion, had to recant and admit that he had spoken under the inspiration of the Evil

[1] *Disquis. Mag.* i. 16.

Spirit, and was either imprisoned for life or burnt.
Such a recantation the theologian De Lure or Edeline
was compelled to make about 1460 ; but it did not
save him. When the priest Cornelius Loos Callidius
affirmed, a century later, that the unhappy women only
confessed under torture what they had never done,
and that thus gold and silver was obtained by a new sort
of alchemy out of men's blood, the Papal Nuncio imprisoned him. He had to recant, but relapsed, and after a
long imprisonment only escaped by his death the fate
of his contemporary Flade, the Trèves counsellor, who
was burnt for assailing the trials of witches on the
strength of the so-called canon of Ancyra.[1] As late as
1623, Gregory XV. ordered that any one who made a
pact with Satan, producing impotence in animals, or
injuring the fruits of the earth, should be imprisoned
for life by the Inquisition. At last, when these mischievous practices of the Inquisition had been carried on
for 170 years, and countless victims had been sacrificed
to the fancies of the Popes and monks, an instruction of
the Roman Inquisition appeared in 1657, containing the
shameful admission that for a long time not a single
process had been rightly conducted by the inquisitors,
that they had wickedly erred through their reckless

[1] *Disquis. Mag.* iii. 58, 227 *seq.*

application of torture and other irregularities, and that most dangerous mistakes were still made daily by them, as by the other spiritual tribunals, and thus unrighteous sentences of death were passed, whereupon certain mitigations and precautions were enjoined.[1] It is even now ordered in the Roman ritual, which, according to Papal injunction, is to be inviolably observed and exclusively used by every priest, that any one who has swallowed charmed articles (*malefica signa vel instrumenta*) must drive out Satan, who has thereby gained possession of him, by an emetic.[2]

§ XVIII.—*Dominican Forgeries and their Consequences.*

How far the principle that Roman decisions are immutable and infallible, had been already introduced, by means of the forgeries and fictions before referred to, at the beginning of the twelfth century, may be perceived from the French Bishop Ivo, who has adopted into his *Decretum* a copious store of such spurious pieces. His logic—and it has been repeated countless times since—comes simply to this: the Popes have asserted that this or that prerogative belongs to them, we must therefore believe that they really pos-

---

[1] It may be found in Piguatelli, *Consultat. Noviss.* i. 123; and without any alterations in Carena, *De Offic. Inquis.*, in the Appendix.
[2] *Rit. Rom.* (ed. Antwerp, 1669), p. 167.

sess it. He observes, naïvely enough, " We are taught by the Roman Church that no one may call in question its decisions, therefore we must flee to it for refuge from itself, *i.e.*, simply submit;"[1] and accordingly it is clear to him that to contradict a Papal ordinance is heresy. This implies that a bishop is orthodox who submits to a Papal injunction, though convinced that it is prejudicial to his Church; a heretic, if he opposes the incipient abuse or usurpation. This view involved momentous results : it has disarmed the Church; it has caused the neglect of that first principle of moral and political prudence, that an abuse should be resisted at the beginning, and thus made the corruption in the Church incurable, and the attempted reformation too late when it was at last undertaken.

About the middle of the thirteenth century a new and comprehensive fabrication was effected, which was not less eventful in its results than the pseudo-Isidorian, though in a different way. As the one served to transform the constitution and canon law of the Church, the other penetrated her dogmatic theology and ruled the schools.

In the twelfth and first half of the thirteenth century,

[1] *Epist.* 159.

theologians had not occupied themselves with the doctrine of Church authority, and, in some cases, had quite remarkably avoided pronouncing on the position of the Pope in the Church. Hugo and Richard of St. Victor, the compilers of "Sentences," Robert Pulleyn, Peter of Poitiers, Peter Lombard, and after them Rupert of Deutz, William of Paris, and Vincent of Beauvais, refrained from entering at all on the subject. The true fathers of scholasticism—Alexander of Hales, Alanus of Ryssel, and even Albertus Magnus, the most fertile of all theologians of that period—have equally abstained from investigating it. Only in one passage, when explaining the well-known prayer of Christ for Peter in St. Luke's Gospel, Albert observes that it implies that a successor of Peter cannot wholly and finally (*finaliter*) lose the faith.

The controversy with the Greeks, which the presence of Dominicans in the East had again brought to the surface, gave occasion for new inventions. To the Greeks, the Isidorio-Gregorian Papacy, which the Dominicans put before them as the sole genuine and saving form of Church government, was utterly unknown and incomprehensible. No attention had been paid at Constantinople to such claims when urged by Nicolas I., and in a more developed form by Leo IX. and Gregory IX.

in their letters to emperors and patriarchs, nor does any
reply seem to have been sent. In Eastern estimation,
"the Patriarch of old Rome" was indeed the first of the
patriarchs, to whom belonged the primacy in the Church,
provided he did not render himself unworthy of it
through heterodoxy ; but the absolute monarchy which
the emissaries of Rome preached was something wholly
different. The Orientals held the Pope's action to be
limited by the consent of the other patriarchs, in all
important concerns affecting the whole Church ; they
could not conceive any arbitrary and autocratic power
existing in the Church. Some special means therefore
had to be found for getting at them.

A Latin theologian, probably a Dominican, who had
resided among the Greeks, composed a catena of spurious passages of Greek Councils and Fathers, St. Chrysostom, the two Cyrils, and a pretended Maximus, containing a dogmatic basis for these novel Papal claims.
In 1261 it was laid before Urban IV., who at once
availed himself of the fabrication in his letter to the
Emperor, Michael Palæologus, discreetly concealing the
names of the witnesses. He wanted to prove from these
newly invented texts, professedly eight hundred years
old, that " the Apostolic throne" is the sole authority

in doctrinal matters.[1] There was this misfortune attending the intercourse of the Popes after Nicolas I. with the Byzantines,—that they always appealed to spurious testimonies and authorities, which did unspeakable injury to the cause of unity.

Urban, evidently deceived himself, sent the document to St. Thomas Aquinas, who inserted the whole of what concerned the Primacy into his work against the Greeks, without the least suspicion of its not being genuine,—for the doubts expressed in his letter to the Pope refer only to the passages on the Trinity and the Procession of the Holy Ghost. At the same time, Buonaccursio, a Dominican residing in the East, translated these passages into Greek in his *Thesaurus*.[2] St. Thomas, who knew no Greek, and, being educated in the Gregorian system, derived all his knowledge of ecclesiastical antiquity from Gratian, found himself at once in possession of this treasure of most weighty testimonies from the early centuries, which left no doubt in his mind that the great Councils and most influential bishops and theo-

[1] Raynald. *Annal.* ann. 1263, 61.

[2] The Dominican Doto, who brought this work into the West about 1330, says Buonaccursio made the Latin translation, and collated it with the Greek text. That, in fact, it was composed in Latin and translated into Greek has been recognised already by Quetif and Echard, *Script. Ord. Prædic.* i. 156 *seq.*

logians of the fourth and fifth centuries had recognised in the Pope an infallible monarch, who ruled the whole Church with absolute power. He therefore did what the scholastics had never done before : he introduced the doctrine of the Pope and his infallibility, as he got it from these spurious passages, and often in the same words, into the dogmatic system of the *Schola*,—a step the gravity and momentous results of which can hardly be exaggerated.

What the Orientals, according to this forgery, are supposed to have taught about the Primacy during the first five centuries, and what St. Thomas developed still further on their authority, is in substance as follows :—

Christ has conferred on Peter his own plenary authority, and thus it is the Pope alone who can command, bind, and loose. Every one is under him as though he were Christ himself, and what he decrees must be obeyed. For " Christ is fully and completely with every Pope in sacrament and authority."[1] The Apostolic See rules, ever remaining unshaken in the faith of Peter, while other Churches are deformed by error, and thus the Roman Church is the sun from which they all receive their light. A Council derives its whole autho-

---

1 That is to say, in a mysterious manner, only to be understood by faith. An infallibility resting on inspiration appears to be intended.

rity from the Pope ; he has the right of establishing a
new confession of faith, and whoever rejects his authority is a heretic, for it belongs to him alone to decide on
every doctrinal question.[1]

It was, then, on the basis of fabrications invented by
a monk of his own Order, including a canon of Chalcedon
giving all bishops an unlimited right of appeal to the
Pope, and on the forgeries found in Gratian, that St.
Thomas built up his Papal system, with its two leading
principles, that the Pope is the first infallible teacher of
the world, and the absolute ruler of the Church.[2]   The
spurious Cyril of Alexandria is his favourite author on
this subject, and he constantly quotes him.

At Rome it was perceived at once how great was the
gain of what had hitherto been taught only by jurists
and codes of canon law becoming an integral part of
dogmatic theology.   John XXII., in his delight, uttered
his famous saying, that Thomas had worked as many
miracles as he had written articles, and could be canonized without any other miracles, and in his Bull he
affirmed that Thomas had not written without a special

---

[1] *Summa,* ii. 2 Q. i. Art. 10 ; Q. xi. Art. 2, 3.
[2] The portion of his work against the Greeks on the Primacy is derived
entirely from these fictions.   In the Paris Dominican edition of 1660, t. xx.,
the parallel passages from his other works are marked in the margin.

inspiration of the Holy Ghost. Innocent VI. said that whoever assailed his teaching incurred suspicion of heresy.[1]

In fact, the new Greek tradition was more necessary and more prized in the West than the East at the time of its appearance. The Church had just been flooded by the stream of new Orders, who were supported entirely on begging, the confessional, and the use of Papal privileges, *i.e.*, preaching indulgences, and absolving from sins reserved to the Pope. In 1215, at his great Roman synod,[2] Innocent III. had for the first time ordered that every Christian should confess once a year to his own parish priest, without whose permission nobody could give absolution. Soon afterwards the Papal See decided to place the new monks everywhere at the side of the bishops and parish priests, as instruments wholly devoted to it, and bearing its direct commission ; and thus the law of 1215 about one's "own parish priest" was made inoperative through privileges accorded to these new wandering confessors, who gained their livelihood chiefly by the confessional. But this required the theory of a universal bishop, acting by his own right throughout the whole Church, and holding concurrent jurisdiction with the diocesan bishops. The

---

[1] Cf. Touron, *Vie de S. Thomas*, p. 593 *seq.*
[2] [The fourth Lateran Council.—Tr.]

title Gregory the Great had rejected with horror was now interpreted in its fullest sense, and St. Thomas asserted, on the strength of his new apocryphal documents, that the Council of Chalcedon had given it to the Pope. The dispute about the privileges accorded to the new Orders raged violently on many points.

Innocent IV. tried, in 1254, to protect the parish priests against this invasion of itinerant monks, who were always ready to absolve. It had been represented to him that the penitential discipline, sufficiently weakened already by the religious wars and the indulgences, would be utterly destroyed in this way. The Pope says it has been proved that the action of the parish priests is thoroughly crippled, and all cure of souls unsettled, that the people learn to despise their priests, and shameful consequences ensue, for men are absolved by a monk who speedily disappears, and perhaps is never seen in the place again, and go on contentedly in their sins.[1] But his ordinance that the monks should not enter the confessional without permission from the parish priest was revoked by his successor, Alexander IV.[2] St. Thomas wrote against

---

[1] See the Bull " Etsi animarum," in Raynald. *Annal.* ann. 1254, p. 70.
[2] Raynald. *ib.* ; Bulæi *Hist. Univ. Paris*, ii. pp. 315-350.

the Paris theologians who defended the parish priests
and the previously existing order and discipline of the
Church ; he deduced from his spurious testimonies of St.
Cyril, that, as regards obedience, there is no difference
between Christ and the Pope, and made the Fathers say
that in fact the rulers of the world (*primates mundi*) obey
the Pope as though he were Christ.[1] He can therefore
annul the ancient order of the Church established by
Councils, for all Councils derive their authority solely
from him. And, on the faith of the fabrications supplied to him, St. Thomas appeals directly to the Council
of Chalcedon for the truth of his Papal absolutism.

The victory of the two Mendicant Orders was
complete, and with it prevailed the view of the
Pope being the real bishop in every diocese, the ordinary of the ordinary, as was said. But every parish
priest found himself powerless in his own village in
presence of a begging monk, dependent on the produce
of his privileges, and could not guard against the
injury and destruction of his pastoral work, resulting
from Papal absolutism. The bishops, whose diocesan
administration was already complicated by the number
of exemptions, were obliged to give free course to troops

[1] *Opusc.* xxxiv. (ed. Paris), xx. 549, 580.

of new religions, with still larger exemptions, and owning no obedience but to their distant superiors. The result was such that even a cardinal, Simon of Beaulieu, said in France, in 1283, that all ecclesiastical discipline was ruined by the privileges of the Begging Orders, and that one might well call the Church a monster.[1] The parish priests were then the most powerless and unprotected of all classes of the clergy; they had no organ and no representation for making their complaints heard. The bishops complained frequently, and the University of Paris made a long resistance; but all had to bow to the united power of the Popes and the Mendicants. The only effect was to convince the monks more clearly that the Papal system, with its theory of Infallibility, was as indispensable and valuable to them as to the *Curia* itself.

§ XIX. *Infallibility Disputed.*

All the alleged grounds for Papal Infallibility, through the older Roman fabrications, the pseudo-Isidore, the Gregorians, and Gratian, and, finally, the Dominican forgeries and the theological authority of St. Thomas, were now admitted almost without contradiction. Yet

[1] *Hist. Lit. de France*, xxi. 24.

it was not generally acknowledged that a Pope was actually infallible in his pronouncements on matters of faith. In countries where the Inquisition was not permanently established, the contrary might be taught, and for centuries opposite views on this point prevailed. That the Roman Church was divinely guaranteed by a special Providence against entire apostasy from the faith was affirmed by Guibert of Tournay about 1250,[1] and Nicolas of Lyra,[2] and was pretty generally believed. But then it was always assumed that a Pope could fall into heresy, and give a wrong decision in weighty questions of faith, and that he might in that case be sentenced and deposed by the Church. Besides the history of Liberius, it was mainly the oft-quoted canon of Gratian, ascribed to St. Boniface, that supplied the rule of judgment here.[3] Even the boldest champions of Papal absolutism, men like Agostino Trionfo and Alvaro Pelayo, assumed that the Popes could err, and that their decisions were no certain criterion. But they also held that an heretical Pope *ipso facto* ceased to be Pope, without or before any judicial sentence, so that Councils, which are the Church's judicature, only attested the

---

[1] *De Offic. Episc.* c. 35, in *Biblioth. Max. Patrum*, t. xxv.
[2] *Ad Lucam*, xxii. 31.   [3] *Si Papa*, Dist. vi. 50.

vacancy of the Papal throne as an accomplished fact.
In that case, according to Trionfo, the Papal authority
resides in the Church, as at a Pope's death.[1] So too,
Cardinal Jacob Fournier, afterwards Pope, thought that
Papal decisions were by no means final, but might be
overruled by another Pope, and that John XXII. had done
well in annulling the offensive and doctrinally erroneous
decision of Nicolas III. on the poverty of Christ, and the
distinction of use and possession.[2] And Innocent III.
had said before,—" For other sins I acknowledge no
judge but God, but I can be judged by the Church for
a sin concerning matters of faith."[3] And Innocent IV.
allowed that a Papal command containing anything
heretical, or threatening destruction to the whole Church
system, was not to be obeyed, and that a Pope might
err in matters of faith.[4] John XXII. had to learn, not
without personal mortification, that his authority was
of little weight when opposed to the dominant belief,
and that a simple recantation was his only resource.

[1] *Summa*, v. 6.

[2] See Eymeric. *Director. Inquis.* p. 295.

[3] De Consec. Pontif. Serm. 3. *Opp.* (ed. Venet. 1578), p. 194. But he
thinks God would hardly suffer a Pope to err against the faith.

[4] *Comment. in Dec.* v. 39, f. 595. " Papa etiam potest errare in fide et
ideo non debet quis dicere, credo id quod credit Papa, sed illud quod credit
Ecclesia, et sic dicendo non errabit." The passage is left in the repertory
of his work, but has been expunged from the text of the later editions.

When he preached at Avignon the doctrine that the blessed do not enjoy the Beatific Vision before the general resurrection, a universal outcry was raised in Paris. The theologians drew up propositions declaring the doctrine to be heretical. The King had it publicly condemned in Paris with sound of trumpets, and commanded the Pope to accept the judgment of the Paris doctors, who must know what was the true faith better than the spiritual jurists, who understood little or nothing of theology.[1] That was the estimate long entertained of the *Curia*. No confidence was felt in their judgment on questions of dogma and theology.

The inseparable connexion between Aquinas and Papal Infallibility was shown in the contest already mentioned between the University of Paris and the Dominican Order, in the person of Montson. The Dominicans said that St. Thomas's doctrine was in all points sanctioned by the Popes, among others by Urban v. in his Bull, addressed to the High School of Toulouse; and thus the Popes bear witness to St. Thomas, and he to the Popes. But St. Thomas teaches, on the authority of his spuri-

[1] As Cardinal D'Ailly stated it to the assembly of the French clergy in 1406, the King's message to the Pope was still ruder and more peremptory, "qu'il se revoquoit ou qu'il se ferait ardre." Cf. Du Chastenet. *Nouv. Hist. du Conc. de Constance* (Paris, 1718), Preuves, p. 153. Villani, whose brother was then in Avignon, does not mention this.

ous Cyril, that it is enough for the Pope alone to declare what is matter of faith, and to sanction or condemn any doctrine. On the other hand, the Faculty enumerated a whole series of errors in St. Thomas, and classed among them this very doctrine of Papal Infallibility.[1] They distinctly call it heresy, it being notoriously the doctrine of the Church that there is an appeal from a Pope to a General Council, and that every bishop, by divine and human right, is qualified to pronounce sentence on points of faith. Thus in 1388 the dogmatic infallibility of the Popes was repudiated by the first and most influential theological corporation in the Church, and the superiority of Councils in matters of faith expressly affirmed, though certainly no Paris theologian doubted the genuineness of the imposing testimonies cited by St. Thomas.

The Popes themselves were constantly bringing their dogmatic authority afresh into suspicion. The most thorough-going and credulous devotee of Roman supremacy could not help feeling uneasy when he found that the Papal See was at a loss for any clear and well-defined principles, on one of the gravest and most practically important questions, involving all certainty of individual and corporate religious life—the doctrine of ordination,

---

[1] D'Argentré, *Collect. Judic.* i. 2, 84.

that the *Curia* was constantly fluctuating on this question, and that it had infected the *Schola* with the same uncertainty since the middle of the twelfth century, as may be seen from Peter Lombard. We mean that since the eighth century, as was before said, ordinations which were valid according to immutable laws, grounded in the very nature of the Church and the Sacraments, had been declared null at Rome, and re-ordinations performed, which had thrown the Italian Church into the most vexatious confusion by the end of the ninth century. And again the increase of simony had given occasion to Popes, as, *e.g.*, Leo IX., to annul a number of ordinations at a Roman Synod, and either to solemnize or order regular re-ordinations.[1] This was based on the double error of supposing that simony, or procuring ordination for money, was heresy, and that heresy made the ordination invalid. The mischief done by the Popes in this way was immeasurable, for there were but few priests and bishops then throughout Italy altogether free from simony, so that millions of the laity became perplexed about the sacraments they had received from clergy said to be invalidly ordained, and

[1] Petri Damiani, *Opusc.* v. p. 419. "Leo IX. plerosque Simoniacos et male promotos tanquam noviter ordinavit."

hatred and feuds between the people and their pastors penetrated every village, nor was it easy to find any way out of this labyrinth of universal religious doubt and interruption or destruction of the succession. Nor was this all. The same confusion was imported into Germany too, and the ordinations of those bishops were declared to be invalid whom the Popes had excommunicated for their loyalty to the Emperor Henry IV. Thus, at the Synod of Quedlinburg in 1085, the Papal legate Otho annulled the ordinations of the bishops of Mayence, Augsburg, and Coire, although Peter Damiani had long since raised his voice against this capricious annulling of ordinations and re-ordaining.[1] Otho, afterwards Pope Urban II., declared that even when there was no simony in the actual ordination, it was rendered invalid if performed by a simoniacal bishop.[2]

At a Synod at Piacenza he annulled the ordinations of his rival, Archbishop Guibert of Ravenna,[3] celebrated after his excommunication by Gregory VII., and thereby gave public evidence of another gross error,

[1] Bernold. in Pertz, *Monum.* vii. 442; Harduin, *Concil.* vi. 1. 614.

[2] This letter of Urban II. has puzzled theologians who dislike seeing a Pope openly teach heresy. Thus, *e.g.*, Witasse (*Tract. Theol.* ed Venet. vi. 51) says it is "intricatissimus et difficillimus locus." Wecilo is the bishop referred to.

[3] [The Antipope Clement III., elected at Brixen in 1080. --TR.]

that the validity of sacraments is affected by Church censures.[1] Even Innocent II. made a great Synod, the second Council of Lateran, an accomplice in his error of declaring invalid the ordinations of " schismatics," *i.e.*, of the episcopal adherents of Pope Anacletus, who had been elected by a majority of the cardinals, but was then dead,—an act of arbitrary caprice and notorious heresy, which cannot be excused, like earlier re-ordinations, by the horror professedly felt for simony.[2]   Hence it was the Roman Church itself which, notwithstanding the protests raised from time to time within its bosom against the terrible disorder caused by these ordinations, was again and again falling into the same error, and disturbing the consciences and belief of the faithful in a way that in the ancient Church would have been found intolerable, and against which a remedy would soon have been discovered.

§ XX.—*Fresh Forgeries.*

Soon after St. Thomas's time, towards the end of the thirteenth century, there arose a need for further inventions, this time in the domain of history, to sustain and further the system.   As the contradictions between

[1] *Concil.* (ed. Labbé), x. 504.   [2] *Ib.* p. 1009.

the older historical authorities and the recent codes of
canon law, Gratian and the Decretals, were obvious to
every one who looked beneath the surface, it seemed
desirable to represent the history of the Popes and
Emperors in such a way as to get rid of those contradictions, and give an historical sanction to the new
canon law.   This task was undertaken, at the command
of Clement v., by Martin of Troppau, called the Pole,
owing to Nicolas III. having made him Archbishop of
Gnesen in 1275.   He was penitentiary and chaplain
to the Pope; all jurists and canonists were said to
bind up his book with Gratian and the Decretals,
and all theologians with the Bible history of Peter
Comestor.[1]   And this book is, of all historical works of
the middle ages, at once the most popular and the most
utterly fabulous.   Many of its fictions simply evidence
the want of any historical sense and the miracle-mon-
gering credulity which had been the rage since the
rise of the Mendicant Orders ; but many also were invented with deliberate intention.   The Popes were to be
exhibited, as in the *Liber Pontificalis*, but still more

---

[1] [Peter Comestor, Chancellor of Paris at the end of the twelfth century, wrote a history extending from the Creation to the birth of Christ.
This work, with the *Sentences* of Peter Lombard and Gratian's *Decretum*,
is said to have made up the average reading of mediæval divines.--Tr.]

conspicuously, as the rulers and legislators of the whole Church, the pseudo-Isidorian fabrications and Gratian were to be confirmed, and history made to reflect the supremacy of Popes over Emperors. The book indicates a great falling off in historical composition; and this is to be accounted for by the general influence of the Begging Monks, especially the Dominicans, with their insatiable hankering after miracles, and their constant endeavour to trace the Papal system to the earliest ages, in materially obscuring historical knowledge, and degrading it below the level it had attained in the twelfth century. The mere fact of so miserable and thoroughly mendacious a book as Martin's gaining such universal currency and influence is an eloquent proof of this decline.

The same object, of adapting the history both of the Empire and the Church to the Gregorian system, was followed by the Dominican Tolomeo of Lucca, Papal librarian, whom John XXII. appointed in 1318 to the see of Torcello. His Church History, up to 1313, is much fuller than Martin's dry compendium, and a far more spirited and artistic composition. This is true also of his continuation of the Political Treatise commenced by Aquinas,[1] and his Annals from the year

¹ St. Thomas only wrote the first book of the *De Regimine Principum,*

1062. His principal work often reads like a commentary on Gratian or the pseudo-Isidore, whom, however, he only knew through Gratian. The purport of his work for the first twelve centuries is to mould the fabrications of these two writers and the Decretals into a coherent history. It may suffice for an illustration of his treatment of ancient Church history, to say that he describes Pope Vigilius as holding the fifth Œcumenical Council at Constantinople in sovereign majesty, with the hearty co-operation of the Emperor Justinian, who manifested an entire devotion to him.[1] So was history written at the Papal Court. One of its main objects was to supply an historical basis for the principles of Rome, and her claims to jurisdiction over the German empire, the elections to the throne, and the emperors.

At that time the Papacy was gradually passing into French hands. The institution of Legates, unknown in the ancient Church, but imported into the ecclesiastical system by means of a spurious canon, and accounted necessary by Gratian,[2] had enabled the Popes to

---

and two chapters of the second. Tolomeo completed the second, and wrote the third and fourth books. Cf. *Quétif-Echard*, i. 543.

[1] *Ptol. Luc.* 8t 5-899.

[2] *Dist.* 94, c. 2, with the title "Excommunicetur qui legatum Sedis Apostolicæ impedire tentaverit." The passage is from pseudo-Isidore, but speaks in very general terms of the episcopal office, which was not to be

dominate and tax the various National Churches, and was now in full bloom. The Popes had overthrown the Hohenstaufen dynasty, and transplanted a French dynasty and French influence into Italy for the sake of the South Italian kingdom. The feudal claim of the Normans was not enough to legitimatize this procedure, and some other title had to be discovered. Tolomeo accordingly related that the Emperor Constantine had presented this kingdom to the Pope as a " manuale," which he could dispose of as he pleased.[1] Thus his whole History is thrown into the shape requisite for the *Curia* and the Dominicans in 1313. He begins by saying that Christ was the first Pope, and keeps to that programme throughout. The second Pope was Peter, who founded, by his disciples, all the principal churches in Italy and Gaul.

Tolomeo was also the first to disseminate, in the Papal interest, the fable about the appointment of the Electors by Gregory v. in 995.[2] This was the complement of the

impeded. By omitting the word "vestram," and with the help of Gratian's title, the Legates are represented as competent to excommunicate any one.

[1] *Ptol. Luc.* 1066.

[2] Not Trionfo, as Friedburg maintains (*De Fin. inter Eccl. et Civit. regund. Judicio*, 1861, p. 25). Nor was the passage interpolated into St. Thomas, as he thinks, and the book does not belong to Ægidius of Columna, as Wattenbach thinks (*Deutschlands Geschichtsquel.* 519), but the passage is in Tolomeo's continuation. Quétif and Echard have already pointed out

theory of translations invented by Alexander III. and ·
Innocent III. It was the Popes, according to Innocent, ·
who took the Empire from the Greeks and gave it to ·
the Franks, and they did this for their own better pro- ·
tection.[1] Charlemagne, by command of the Church,
put an end to the empire of the Greeks, says Tolomeo.[2]
Boniface VIII. brought the German emperor Albert to
acknowledge formally that the Popes had transferred
the Empire; that it was they who had conferred the
right of election on certain princes, and given to kings
and emperors the power of the civil sword.[3] And to
this were added the new claims, first put in force by
Clement V., that the Pope succeeds during a vacancy to ·
the Imperial power, and that every Emperor is bound to ·
take an oath of fealty to him,—claims which John XXII. ·
acted upon in his contest with the Emperor Louis, and
from whence he drew the further corollary, which he at ·
once put into practice against Louis, that he, as Pope, ·
was administrator of the Empire during a vacancy.[4]
The *Curia* found Gratian and the Decretals insufficient

this addition of Tolomeo's to St. Thomas's work, and shown that he was the
first to disseminate the fable, and probably himself invented it.
  [1] *Registr.* Epp. 29, 62 ; *Decret.* c. 34, De Elect. i. 6.
  [2] *Ptol. Luc.* 974.   [3] Raynald. *Annal.* ann. 1303, 8.
  [4] Cf. "Processus in Ludovic. Bav." in Martene, *Thes. Anecd.* ii. 710,
seq., where a whole series of fables and falsifications, like Martin's and Tolo-

for these purposes, and so to the numerous class of
Papal Court jurists and Court theologians, like Trionfo
and Ægidius Columna, must be added the Court historians Martin and Tolomeo.

Besides these, special fictions were wanted to meet
the circumstances of particular countries and National
Churches, so as to adapt their history to the requirements of the Papal system. This was eminently true of
Spain. The business of cooking history was carried on
in her case more systematically than anywhere else.
The ancient Spanish Church, without ignoring the
Roman primacy,[1] had yet maintained an independent
attitude towards it. Her Synods, regularly held, exercised judicial power over bishops and metropolitans, and
sometimes opposed even Popes in questions of faith, as,
e.g., the Synod of Toledo in 688 subjected Pope Benedict's letter to severe criticism, and did not scruple to
charge him with "barefaced contradiction of the Fathers."
At the time of the Arabian invasion, and till towards
the end of the eleventh century, the Spanish Church

---

meo's, are produced as weapons against the Emperors and their adherents,
as, *e.g.*, Pope Innocent's excommunication of the Emperor Arcadius, the
legends of Constantine and Theodosius, and many more.

[1] Thus the most influential of Spanish prelates and theologians, Isidore
of Seville, in his letter to the Duke Claudius, asserts his subjection to the
Roman See more emphatically than was usual with bishops of that age.

preserved her independent life.[1] Roman influences were seldom felt, and only at long intervals. Archbishop Diego Gelmirez, a zealous advocate of the Gregorian system, testifies, at the beginning of the twelfth century, that no Spanish bishop then (in the previous century) paid to the Roman Church tribute or obedience, and that the Spanish Church followed the laws of Toledo, not of Rome.[2]

A change in the interests of Rome was effected through the influence of the monks of Clugny, who received abbeys and bishoprics, through the action of French queens, and the policy of some kings who were seeking support at Rome. Even Gregory VII. asserted that all Spain had from ancient times been the property of the Popes, as he expected also to be able to demand Hungary, Russia, Provence, and Saxony. And this claim had one result, in the suppression of the Mozarabic and substitution of the Roman rite in 1085. A French Cluniac monk became Archbishop of Toledo, and for 150 years, up to the middle of the thirteenth century, a con-

---

[1] Masdeu, *Hist. Critic. de España*, xiii. 258 *sqq.* Here it is observed that, according to a letter issued by Adrian I. about 790, denouncing certain abuses, there had for two centuries been no correspondence of the Popes with Spain. Nor was there any even in the eleventh century, before Gregory VII.'s time, except on a few unimportant points.

[2] Hist. Compost. 253, in vol. xx. of Florez' *España Sagrada.*

stant struggle went on for the subjugation of the Spanish
Church. This was the aim of the historical fictions first
perpetrated by Bishop Pelayo of Oviedo, and then by
Bishop Lucas of Tuy. The former adulterated Sam-
piro's Chronicle by inventing an embassy of the Spanish
Church to John VIII., some decrees of that Pope, and a
Synod held by his order at Oviedo, besides other things.[1]
More comprehensive and still more influential were
the inventions of Lucas, who thoroughly corrupted the
ancient history of Spain. In order to give an appearance of early and complete dependence on Rome to
the Spanish Church, he represented Archbishop Leander
as a legate of the Pope, and falsified the whole history
of Isidore, whom he converts into a vicar of Pope
Gregory.[2] The misfortunes of Spain and the overthrow
of the Gothic kingdom are explained by a purely fabulous history he invented of King Witiza, who is said
to have forbidden the Spaniards, on pain of death, to
obey the Pope.[3]

[1] Florez' *España Sagrada,* xiv. 440.
[2] *Ib.* ix. 203-204.
[3] " Chronicon Mundi" in Schotti *Hisp. Illustrat.* iv. 69. " Istud quidem
causa pereundi Hispaniæ fuit," says Lucas. The moral to be drawn was
that the prosperity of Spain depended on obedience to the Pope. The
whole Chronicle, written about 1236, is a tissue of lies, exceeding anything
previously known, or at least published, in Spain.

In theology, from the beginning of the fourteenth century, the spurious passages of St. Cyril and forged canons of Councils maintained their ground, being guaranteed against all suspicion by the authority of St. Thomas. Since the work of Trionfo in 1320, up to 1450, it is remarkable that no single new work appeared in the interest of the Papal system. But then the contest between the Council of Basle and Pope Eugenius IV. evoked the work of Cardinal Torquemada, besides some others of less importance. Torquemada's argument, which was held up to the time of Bellarmine to be the most conclusive apology of the Papal system, rests entirely on fabrications later than the pseudo-Isidore, and chiefly on the spurious passages of St. Cyril. To ignore the authority of St. Thomas is, according to the Cardinal, bad enough, but to slight the testimony of St. Cyril is intolerable. The Pope is infallible; all authority of the other bishops is borrowed or derived from his. Decisions of Councils without his assent are null and void. These fundamental principles of Torquemada are proved by the spurious passages of Anacletus, Clement, the Council of Chalcedon, St. Cyril, and a mass of forged or adulterated testimonies.[1] In the times of

---

[1] *De Pontif. M. et Gen. Concil. Auctorit.* (Venet. 1583), p. 17; *Summa de*

Leo X. and Clement III., the Cardinals Thomas of Vio, or Cajetan, and Jacobazzi, followed closely in his footsteps.[1] Melchior Canus built firmly on the authority of Cyril, attested by St. Thomas, and so did Bellarmine and the Jesuits who followed him. The Dominicans, Nicolai, Le Quien, Quétif, and Echard, were the first to avow openly that their master, St. Thomas, had been deceived by an impostor, and had in his turn misled the whole tribe of theologians and canonists who followed him.[2] On the other hand, the Jesuits, including even such a scholar as Labbé, while giving up the pseudo-Isidorian decretals, manifested their resolve still to cling to Cyril.[3] In Italy, as late as 1713, Professor

Eccl. (Venet. 1561), p. 171 ; *Apparat. super Decr. Union. Grœc.* (Venet. 1561), p. 366, and in many other places.

[1] *Opera* (ed. Serry), Patav. 734, p. 194, " Cyrillus . . . multo evidentius. quam cæteri auctores huic veritati testimonium perhibet," viz., that the Pope is the infallible judge of doctrine. Those who wish to get a bird's-eye view of the extent to which the genuine tradition of Church authority was still overlaid and obliterated by the rubbish of later inventions and forgeries about 1563, when the *Loci* of Canus appeared, must read the fifth book of his work. It is indeed still worse fifty years later in this part of Bellarmine's work. The difference is that Canus was honest in his belief, which cannot be said of Bellarmine.

[2] Le Quien speaks out with peculiar distinctness on the point in the Preface to his *Panoplia contra Schisma Græcorum,* published at Paris in 1718 under the name of Steph. de Altimura, pp. xv.-xvii.

[3] Cf. Labbé, *De Script. Eccles.* (Paris, 1669), i. 244. He and Bellarmine sheltered themselves under the pretext that the *Thesaurus* of Cyril has come to us in a mutilated condition; Dupin, Ceillier, Oudin, and others have long since shown the falsehood of this assertion.

Andruzzi of Bologna cited the most important of the interpolations in St. Cyril as a conclusive argument in his controversial treatise against the patriarch Dositheus.[1]

§ XXI.—*Interdicts.*

To all these means for supporting the universal supremacy of the Popes, and bringing the belief of their infallibility into more general acceptance, were added the Interdicts to which whole countries were frequently subjected. God's Vicar upon earth, it was said, acts like God, who often includes many innocent persons in the punishment of the guilty few; who shall dare to contradict him? He acts under Divine guidance, and his acts cannot be measured by the rules of human justice. And thus from the Divine inspiration which guided their action was inferred the doctrinal infallibility of the Popes, and *vice versa*, just as is the case now with the people, and even the clergy, especially in countries of the Latin race. The Popes had indeed themselves declared, in their new code, in the sixth book of the Decretals, that interdicts produced the most injurious effects on the religion of the people, strength-

---

[1] *Vetus Græcia de Rom. Sede præclare sentiens*, Venet. 1713, p. 219.

T

ening their impiety, eliciting heresies, originating numberless dangers to souls, and depriving the Church of her rightful dues.[1] But notwithstanding this confession, they made more copious use of interdicts than ever; their proceedings against Germany during the long struggle against the Emperor Louis the Bavarian exceeded, through the long duration of the interdict, anything that had happened there before. It really seemed as if they wished to root out from the minds of men the gospel teaching about the rights of baptized Christians, and teach them instead to regard themselves as mere herds of cattle belonging to the Pope, with no will of their own, or, as Alvaro Pelayo said, teach them to fly from his wrath to his mercy, which, however, had been refused to them. The results of this conduct varied greatly according to differences of national character. While it led some nations to question more and more the Divine right of an authority so horribly abused, and thus scattered seeds which bore fruit a century and a half later; others were confirmed in the notion that the Papacy is a mysterious power like the Godhead, whose ways are unsearchable, and which must not be too closely scrutinized, but must always be blindly

---

[1] Cap. ult. de Excom. in *Sexto Decr.*

trusted as being enlightened from on high, and acting under Divine inspiration.

Paradoxical as it may sound, it is an historical fact that the more suspicious and scandalous the conduct of the Popes—with their exemptions, privileges, indulgences, and the like, and the consequent confusion in the Church—appeared to pious men, the more inclined they felt to take refuge from their own doubts and suspicions in the bosom of Papal infallibility. Tested by simple Christian feeling, they would have been obliged to condemn this, and much else, as an abuse and heinous sin against the Church. But that feeling had to contend with the notion, instilled into them from youth, that the Pope is the lord and master of the Church, whom none may contradict or call to account. This may be illustrated by the language of Peter Cantor, as early as the end of the twelfth century. He says there would indeed be just reason to apprehend that the Papal corruptions might produce a general separation from the spiritual empire of Rome, for there is no scriptural justification for them; but then it would be sacrilegious to find fault with what the Pope does. God suffers not the Roman Church to fall into any error, and we must assume that the Pope does these things under inspiration of the Holy Ghost, by virtue of which he is in the last instance the sole ruler of the Church, to the exclusion of all others.[1]

§ XXII.—*The Schism of the Antipopes.*

In the fourteenth century, the Church was brought into a condition which forced doubts upon the minds of even the most zealous votaries of the Papal system.

The long schism which for above forty years presented to the world the novel spectacle of rival Popes mutually anathematizing one another, and two *Curias,* —a French one at Avignon, and an Italian,—shook an authority still commonly regarded as invincible under the last Popes before 1376. For the discomfiture suffered by the Papacy at the beginning of the century, in the person of Boniface VIII., was soon blotted out of men's remembrance by the complete victory it gained soon afterwards over Germany and the Emperor Louis; and the practical effects of that first humiliation were inconsiderable,—it left its mark rather on the *Schola* and the writings of the French jurists. The wounds inflicted by the persistent policy of the Popes for centuries on the Empire and the national unity of Germany long continued to bleed. The German Church had lost the

---

[1] *Verbum Abbrev.* (ed. Galopin), p. 114.

very idea of regarding itself as an organic whole; that there had ever been such a thing as German National Synods was utterly forgotten. The experiment of "divide et impera" had been first tried upon the German Church, and had proved a complete success.

The Schism arose from the struggle between two nations for the possession of the Papacy: the Italians wanted to regain and the French to keep it. And thus it came to pass that from 1378 to 1409 Western Christendom was divided into two, from 1409 to 1415, into three, Obediences. A Neapolitan, Urban VI., had been elected, and his first slight attempt at a reform gave immediate occasion to the outbreak of the schism. Soon after entering on his pontificate, he excommunicated the Cardinals who were guilty of simony. But simony had long been the daily bread of the Roman *Curia* and the breath of its life; without simony the machine must come to a stand-still and instantly fall to pieces. The Cardinals had, from their own point of view, ample ground for insisting on the impossibility of subsisting without it. They accordingly revolted from Urban and elected Clement VII., a man after their own heart.[1] Nobody knew at the time whose election was the most regular, Urban's or Clement's. Things had

---

[1] Thom. de Acern. *De Creat. Urbani.* See Muratori, iii. 2, 721.

in fact occurred in both elections which made them legally invalid. The attorneys on both sides urged irrefutable arguments to show that the Pope of the opposite party had no claim to their recognition. There were persons on both sides, since accounted as Saints throughout the whole Church, but who then anathematized one another : on the French side, Peter of Luxemburg and Vincent Ferrer, on the Italian, Catherine of Sienna and Catherine the Swede. Meanwhile there were two Papal Courts and two Colleges of Cardinals, each Court with diminished revenues, and determined to put on the screw of extortion to the utmost,— each inexhaustible in the discovery of new methods of making gain of spiritual things, and the increased application of those already in use.

The situation was a painful one for all adherents of Papal infallibility, who found themselves in an inextricable labyrinth. Their belief necessarily implied that the particular individual who is in sole possession of all truth, and bestows on the whole Church the certainty of its faith, must be always and undoubtingly acknowledged as such. There can as little be any uncertainty allowed about the person of the right Pope as about the books of Scripture. Yet every one at that period must at bottom have been aware that the mere accident of what country he lived in determined which Pope he adhered to, and that all he knew of his Pope's legitimacy was that half Christendom rejected it. Spaniards and Frenchmen believed in Clement VII. or Benedict XIII., Englishmen and Italians in Urban VI. or Boniface IX. What was still worse, the old notion, which for centuries had been fostered by the Popes, and often confirmed by them, of the invalidity of ordinations and sacraments administered outside the Papal communion, still widely prevailed, especially in Italy. The Papal secretary Coluccio Salutato paints in strong colours the universal uncertainty and anguish of conscience produced by the schism, and his own conclusion as a Papalist is, that as all ecclesiastical jurisdiction is derived from the Pope, and as a Pope invalidly elected cannot give what he does not himself possess, no bishops or priests ordained since the death of Gregory XI. could guarantee the validity of the sacraments they administered.[1] It followed, according to him, that any one who adored the Eucharist consecrated by a priest ordained in schism worshipped an idol.

[1] See his letter to the Count Jost of Moravia, in Martene, *Thes. Anecd.* ii. 1150, "Quis nescit ex vitiosâ parte veros episcopos esse non posse?" And the point is then further worked out.

Such was the condition of Western Christendom. A happier view prevailed in France, England, Germany, and Spain, than in Italy and at the Papal Court, about the conditions of valid ordination and administration of sacraments. ˙

Those who had any knowledge of the constitution of the ancient Church perceived now that the confusion for which no remedy had been discovered for thirty years, could only be traced ultimately to the development of the Gregorian system. A strong and earnest desire was aroused for the restoration of the episcopal system, so far as it could then be distinguished through the accumulated rubbish of fabrications it was overlaid with, and the distortions and obscuring of Church history. It was felt that the old system would have made such a degradation and devastation as the Church had now experienced impossible. The conviction grew stronger and stronger that a General Council was the only effectual means for the restoration of harmony in the Church, as also for limiting Papal despotism. Germans, like Henry of Langenstein and Nicholas Cusa; Frenchmen like D'Ailly, Gerson, and Clemange; Italians like Zabarella; Spaniards like Escobar and John of Segovia, came, in the end of the fourteenth and beginning of the fifteenth century, to substantially similar conclu-

sions,—that the Church must recover herself, break the
chains the Curialistic system had fastened upon her,
and reform herself in her head and her members. And
indeed for some time, all who were eminent in the
Church for intelligence and knowledge had declared
themselves in favour of her rights, and the rights of
free Councils, against the Papacy. Even the voices of
those who thought so terribly degenerate and misused
an institution as the Roman See had now become was
nevertheless indispensable, were loudly raised, but without producing any result. Public opinion still recognised the necessity of its existence, but also the urgent
need for its limitation and purification.

The first attempt to bring about the assembling of a
real, free, and independent Council succeeded. Instead
of the mock Synods which had been customary for the
last 300 years, when the bishops only came to hear the
Pope's decrees read and go home again, a Synod from
all Europe was assembled at Pisa in 1409, at which men
could dare to speak openly and vote freely. It seemed
a great point to contemporaries that two Popes, Gregory
XII. and Benedict XIII., were deposed, and a third, Alexander III., was elected. But these proceedings exhausted
the strength of the Synod; the mere presence of a Pope,
with the Cardinals now again adhering to him, though

he was the creation of the Synod, prevented even the attempt or beginning of a reformation of the Church. The reforms conceded by Alexander were insignificant. As the other two Popes did not submit to the decision of the Synod, there were now three heads of the Church, as before in 1048, but the Pope elected by the Council received far the most general recognition.

§ XXIII.—*The Council of Constance.*

To bring about the actual downfal of the system, it was necessary that it should be represented in the person of a Pope who was the most worthless and infamous man to be found anywhere, according to the testimony of a contemporary.[1] This Pope, recognised up to the day of his deposition by the great majority of Western Christendom, was Balthasar Cossa, John XXIII. Now was the first real victory won, not only over persons, but over the Papacy, and for this was required such an assembly as was the Council of Constance (1414-1418), the most numerous ever seen in the West, at which, besides 300 bishops, there were present the deputies of fifteen universities, and 300 doctors, men who were not

---

[1] Justinger, *Berner-Chronic.* p. 276. "The worst and most abused man to be found, when his badness had been thoroughly exposed in the Council at Constance."

in the ambiguous position of having to reform abuses to which they owed their own dignities and emoluments. And this assembly had to introduce the new plan of voting by nations in place of the old one of voting by individuals, or all would have been wrecked through the great number of Italian bishops, the majority of whom considered it their natural duty to uphold the Papal system, the *Curia*, and the means of revenue thence accruing to the Italians. The corruption of the Church, and the demoralization which was its result, had penetrated deeper in Italy than elsewhere, and then, as afterwards, it was remarked, that the Italian bishops were the most steady opponents of every remedy and reformation.

With the Council of Constance arose a star of hope for the German Church. Well were it if she had possessed men capable of taking permanent advantage of so favourable a situation. The new Emperor, Sigismund, full of earnest zeal to help the Church in her sore distress, managed so skilfully to persuade and press Pope John, who was threatened in Italy, that he chose the German city of Constance for the Council, and came there himself, though not by his own goodwill. For three centuries the Germans had been thrust out by the Italians and French from all active part in the general affairs of the Church. They were the nation least responsible, next to the English, for the evils of the schism,—for the *Curia* had always been purely French and Italian, and had contained no single element of German representation. The German clergy were more sinned against than sinning. It is true that even in Germany the corruption of the Church had become intolerable, and cried to Heaven, but it was no native product of the German people; it had been imported from the south, like a foreign pestilence, and become permanent through the destruction of the organic life of the national Church.

In the famous decrees of the fourth and fifth sessions, the Council of Constance declared that " every lawfully convoked Œcumenical Council representing the Church derives its authority immediately from Christ, and every one, the Pope included, is subject to it in matters of faith, in the healing of schism, and the reformation of the Church." The decree was passed without a single dissentient voice,—a decision more eventful and pregnant in future consequences than had been arrived at by any previous Council, and accordant in principle with primitive antiquity,—for so the Church held before the appearance of the pseudo-Isidore. But at the time it must have looked like a bold innovation ; so strongly had the current set in the opposite direction for a lengthened period, and so loftily had the Popes towered above the humble attitude of the silent and submissive Synods from the third Lateran to the Council of Vienne. That the Council had a full right to call itself Œcumenical was obvious. The small and divided fractions of the other two Obediences could not prejudice its claims. Gregory XII. and Benedict XIII. had been deserted by their Cardinals, and all that could be held to constitute the Roman Church took part in the Council.

If a Pope is subject to a Council in matters of faith he is not infallible ; the Church, and the Council which represents it, inherit the promises of Christ, and not the Pope, who may err apart from a Council, and can be judged by it for his error. This inference was clear and indisputable. But it was not the article in the decrees concerning faith, but that concerning reformation, which excited the suspicion of the Cardinals. That a Pope who became heretical fell under the judgment of the Church, and therefore of a Council, was the commonly accepted and admitted theory since the so-called canon of St. Boniface had been received into the codes, though it could not really be reconciled with the doctrine of infallibility assumed in the same codes of canon law, and disseminated by Aquinas. Yet the Cardinals dared not refuse their assent to the decrees which were so menacing to the interests of the *Curia*.

These decisions of Constance are perhaps the most extraordinary event in the whole dogmatic history of the Christian Church. Their language leaves no doubt that they were understood to be articles of faith, dogmatic definitions of the doctrine of Church authority. And they deny the fundamental position of the Papal system, which is thereby tacitly but very eloquently signalized as an error and abuse. Yet that system had prevailed in the administration of the Church for centuries, had been taught in the canon law books and the schools of the Religious Orders, especially by Thomist divines, and assumed or expressly affirmed in all pronouncements and decisions of the Popes, the new authorities for the laws of the Church. And now not a voice was raised in its favour; no one opposed the doctrines of Constance, no one protested !

But the state of the Church had become so unnatural and monstrous,—the measure of human infirmity and sinfulness which must be reckoned upon in every,

even the best, community was so largely exceeded,—
and the habitual transgression of the laws of God and
the ordinances of the ancient Church was so open and
universal, that every one could perceive that the whole
dominant system, rather than particular individuals,
was responsible for this perversion of Church-government into a vast engine of finance and money-getting,—
this transformation of a free Church arranging its affairs
by common consultation into a subject empire under
absolutist rule, and made the prey of an oligarchy.
When the Cardinals said, in the letter they addressed
to their Pope, Gregory XII., in 1408, that there was no
soundness in the Church from the sole of the foot to
the crown of the head,[1] they should have added, if they
wished to tell the whole truth, " It is we and our colleagues, and your predecessors, it is the *Curia*, who
have gone on saturating the body of the Church with
moral poison, and therefore is it now so sorely diseased."

There were certainly but few who clearly understood
all the real causes as well as the greatness of the
evil, but those few spoke out distinctly what every
one dimly felt.   Reform in the head and the mem- .
bers was the universal watchword throughout Europe, -

[1] Raynald. *Annal.* 1408.

and was understood by every one to mean that the head, the Papal See, needed reform first of all, and that only then and thus would a reform of the members be possible. It was notorious to all that the good dispositions of this or that individual Pope, even if they continued, were utterly powerless, and that reformation in the present case meant an entire change of system. In face of this evidence all the wisdom of both schools—of the canonists and the monkish theologians—was dumb, built, as it was, on rotten foundations. They were reduced to silence, or had, like Tudeschi and many Dominicans, to assent to the decrees of Constance. The public opinion of the whole Christian world, directed and matured by the discussions carried on for the last forty years at Paris, Avignon, Rome, Pisa, and the German universities, was too strong for them.

Even the new Pope elected at the Council of Constance was obliged to declare himself in accord with this feeling. He had indeed been a zealous adherent of John XXIII., and had only at the last moment deserted him, and given in his adhesion to the Council. But he was now Pope by virtue of this deposition of his predecessor, which depended entirely on the decree passed at the Council, and therefore on the Episcopal system. John had not been deposed on account of his opposition to the Council, but only on account of his breaking his oath of obedience to it, and his crimes, after a formal investigation. An express confirmation of this decree by Martin V. seemed at the time not only superfluous, but objectionable. It would have been like a son wanting to attest the genuine paternity of his own father, for this decree had made him Pope. Had he wished to assail its validity in any way he would have been bound at once to resign, and let the deposed Pope again take his place. It was clear to him that he could no longer act upon the right, claimed and exercised by his predecessors for 200 years, to be the ruler of the whole Church assembled and represented at the Council, and he distinctly said this in his Bull against the doctrine of Wicliffe, where he asserted the proposition that the supremacy of the Roman Church over the rest is no part of necessary doctrine, to be an error, because Wicliffe understood by the Roman the universal Church, or a Council, or at least denied the primacy of the Pope over the other particular Churches.[1]

[1] "Super alias ecclesias particulares," *i.e.*, no primacy over the universal Church or a general Council, in strict accordance with the decrees of Constance. So, again, in the questions addressed by Martin's direction to the Wicliffites or Hussites, they were asked whether they believed the Pope

U

He took occasion to declare, towards the end of the Council of Constance, that he confirmed all its "conciliar" decrees, meaning by this phraseology to withhold his approval from two decrees, on Annates, and on a book by the Dominican Falkenberg, not passed by the Council in full session, but in the congregations of certain nations.[1] The two other Obediences also,[2] in giving in their adherence to the Council afterwards, assented to its decrees, as is clearly shown by the Concordat of Narbonne, in the twentieth session, which enumerated the subjects coming within the competence of the Council in accordance with the decrees of the fourth and fifth sessions.

After the deposition of John XXIII., and the resignation of Gregory XII., there occurred a significant division and struggle between the Latins and Germans. The Germans and English wanted the reformation of the Church, which was the most important and difficult task of the Council, to be undertaken before proceeding to the election of a new Pope. The experience of the Council of Pisa had proved that the election of a new Pope at once put an end to every scheme of reformation.

to be Peter's successor, "habens supremam auctoritatem in Ecclesiâ (not Ecclesiam) Dei," and that every General Council, including that of Constance, represents the universal Church.

[1] "Conciliariter" is opposed to "nationaliter."

[2] [The adherents of Benedict XIII. and Gregory XII.—TR.]

But the Cardinals, and with them the Italians and French —the latter from jealousy of the lofty position held by the German King Sigismund,—pressed for the election taking precedence of the reformation. Sigismund contended skilfully, bravely, and perseveringly for the interests of the Church, the Empire, and the German people, who then with good reason called themselves "the godly, patient, humble, and yet not feeble nation."[1] Had they been somewhat less patient and humble, and had something more of that strength which union bestows, the ecclesiastical and national discomfiture of 1417 would not have been followed by the revolt of 1517, the religious division of the nation, the Thirty Years' War, and many other disastrous consequences. But the Cardinals and Latins carried the day by gaining over the English, and corrupting some German prelates, as, for instance, the Archbishop of Riga, and the Bishops of Coire and Leutomischl.[2] And before the new Pope, Martin v., had been elected above a few weeks, the *Curia* and "curialism" were again in the ascendant. The new rules of the Chancery, at once published by Martin, must have opened the eyes of the short-sighted French, and have shown them that in the

---

[1] See De Hardt, *Acta Conc. Const.* iv. 1419.   [2] *Ib.* iv. 1427.

disposal of benefices the whole network of abuses and corrupt trading upon patronage was to be maintained.[1]

Only a few reforming ordinances came into force; the worst wounds and sores of the ecclesiastical body remained for the most part untouched. Martin understood how to divide the nations by pursuing a different policy towards each. His two Concordats, with the German States and the Latin nations, chiefly related to the possession of offices, and expressly reserved to the Pope what a long and universal experience had proved to be hateful abuses, as, *e.g.*, the annates, which were so demoralizing to the character of the clergy, and compelled them to incur heavy debts. And most of the articles were so drawn as to leave open a door for the renewal of the abuse. In the life and practice of the Church, the Papal system, with all its attendant evils, was restored.

§ XXIV.—*The Council of Basle.*

The Episcopal system, which was the true principle of reform, still survived in the decrees of the fourth and fifth sessions of Constance, and for a long time no one dared to meddle with them. One other hope re-

[1] See De Hardt, *Acta Conc. Const.* i. 965 *seq.*

mained : the Synod had decided that another should be held after five years, and that for the future there should be an Œcumenical Council every ten years. Here again Martin V. showed that he felt bound to observe the decrees of Constance, for he actually summoned the Council, in 1423, to meet, first at Pavia, and then at Sienna. But the moment any signs of an attempt at reform manifested themselves, he dissolved it, " on account of the fewness of those present." However, shortly before his death, he summoned the new Council to meet at Basle. Eugenius IV. could not avoid carrying out the duty he had inherited from his predecessor, to which he was already pledged in conclave. When the earliest arrivals at Basle took place at the appointed time, the citizens laughed at the new-comers as dreamers, so little could they now conceive the Pope's being in earnest in convoking the Council after the course events had taken since 1417.[1] In fact, Eugenius ordered the dissolution of the still scanty assembly immediately after its first proceedings, December 18, 1431, on the most transparently frivolous pretexts, with a view to its resuming its sittings a year and a half later at Bologna, under his own presidency. And yet the need for a Council had

---

[1] Æn. Silv. *Commentar. de Rebus Basil. Gestis* (ed. Fea. Rom. 1823), p. 39.

never seemed more urgent than at that moment, on account of the triumphs of the Hussites. The assembly, relying on the decrees of Constance, which had been repeatedly promulgated, remained united, and profited by the warning of the evil consequences resulting at Constance from the sharp division of nations to frame a better organization for itself, by forming four deputations, in which different nations and orders were represented. And thus the contest with the Pope began, at first under favourable circumstances, for public opinion throughout Europe was already enlisted on the side of the Council. Moreover, it received strong support from King Sigismund, and Eugenius found himself hard pressed in Italy, and deserted by many Cardinals, and even by the Court officials, hundreds of whom had run away from him. In vain he pronounced excommunication against the prelates who were on their way to Basle. Letters of adhesion poured into Basle from kings, princes, and prelates, from bishops and universities ; it seemed as if once again the spell was broken whereby the Papal system had held men's minds enthralled. Eugenius saw that he must give in, and he signified his assent to the continuance of the Council in his Bull of February 4, 1433, and named four cardinals to preside over it.

But this Bull, again, did not satisfy the Council, though Eugenius expressly declared that he regarded it as having never been interrupted, and thereby absolutely retracted his former decree for its dissolution. There was a design of suspending him, when Sigismund, now become Emperor, arrived unexpectedly, and, through his exertions, effected a reconciliation between the Pope and the Council. Eugenius transcribed word for word the form of approval drawn up by the Council in his Bull of December 15, 1433, and recalled his three former Bulls ; he was now - ashamed of the third, in which he had most vigorously assailed the authority of the Council, and on the principles of the Papal system, and affirmed that he had not sanctioned its publication.[1]   He admitted that the Council had been fully justified in continuing in session, and passing decrees, in spite of his Bull of dissolution, and promised to adhere to it " with all zeal and devotion."[2]   " We recall the three Bulls," he said, " to show clearly to the world the purity of our intentions and sincerity of our devotion to the universal Church and the holy Œcumenical Council of Basle."   The

---

[1] The style and tone of this Bull, *Deus novit*, betray unmistakeably the hand of the Papal Court theologian, and Master of the Palace, Torquemada, who was in Basle in 1433, by commission of the Pope, but seems soon afterwards to have returned to him.

[2] Mansi, *Concil.* xxix. 78.

humiliation of the man and the discomfiture of the system were complete. It was no isolated act of condescension for the sake of peace, but the most definite
and indubitable acknowledgment of the superior authority of the Council, and his own subjection to it.

The Synod had from the first taken the decrees of
Constance on the supreme authority of Councils as its
basis, and expressly published them anew as articles of
faith, which in fact they were expressly declared to be
by the Council of Constance. Pope and Council in
common enjoined Western Christendom to believe these
doctrines, and it certainly appeared incredible to every
one then that a time could ever come when the attempt
would be made to overthrow them.[1]

Even in his former Bulls, condemning and annulling

---

[1] Ultramontanes, from Torquemada and Bellarmine to Orsi, have discovered but one escape from this dilemma, by saying that Eugenius's concessions were made under sheer pressure of fear. But he was perfectly free per-
sonally. Sigismund was at Basle, Eugenius in Italy, and they corresponded
by letter. If Eugenius was afraid, it was simply the conviction of the
whole Church, the public opinion of princes, clergy, and nations, he was
afraid of. And if this feeling is to be called fear, then every Pope lives in a
chronic state of fear. Eugenius had in deed first sent about his ambassadors
to investigate the state of opinion. But even the Religious Orders, always
devoted to Rome, refused their services then. Gonzalez, General of the
Jesuits, who thought the argument from fear too absurd, took refuge in
the pretext that Eugenius sought to deceive the Council by the ambiguous
language of his Bull (*De Infallib. Rom. Pontif.* Romæ, 1689, p. 695),—an
unjust imputation on the Pope, for the Bull is clear and unambiguous from
beginning to end.

the decisions of the Fathers at Basle, Eugenius had not
ventured to touch the decrees of Constance on which
they were based, and he had, moreover, recognised the
second session, in which those decrees were renewed ;
he had only attacked what was done after the issue of
his decree for the dissolution of the Council. So completely and irrevocably was the Papal See bound, as we
must believe, to the decisions of Constance on Church
authority,—for if Eugenius erred in confirming them
he was not infallible, and the gift must rest with the
Council, while, on the other hand, if he was right, his
subjection in matters of faith to the Council, and therefore his fallibility, was again affirmed. Moreover,
Eugenius had maintained his right, as Pope, to dissolve
or suspend any Council at his pleasure; this he now
retracted, and acknowledged the legitimacy of a General
Council carried on in defiance of a Papal decree for its
dissolution.

For three years and a half, from the fourteenth session
of November 7, 1433, to the twenty-fifth of May 7, 1437,
an external harmony at least was maintained between
the Council and the Pope, as represented by his legates
and by Cardinal Cæsarini. The decrees of reform only
included matters long since universally recognised as

necessary, and forbade nothing which had not been regarded as a public scandal for the Church. The regular method of conferring spiritual offices was restored, reservations of elective benefices and reversionary rights in them were abolished, simony and pluralities were forbidden, some regulation and limitation of appeals was introduced, and the frequency and severity of interdicts diminished. All this was so reasonable, so just, and so ecclesiastical, that it was received with general applause. The Synod acted so considerately, that of the numerous rights claimed by the Popes in the Decretals of the *Corpus Juris,* no single one was abrogated. And besides, by adding the exception, " for weighty and prudent reasons," the Synod had left open a wide door for the Pope, notwithstanding its prohibitions, which gave occasion to the University of Paris to blame them sharply.[1]

Eugenius himself had declared his entire agreement with the decrees of reformation, even after the twentieth session of January 23, 1435,[2] and he repeated this on June 15 of the same year to the deputy of the Synod, John of Brekenstein.[3] Yet he had a grudge against

[1] Bulæi, *Hist. Univ. Paris,* v. 246.
[2] " Se Concilii decreta semper suscepisse et observasse." Aug. Patric. *Hist. Concil. Basil.* c. 46, in Labbé, *Concil.* xiii. 1533.
[3] Labbé, *ut supra,* p. 865.

the Council for not giving him the means of obtaining money, which he asserted his need of, for abolishing annates, and for disputing his right to the patronage of benefices reserved by the last Popes. Before finally breaking with them, he had a charge brought against the Council, through his agents, who travelled about to the different Courts furnished with secret instructions, that they had appointed a President, and given far too sweeping an interpretation to the decrees of Constance, which, however, he had himself three years before acknowledged as the true one. The payment of annates, he said, was an immemorial usage—the fact being that the Popes had introduced it about forty years before, during the schism.[1] His nuncios were further instructed that, as the abuses of the Court of Rome were constantly cast in its teeth, and this produced a great impression, they should carry with them a scheme of reformation of a certain sort, in the shape of a Bull, to be produced for the edification of the sovereigns, and to shut the mouths of accusers.[2] They were at the same time fur-

[1] The annates amounted to half, and often more than half, the annual income of a see or a benefice, which every fresh occupant had to pay once, and to pay in advance, to the Papal treasury. This excluded all poorer men, unless their families could raise the money, from the higher dignities in the Church, and placed the clergy generally in the position of having to enter on their posts under pressure of heavy debts. In some German bishoprics the annates amounted to 25,000 florins (£2000).

[2] " Per hanc reformationem, etiamsi usquequaque plena non foret, modo

nished with special powers, *in foro conscientiæ* (dispensations and absolutions), by the use of which they might gain over the sovereigns to the Pope.[1]

The Council, on the other hand, had some weak points. Carried on and encouraged by the general confidence and assent accorded to it, it was under the temptation of entering upon a mass of details, processes, and local concerns, which were brought before it chiefly from France and Germany; it got involved as umpire in political intrigues, and made enemies here and there even among the sovereigns. And the final decision naturally rested with them, when the struggles between the Council and the Pope broke out afresh.

The negotiations with the Greek Emperor about the reunion of the Churches gave the Pope the desired pre-

---

esset aliqua, eorum ora obstruerentur, qui continue lacerant et carpunt Romanæ Curiæ famam—redderenturque tunc reges et principes melius ædificati et magis proni ad condescendendum petitionibus Papæ et Cardinalium," etc. Raynald. *Annal.* ann. 1436, 15. Had the Roman encomiast, who has been so discreetly reticent elsewhere, gone to sleep when he let this passage get into print?

[1] The Bull does not specify the extent of graces of this kind, such as were used for detaching the princes from the side of the Council; but they must have been very large; for a century earlier, *e.g.*, Clement v. had granted to King John of France and his wife the privilege of being absolved by their confessor, retrospectively and prospectively, from all obligations, engagements, and oaths, which they could not conveniently keep. "Sacramenta per vos præstita et per vos et eos præstanda in posterum, quæ vos et illi servare commode non possetis."—D'Achery, *Spicil.* (Paris, 1661), iv. 275.

text for setting up a rival Synod in Italy. He had already obtained a decision from the minority friendly to him at Basle in favour of removing into Italy, when, at the end of 1437, he proclaimed the adjournment of the Council, or rather, as the event showed, the opening of a new one at Ferrara. As the Greeks took his side, and the Emperor, the Patriarch, and the Bishops of the Eastern Church, really came to Ferrara (as afterwards to Florence), his design succeeded.

It was well known at Basle that the Synod opened on Italian soil would at once be flooded by the local bishops, the officials of the *Curia*, and the clerical vagrants and place-hunters, and all hopes of reforming the Church would be lost. In fact, during the two years the Council sat at Ferrara and Florence, which the Pope prolonged to two years more, until 1442, after the departure of the Greeks, not a single genuine decree of reform was framed or promulgated.

Meanwhile the breach between the Fathers of Basle and the Pope was not obvious on the surface from the beginning, for Eugenius worded his original Bull as though it were based on that decree of the minority which professed to emanate from the whole Council, and thus the Synod of Ferrara at first appeared to be simply a continuation of that at Basle, and its decrees were supposed to form one body with those enacted there up to the time of the adjournment of the Synod after the twenty-fifth session. Both parties in the meantime adopted the extremest measures. The Synod of Basle, on the strength of the canon of Constance, declared it an article of faith that the authority of a General Council is higher than the Pope's, that none can dissolve or remove it against its will, and that to deny this is heresy. Thereupon Eugenius IV. was deposed, against the advice of the Emperor, and a new Pope, Duke Amadeus of Savoy, chosen, who took the name of Felix V.,—a grievous mistake and presumption, for the horror of a two or three headed Papacy and an European schism were still only too fresh in men's memory. Moreover, when the Synod ventured on these steps, at the instigation of its leader, Cardinal Allemand of Arles, it had already become insignificant in numbers and personal weight. It was too like a tumultuous multitude composed partly of impure and incongruous elements, though it manifested good discipline and steady perseverance under the leadership of the presiding Cardinal, whom it implicitly obeyed.[1]

[1] To the constantly repeated charge that the few bishops had been out-

§ XXV.—*The Union with the Greek Church.*

Eugenius had to give up all hopes of the non-Italian
bishops attending his Italian Council; not one of them
came, except that the Duke of Burgundy compelled
two of his Bishops to appear. But at Ferrara and
Florence he at last induced the Greeks, after long
resistance, to accept—to be sure only for the moment—
those conditions of reconciliation which he insisted upon,
and to subscribe the act of union. The Emperor, in
presence of the threatened destruction of his capital and
the last remaining fragments of his empire, yielded at
last. One of the main difficulties concerned the question
of the primacy, and that at the moment was the most
important point for the Pope, for if he could meet the
efforts of the Synod of Basle by producing the testimony of the re-united Eastern Church on his side, it
would greatly strengthen his case in the public opinion
of the whole West. A general recognition of the
Roman primacy was a matter of course for the Greeks,
according to their own tradition, as soon as the charge

voted by the numerous presbyters, D'Allemand might have well replied,
that had bishops only voted, the will of the Italian nation must have
always prevailed, for their bishops outnumbered or equalled those of all
other nations.—(Æn. Silv. *De Conc. Basil.* 1791, p. 87.)

against the Holy See of having become heretical or schismatical was disposed of. The Easterns had been familiar for nearly a thousand years with the Patriarchal theory, according to which the five Patriarchs, among whom the Patriarch of old Rome was the first and chief in rank, stood at the head of the whole Church, so that nothing could be separately decided on questions of doctrine and the common interests of the Church without the consent of all five of them. But this view of the precedence of the Roman "Pope" (the Patriarch of Alexandria had the same title with them) had at bottom as little in common with that universal Papal monarchy invented in the West in 845, and carried out in practice since 1073, as the position of a Venetian Doge has with that of a Persian Shah. To the Greeks, at all events, the notion of such theocratic sovereignty, interfering forcibly in all the details of the Church's life, and systematically ignoring all legal limitations, such as existed in the West, was strange and incomprehensible. Their Patriarchs moved within a far narrower sphere, and acted by fixed rules. The whole Papal system of indulgences was entirely unknown to them. Many rights and means of power gradually acquired by the Popes could never have come into use in their simple system of Church-government. And it was just these very claims of the Papal system which for centuries had been their main ground for resisting any overtures for reunion. As early as 1232 the Patriarch Germanus had written to the Cardinals,—"Your tyrannical oppression and the extortions of the Roman Church are the cause of our disunion."[1] Humbert, General of the Dominicans, made the same statement in the memorial he drew up for the Council of Lyons in 1274 :—"The Roman Church knows only how to make the yoke she has laid on men's shoulders press heavily; her extortions, her numberless legates and nuncios, and the multitude of her statutes and punishments, have deterred the Greeks from reunion."[2] And this was the universal opinion in the West.[3] The French clergy appealed to it in their representation to Clement IV. in 1266 ;[4] and Bishop Durandus of Mende urged it upon Clement V.[5] The English Sir John Mandeville related, after his return from the East, that the Greeks had answered laconically to John XXII.'s

---

[1] Matt. Par. *Hist. Angl.* p. 461. [2] Brown, *Fascic.* ii. 215.

[3] So Gerhoch (*De Invest. Antichr.* p. 171) said about 1150, "Græci a Romanis propter avaritiam, ut dicunt, se alienaverunt."

[4] Marlot, *Metrop. Rhemens,* ii. 557, "Quod propter ejusmodi exactiones Orientalis Ecclesia ab obedientiâ Romanæ Ecclesiæ recesserit, patet omnibus." [5] *Tractat. de Conc.* p. 69.

demand for their submission, "Thy plenary power
over thy subjects we firmly believe; thine immeasurable pride we cannot endure, and thy greed we cannot
satisfy. With thee is Satan, with us the Lord."[1] In
1339, the Minorite John of Florence sent to the East
by Benedict XIII., had an interview with the Patriarch
of Constantinople and his Synod, and it was again said
that the cause of the disunion was the insatiable pride
of the Bishop of Rome.[2]

That notion of the Papacy according to which all
Church authority is exercised by the Pope, and belongs
by inherent right to him alone, in whom are centred all
the rights of the episcopate, was a special stumblingblock to the Greeks;[3] and if they regarded the number
of oaths in use among the Latins as unchristian, the
demand that they should take an oath of obedience to
the Pope was doubly hateful to them. But the hope-
lessness of their situation had broken their spirit; they
were living during the Council on the alms of the Pope,
and could not return home with their work unaccom-
plished. Eugenius wanted them to acknowledge his

[1] *Itinerar. Zwollis*, 1487, i. 7.
[2] Joh. Marignol. *Chronic.* in Dobner's *Script. Ter. Bohem.* ii. 85.
[3] Thus in the *Crimen contra Eccl. Lat.*, written about 1200, and found
in Coteler, *Monum. Eccl. Grcc.* iii. 502, we read, ἕνα συνεκτικὸν τῶν
ἀπάντων ἀρχιέρεα τὸν Πάπαν. That they could not comprehend.

monarchical power over the whole Church in the form usual in the West, and, when the Papal theologians overwhelmed them with a mass of forged or corrupted passages derived from the pseudo-Isidore and Gratian, they answered shortly and drily, "All these canons are apocryphal."[1] The Emperor said that if the Pope insisted on this point, he would depart with his bishops. At last a compromise was effected; the Pope waived - his demand for a recognition of his supremacy over the Church "according to Scripture and the sayings of the saints."[2] The Emperor had observed on that point, that the courtly rhetoric to be found in the letters of ancient bishops and emperors could not be transmuted into the logic of strict law, and that the canons of Councils should rather be taken as the rule. The article was accordingly worded to this effect, that "the Pope is the vicar of Christ, the head of the whole Church, the Father and teacher of all Christians, and has full authority from Christ to rule and feed the Church in the manner contained in the acts of the Œcumenical Councils and in the Canons." This language defined the limits of the Papal authority, and the

[1] Harduin, *Concil.* ix. 968-974.

[2] This meant, as the acts show, the strongest of the spurious passages in pseudo-Isidore and St. Thomas.

rules for its exercise, and moreover reduced it within
such narrow and moderate boundaries that Eugenius
and his theologians would never have agreed to it had
they known the true state of the case, and not been
misled by the old and new forgeries into a very mistaken estimate of the ancient Councils, and the position
the Pope occupied in them. The Greeks understood
by the Œcumenical Councils those only which were
held in the East during the first eight centuries, and
before the division of the two halves of the Church,
the Eastern and Western, and this was recognised at
Rome as self-evident, so that in the first edition printed
there, as well as in the *Privilegium* of Clement VII.,
and even in the Roman edition of 1626, the Council of
Florence is called the eighth Œcumenical.[1]   But in the
first seven Councils nothing was said of any special
rights of superiority in the Pope ; only his precedence
over all other patriarchs was recognised in the twenty-
eighth canon of Chalcedon.   The appeals, which Eugenius wanted, were expressly forbidden by the ancient
Councils.   But the Latins, to whose minds the mention
of the ancient Councils only suggested the legends of

---

[1] [It is also quoted as the eighth in Cardinal Pole's *Reformation of England*, dated Lambeth, 1556.—Tr.]

Silvester, Julius, and Virgilius, etc., and the spurious canons, thought they had provided sufficiently for the interests of the Pope by this formula.

The original Latin translation rendered the Greek text faithfully, for after the long controversy with the Greeks over every word, it had been necessary to draw up the decrees first in Greek. Flavio Biondo, the Pope's secretary, gives a correct version.[1] But in the Roman edition of Abraham Cretensis, by the unobtrusive change of a single word, what the Greeks intended to have expressed by it had disappeared, viz., that the prerogatives attributed to the Pope are to be understood and exercised according to the rule of the ancient Councils.[2] By this change the rule was trans-

---

[1] The Greek version runs, "καθ' ὃν τρόπον καὶ ἐν τοῖς πρακτίκοις τῶν οἰκουμενίκων συνόδων καὶ ἐν τοῖς ἱεροῖς κάνοσι διαλαμβάνεται." This is honestly rendered in the original Latin text, "quemadmodum (better 'juxta eum modum qui') et in gestis Œcum. Concil. et in sacris canonibus continetur." So Biondo quotes it in his History (l. x. Dec. 3), and so Cardinal Marcus Vigerius, Bishop Fisher of Rochester, Eck, and Pighius have quoted it after him. But the Dominican Antoninus had already substituted "etiam." ["Continetur" is, however, an inadequate rendering, to say the least, of διαλαμβάνεται, which rather means "is determined" than "is contained." See an article on the Council of Florence in the *Union Review*, vol. iv. pp. 190 *sqq.* and cf. vol. iii. pp. 686, 687.—Tr.]

[2] "Quemadmodum etiam," instead of "et—et." It is one of the many disingenuous statements Orsi has made himself responsible for, when he says (*De Rom. Pont. Auctor.* vi. 11), in the teeth of the facts as evidenced by the record of proceedings, that the Greek text was translated from the Latin, which, however, had not "etiam" originally. His ignorance of

formed into a mere confirmatory reference, and the sense
of the passage became, that the prerogatives enumerated there belonged to the Pope, and were *also* contained
in the ancient Councils. And the decree of Union
has since been printed in this corrupted form in the
collections of canons, and elsewhere.[1]

After the departure of the Greeks, Eugenius severely
denounced the Synod of Basle in his Bull issued from
Florence, but this censure only touched the sessions
held after its prorogation, and the "false interpretation
put upon the decrees of Constance."[2] In this reserved
and tortuous document he did not venture to make
any direct attack on the decrees of Constance, then so
highly reverenced throughout the Christian world, but
he tried to damage their credit by observing that they

Greek may excuse him for saying, on the authority of a young man, that
καί—καί may be translated by "etiam." Launoy, Bossuet, Natalis Alexander, De Marca, the Jesuit Maimbourg, and Duguet, have long since
exposed the fraud. But in the Greek version, sent directly from Florence
by the Pope to the King of England, all the words after "primacy over
the whole Church" are missing, so that there is reason to suspect an interpolation even in the Greek text. Brequigny has shown (*Mémoires de
l'Académ. des Inscr.* t. 43, p. 306 *sqq.*) how suspicious are all the copies of
the decree of Union, nine in number, now extant, except the British.
None of them are original documents. The five original copies have disappeared.

[1] [It is also printed in some theological manuals, and often quoted for
controversial purposes, with the words about the canons of Councils suppressed altogether.—Tr.]

[2] In the Decretal "Moyses Vir Dei." Cf. *Concil.* (ed. Labbé), xiii.
1030.

had been passed during the time of the schism by one Obedience only, and after the departure of Pope John. Yet it was not the loss of his infallibility through these decrees that so deeply grieved him. That he had already recognised. Torquemada had made him say in the former Bull (*Deus novit*) that the Pope's sentence must always take precedence of that of a Council, except in what concerned questions of faith, or rules necessary for the good of the whole Church, and in that case the decision of the Council must be preferred.[1]

§ XXVI.—*The Papal Reaction.*

The French nation assumed the most dignified and consistent attitude in view of the altered condition of the Church and the renewal of the schism. In 1438 the King opened a mixed assembly of ecclesiastics and laymen at Bourges. The deputies both of the Pope and the Council of Basle were heard, and it was decided to receive the decrees of the Council, with certain modifications required by the circumstances of France. Thus originated the Pragmatic Sanction of Bourges, which included the freedom of Church elections, the principle of the superior authority of General Councils, and the

[1] See *Concil.* (ed Labbé), xii. 537.

rejection of the disorderly proceedings of the *Curia*, with its expectancies, reservations, appeals, and manifold devices for extorting money. It was the first comprehensive codification of what have since been called the Gallican Liberties. Detested at Rome, it became the butt for the attacks of every Pope after Eugenius IV., until at last Leo X. succeeded in abolishing it by the Concordat of 1517, in which the Pope and the King shared the spoils of the French Church ; the lion's share falling, however, to the King.

England, involved at the time in political troubles, neglected to take a side. Few only would acknowledge the Savoyard Pope, even if they would not resolve on giving up the Council. Alfonso, King of Aragon and Naples, hitherto the main support of the Council of Basle, but who had now been won over by the large offers of the Pope, recalled his bishops, and together with the Venetians, who were the countrymen of Eugenius, was his great support in Italy. The German nation, under the lead of the Electors, maintained neutrality between the Synod of Basle and the Pope, but in a sense practically favourable to the Council; and they solemnly accepted its decrees of reformation in 1439 at the imperial Diet of Mayence, whereby

Germany bound itself, like France, to the recognition
of the doctrine of Church authority laid down in the
canons of Constance.[1] There was no man of mark in
all Germany at that time who expected any good from
the Court of Rome for the Church or for his country.
Most of the clergy, the Universities of Vienna, Erfurt,
Cologne, Louvain, and Cracow, besides Paris,[2] the
sovereigns and their counsellors, and all the people,
were for the Council and its doctrine against the
Papal system.

But Eugenius understood well how to gain over
converts to his side, by bestowing privileges and grants
of all kinds, and for this he was much more favourably
situated than the Council, which was bound by its own
principles, and the decrees it had published, and had
little or nothing to give in the way of dispensations,
privileges, and exemptions, but was obliged to confine
itself within the limits of the ancient Church, while
Eugenius, according to the tradition of the *Curia*,
was not bound to the laws of the Church. To the
Duke of Cleves he gave such important ecclesiastical

[1] See, for the document of acceptance, Koch, *Sanctio Pragmat. Germ.*
p. 93.
[2] Launoy (*Opp.* vi. 521 *seq.*) has had their judgments printed from Parisian
manuscripts.

rights, at the expense of the bishops, that he made him master of the Church and the clergy of his country, so that it became a proverb, "The Duke of Cleves is Pope in his own land."[1] As early as 1438, Eugenius had not only deposed and anathematized the members of the Council, but laid Basle under interdict, excommunicated the municipal council, and required every one to plunder the merchants who were bringing their wares to the city, because it is written, "The righteous hath spoiled the ungodly." For a long time, indeed, his acts produced no result; there was too strong a feeling in favour of the Council, which had shown so sincere a desire to benefit the Church. For some years the Electors vacillated in their policy between Rome and Basle. At last their decision came, in 1446. King Frederick, acting under the advice of his secretary, the accomplished rhetorician Æneas Silvio Piccolomini, sold himself to Pope Eugenius, who could offer him more than Felix, since the latter was bound to the decisions of the Council. The generous Eugenius pledged himself to pay the King 100,000 florins for his journey, together with the imperial crown, assigned tithes to him from all the German

---

[1] Teschenmacher, *Annal. Cliviæ* (Francof. 1729), p. 294.
[2] Raynald. *Annal.* anno 1438, 5.

benefices, the patronage for one vacancy of 100 benefices in his hereditary territories, and the appointment of bishops to six dioceses, and, finally, gave full
powers to his confessor to give him twice a plenary absolution from all sins.[1] Thereby the cause of the Council
and of Church reformation was lost in Germany, and the
German Church sank back, step by step, into its former
bondage. Æneas Silvius, who had meanwhile entered
the Papal service, bribed two ministers of the Elector
of Mayence, who won over their master to the side of
the Pope. Thus the body of German princes was
divided, and the previous demand for a new Council
was reduced to a mere petition, which people did not
trouble themselves about at Rome. The victory of
Eugenius was complete. When on his death-bed he
received the homage of the German ambassadors, the
event was celebrated (Feb. 7, 1447) in Rome with ring-
ing of bells and bonfires. Even the slight concessions
the Pope had made to the Germans he thereupon at
once recalled in secret Bulls, " so far as they contained
anything prejudicial to the Papal See." A fortnight
later he died, after triumphing over the Council and

---

[1] Chmel, *Geschicht. Friedr.* IV. (Hamburg, 1839), ii. 385 ; *Material.* ii.
195 *sqq.*

over Germany; but the means he had employed wrung from him in his agony of conscience the words, " O Gabriel, how much better were it for thy soul's salvation hadst thou never become Cardinal and Pope!" Meanwhile, however, he had acknowledged in his public Bull the decrees of Constance on the superiority and periodical convocation of Councils.[1]

When Frederick III., in 1452, received the imperial crown from the hands of the Pope, Æneas Silvius was able to declare in his name and his presence that another Emperor would, no doubt, have desired a Council, but the Pope and the Cardinals were the best Council.[2]

The new Pope, Nicolas V.—that same Thomas of Bologna who had been so successful in his dealings with King Frederick—added a fresh conquest to the hardwon victory of his predecessor in the Concordat of Vienna (of Feb. 17, 1448), restoring to the Pope the right of appointing to a great number of German benefices—a compact concluded with King Frederick, as plenipotentiary of the German princes, who came into his portion of the gains and influence shared between them and the Papal Court. The princes had been the

---

[1] Raynald. *Annal.* ann. 1447, 4; Müller, *Reichstags-Theatrum*, pp. 347, seq. ; Koch, *Sanctio Pragm.* pp. 81 *seq.*

[2] Æneæ Silvii *Hist. Fred. III.* in Kollar's *Analecta*, ii. 317.

more readily won over at an earlier period by various privileges, because the observance of the reforming decrees of Basle would have considerably diminished their power over the churches in their dominions. Not long after the compact had been agreed upon, Pope Calixtus III., in 1457, declared to the Emperor that it was obvious the Pope was not bound by the Concordat, for no agreement could bind or limit in any way the full and free authority of the Papal See, and if he paid regard to it, that was only out of favour, friendliness, and tender affection for the German nation.[1] And this has been a Roman maxim from that day forward. It was taught that an authority like the Papal cannot bind itself, for that would be inconsistent with its plenary power; least of all can it lay an obligation on future Popes, since all have equal rights, and an equal has no power over his equal. The nation therefore is bound by the Concordat, but not the Pope. And thus the Bolognese jurist, Cataldino de Buoncampagni, who wrote for the Pope against the Synod of Basle, had already determined that whatever promises the Pope might make, he was never bound by them in the fulness

---

[1] "Quamvis liberrima sit Apostolicæ Sedis auctoritas nullisque debeat pactionum vinculis coerceri," etc.—*Æneæ Silvii Epist.* 371, *Opp.* (ed. Basil. 1551), 840.

of his power, for as every one is his subject, every compact or engagement bears the character of a gracious condescension only, and can, as such, be at any moment retracted,[1] and therefore the Pope, in spite of his promises, was not bound to the decrees of the Council.[2] It was roundly affirmed in the Roman Court of the Rota in 1610, in reference to the German Concordat, that for the Pope and the *Curia* its only validity was as a privilege graciously bestowed, and that it had no binding force.[3]

But the hatred and contempt of both Pope and Emperor, which had become deeply fixed in the minds of the

---

[1] Thus, *e.g.*, says the Roman canonist and assessor of the Inquisition, Pirro Corrado, *Praxis Dispens. Apost. de Concord.* Quæst. 8.

[2] *De Translat. Concil.* in Roccaberti's *Biblioth. Max.* vi. 27. That was allowed to be again printed in 1697, notwithstanding the Roman censorship. It was maintained still later by the famous canonist, Felino Sandei, whom the Pope rewarded with bishoprics for his commentary on the Decretals, "ad cap. xiii. de Judiciis."

[3] Nicolarts, *Ad Concord. Germ.* Tit. 3. dub. 3, § 6. It was the received doctrine of the *Curia*, that Concordats could not bind the Pope. Thus the Benedictine Zallwein (*Princip. Jur. Eccl.* iv. 300) says, "Passim docent assentatores Romani Pontificis et curiales Romani apud quos ipsum nomen Concordatorum pessimè audit." Hence all German canonists, with the exception of course of the Jesuits, have felt it necessary to prove, from the laws of nations and of the ancient Church, that a Pope is bound to keep his word and the engagements of his predecessors. Thus Barthel, Schramm, Schrodt, Dürr, Schmidt, Schlör, Oberhauser, Zallwein, etc. Benedict xiv. himself alone declared, Dec. 14, 1740, in a Brief to the Chapter of Liége, that he did not hold himself bound by the Concordat. Cf. Endres, *De Libert. Eccl. Germ.* 1774, p. 60; Theod. a Palude (Hontheim) *Flores Sparsi*, 1770, p. 452; Barthel, *Opusc. Jurid.* 1756, ii. 373 *seq.*

Germans, broke out at the Imperial Diet at Frankfort
in 1454, and later, when the question of contributions
for the war against the Turks was raised. Nobody was
willing to trust a word said by them or their ambas-
sors, since the extortion of money was the only thing
aimed at. "All," says Æneas Silvius, who was soon as
Pope to experience similar treatment, "cursed the Emperor and the Pope, and treated the legates with contempt."[1] But the summoning of a General Council
was still sometimes talked of at these Diets, and the
very notion had become such a bugbear of the Popes,
that they made it a primary condition in their dealings
with some German princes, as, *e.g.*, with Diether of
Isenberg, that they should never moot the question.
Meanwhile every appeal to a General Council was
promptly visited with excommunication in the most
decisive manner by Pius II.

At the close of his life, the Emperor Frederick seems
to have repented of his share in this work of destruction. The instructions he gave his ambassador for the
Diet at Frankfort, in 1486, contain words to the effect
that he knew what immense sums passed to Rome
in the shape of annates, indulgences, and the like, and

[1] Pii *Commentar.* a Joh. Gobellin (Fcf. 1614), p. 22.

what abject obedience and subjection to the Papal See the German nation had exhibited, above all others. These services were received thanklessly and haughtily by the Pope, Cardinals, and Court officials, and the German nation was contumeliously treated in all dealings, from the highest to the lowest, so that it would be against the common nature and reason of mankind to endure such piteous treatment any longer. It was therefore to be impressed on the princes that they should no longer show obedience and submission to the Pope, in order that the German nation might no more be despised and humbled beyond all others."[1]

Felix (the Antipope) was now induced by the French King to resign, and was made the chief Cardinal, with extensive jurisdiction over several dioceses. The remnant of the Synod of Basle, which had at last been driven to Lausanne, dissolved itself, and the Cardinal of Arles, that "adept in iniquity and son of perdition," as Eugenius had termed him, was restored without ever retracting any of his principles. This did not prevent Clement VII. from canonizing him after his death, " since his sanctity had been proved by miracles, and he had always led a heavenly, chaste, and blameless life."

[1] Schlözer, *Briefwechsel*, x. 269.

§ XXVII.—*Temper and Circumstances of the Fifteenth Century.*

Some time had elapsed after the disastrous year 1446, before it was understood in Germany that all hope of reforming the Church by means of Councils was at an end. Even so late as 1459, men could not and would not believe in this utter wreck of all schemes of reformation. The Carthusian Prior, Vincent of Axpach, thought that if but one king would issue safe-conducts for the assemblage of a Council in his dominions, and but one bishop were to summon it, it would meet in spite of the reclamations or anathemas of the Court of Rome; and that was the last remaining hope, for the experience of the last fifty years proved that no help could be looked for from the See of Rome. It was a far worse error than the Hussite heresy, to deprive the Church of General Councils, which are its best possession. And Vincent then relates how Eugenius succeeded in alluring over nearly all the educated to his side by the offer of benefices.[1] An anonymous German writer, as early as 1443, had also lamented this falling away of the learned, such as Nicolas Cusa and Archbishop

---

[1] Pez, *Codex Epistol.* iii. 335.

Y

Tudeschi. "The Roman harlot has so many para-mours drunk with the wine of her fornications, that the Bride of Christ, the Church, and the Council represent-ing her, scarcely receive the loyal devotion of one among a thousand. And yet Germany, in the person of its Emperor, has been worse used by the Popes than any other kingdom; the German Emperor alone was compelled, in accordance with 'legendary and forged decretals,' to swear obedience to the Pope."[1]

At last, at the very moment of its dissolution, the much-abused Synod of Basle had obtained a conspicuous satisfaction; Councils were still held in such high esteem in Rome, even after the death of Eugenius, that the new Pope, Nicolas V., by advice of the Cardinals, issued a Bull, declaring all documents, processes, decrees, and censures of his predecessor against the Council void and of no effect, even though issued with the approval of the Council of Ferrara or Florence, or any other.[2] They were to be regarded as having never existed, and were expunged from the writings of Eugenius as com-

[1] *Tractat. missus March. Brandenburg.* 1443. See MSS. of vol. 31 of *Hardtisch* collection in the library of Stuttgart. What is said of the de-cretals is surprising at that early date. Yet Nicolas of Cusa also had just then for the first time recognised the spurious character of certain Isidorian decretals.

[2] See Bull *Tanto Nos*, in the Jesuit Monod's *Amadeus Pacif.* (Paris, 1626), p. 272.

pletely as the Bulls of Boniface VIII. against France and
the French king had been expunged on a former occasion by command of Clement V.[1] And thus the principles of the two reforming Councils, on the superiority
of General Councils to Popes, completely triumphed
after all; the attempts of Eugenius, acting under inspiration of Cardinal Torquemada, to bring the Synod
of Constance into bad odour, were entirely foiled, and
the *Curia* itself bowed to the superior claims of a
General Council. As regards the reforming decrees of
the Fathers of Basle, so far as they prejudiced the
power and finances of the *Curia*, they were surrendered
to destruction, but the dogmatic decisions of the Pope's
inferiority to a Council, on which they were based,
remained untouched.

Pius II., indeed, who in his former position of rhetorician and scholar had defended the interests of the
Synod of Basle, made the most desperate attempt to
directly condemn the decisions of Constance, which
hung like a Damocles-sword over the uneasy heads of
the Court officials, and disturbed their enjoyment of
Papal autocracy. But public opinion was too emphatically on the side of the Council, and he not only

---

[1] The Bull says, "Tollimus, cassamus, irritamus et cancellamus."

did not dare to go against it, but on the contrary found it prudent, in his Bull of retractation in 1463, to add expressly that he acknowledged the authority and power of an Œcumenical Council, as defined by the Council of Constance, which he reverenced.[1]

But the race of Torquemadas was not yet extinct. By degrees works appeared from the pens of monks and cardinals, or those who hoped to become such, designed to raise the Papal system from the humiliation it had suffered through the Councils. This was not difficult, for they had merely to arrange and systematize, in the form of axioms and deductions, the rich materials provided by the forgeries of Isidore, Gratian, and St. Thomas, in order to prove the groundlessness of the two closely connected doctrines, of the authority of the episcopate and of Councils. In this way originated the writings of Capistrano, Albanus, Campeggi, Elisius, Marcellus, and Lælius Jordanus, between 1460 and 1525. The character of the whole series may be judged from any one of them, for one is copied from another, and the same falsified or spurious testimonies, canons, and statements of fact, are reproduced in all of them.

When that holy and highly favoured soul, St. Cathe-

---

[1] *Concil.* (ed. Labbé), xiii. 1410.

rine of Sienna, came to Gregory XI., she told him that she found in the Court of Rome the stench of infernal vices, and on his replying that she had only been there a few days, the virgin, humble as she was, rose majestically, uttering these words, "I dare to say that in my native city I have found the stench of the sins committed in the *Curia* more oppressive than it is to those who daily commit them."[1]

It was the same everywhere; it seemed as though, through the state of things gradually brought about, and the dominant system in Rome, a new art had been discovered among men, of making corruption and vice omnipresent, and diffusing it like some subtle poison from one centre and workshop, throughout every pore of the vast organization of the Church. Every one who looked over the Christian world for advice and aid against the general corruption, or who only tried to effect an improvement within his own immediate sphere, found himself hampered at once by a Papal ordinance, and gave up the attempt as hopeless. Papal bulls, fulminations, begging monks, clerical place-hunters,[2] and inquisitors, were everywhere. Even

[1] *Acta Sanct. Bolland.* 30 April, p. 891.
[2] "Curtisanen," a name given to clerical vagrants who came to Rome to barter or beg for benefices. Wimpheling has accurately described them.

Erasmus could say, in his letter to Bishop Fisher of Rochester, "If Christ does not deliver His people from this multiform ecclesiastical tyranny, the tyranny of the Turks will at last become less intolerable."[1]

And thus from the middle of the fifteenth century every accent of hope disappears from the literature of the Church, clearly as these accents had again rung out at the beginning of the century, and about the time of the Synods of Constance and Basil, both in speech and writing. Men's thoughts could only revolve within the same narrow circle—a reformation of the Church is impossible as long as the Court of Rome remains what it is; there every mischief is fostered and protected, and thence it spreads, but there, unless by a miracle, there is no hope of reformation. So says the Abbot Jacob of Junterberg, "A reformation of the Church is to me almost incredible, for first the Court of Rome must be reformed, and the course things are taking shows how difficult that is. Yet no nation so vehemently opposes reform as the Italian, and to them all who have cause to fear it attach themselves."[2] The most highly reverenced theologian of the Netherlands, " the

---

[1] Erasm. *Epp.* vi. 8, p. 353 (ed. Londin. 1642).
[2] *De Sept. Stat. Eccl.* about 1450, in Walch, *Monum.* ii. 2, 42.

ecstatic doctor," as he was called, the Carthusian Prior
Dionysius Ryckel, related how it was revealed to him
in a vision, which he communicated to the Pope himself, that the whole choir of the blessed in heaven had
offered intercessions for the Church on earth, which
was threatened with the severest judgments, but had
received answer that even if the Pope, the cardinals,
and the prelates, with the rest, swore in God's name,
that they wished to reform themselves, they would be
perjured; from head to foot there was no soundness in
the Church.[1]

It was pretty generally felt that it was with the reformation of the Church as with the Roman king and
the Sibylline books; since the seed of corruption sown
everywhere by the *Curia* had so plentifully sprung up
during the last fifty years, while the Church made no
efforts for her deliverance, reform could only be purchased at a much dearer price, and with far less hope
of satisfactory results. Many thought, like the Dominican Institoris, about 1484, "The world cries for a
Council, but how can one be obtained in the present
condition of the heads of the Church? No human power
avails any longer to reform the Church through a

[1] Petri Dorlanc. *Chron. Cartus.* (Colon. 1608), pp. 394-9.

Council, and God himself must come to our aid in some way unknown to us."[1]

The Germans at that period looked with great envy on the French, English, Scotch, and other nations, who were not so shamefully abused and recklessly plundered as the barbarous but "humble and patient" Germans, who were sacrificed by their own princes. Æneas Silvius, or Pius II., had reminded them before, that, considering their barbarism, they must account it properly an honour they had to be thankful for, that the Court of Rome, in virtue of its long attested civilizing mission for Germany, was undertaking their affairs, and indemnifying itself richly for the trouble.[2]

When the Elector, Jacob of Trèves, advised King Frederick to gain the favour of the German nation by urging the new Pope, Calixtus III., to remedy their grievances, Æneas Silvius persuaded him rather to unite himself with the Pope than with the German people for a common object, for, said the Italian, between king and people there is an inextinguishable hatred, and it is

---

[1] Cf. Hottinger, *Hist. Eccl. Sæc.* xv. p. 413.

[2] *Respons. et Repl. Wimphel. ad Æneam Silvium,* in Freher, *Script. Rer. Germ.* (ed. Struv.) ii. 686-98. As late as 1516 the patriotic Wimpheling thought it necessary to defend his country and its spokesman, Chancellor Martin Maier of Mayence, against the Siennese Pope.

therefore wiser to secure the favour of the new Pope by rendering services to him.[1]

Rome thus became the great school of iniquity, where a large part of the German and Italian clergy went through their apprenticeship as place-hunters, and returned home loaded with benefices and sins, as also with absolutions and indulgences.

There is something almost enigmatical about the universal profligacy of that age. In whole dioceses and countries of Christian Europe clerical concubinage was so general that it no longer excited any surprise ; and it might be said of certain provinces that hardly one clergyman in thirty was chaste, while in our own day there are countries where the great majority of the clergy are free even from the suspicion of incontinence. This distinction is to be explained by the universally corrupt state of the ecclesiastical administration. There could be no thought of any selection or careful training for the ministry where everything was matter of sale, where both ordination and preferment were bought and begged in Rome, where the conscientious, who would not be tainted with simony, had to stand aside, while the men of no conscience prospered, and rapidly attained

---

[1] Gobellin. *Comment.* Pii II. p. 25.

the higher positions, and the clerical profession was that of all others which offered the easiest and idlest life, with the largest privileges and the least of corporate obligations. The *Curia* had abundantly provided for the universal security and impunity of the clergy. Where the heads themselves gave the example of contempt for all laws, human and divine, it could not be expected that their subordinates would submit to the oppressive yoke of continence, and so the contagion was sure to spread. Every one who came from Rome brought back word that in the metropolis of Christendom, and in the bosom of the great mother and mistress of all Churches, the clergy, with scarcely an exception, kept concubines.[1]

§ XXVIII.—*The Opening of the Sixteenth Century.*

At the beginning of the sixteenth century, under Julius II., events took a turn which suggested an opportunity to the *Curia* for recovering the ground they had in theory lost. Louis XII. of France, and the German emperor Maximilian, who were at political

---

[1] When the vicar of Innocent VIII. wanted to forbid this, the Pope made him withdraw his edict, "propter quod talis effecta est vita sacerdotum et curialium ut vix reperiatur qui concubinam non retineat vel saltem meretricem." So too the Roman annalist, Infessura, in his diary, given in Eccard. *Corp. Hist.* ii. 1997.

enmity with the Popes, had recourse to the plan of
holding ecclesiastical assemblies. First, a French
National Synod was assembled at Tours, and then a
General Council summoned to Pisa, which being almost
entirely composed of French prelates, imitated the conduct of the Council of Basle towards the Pope. The
quarrel, as all the world knew, was purely political,
regarding the sovereignty in Italy, and thus the scheme
of the Council came to nothing. Julius II., and Leo. X.
after him, assembled their Lateran Council, with about
sixty-five bishops, in opposition to it. The utter failure
of the attempt made at Pisa encouraged the *Curia* in
its turn to strike a blow at Councils, since during the
period of increased confusion and uncertainty, from 1460
to 1515, the names of Constance and Basle were become
obsolete. Francis I. surrendered the Pragmatic Sanction
in return for the Church patronage bestowed upon him,
whereby elections were abolished, and the fortunes of
the superior clergy, who aimed at dignities and benefices, were placed absolutely in the hands of the
King. Thus fell the main support of the authority
of the Council of Basle in France, as it had already
fallen in Germany through the Concordat of Vienna.
Maximilian, herein a worthy son of his father, had

shortly before sacrificed the Council of Pisa, and given in his adherence to Julius II. and the Lateran Synod. But in Rome the *Curia* seized the opportunity to raise the clergy, who in France had just been so completely made dependent on the favour of the Court, from all subjection to civil ties, and accordingly, in the ninth session of the Lateran Council, it was ruled by the Pope and bishops that "by divine as well as human law the laity have no jurisdiction over ecclesiastical persons." This was a confirmation of the former decree issued by Innocent III. at the Synod of 1215 (the fourth Lateran), that no cleric should take an oath of fealty to the princes of whom he held his temporalities. It was next declared to be an obvious and notorious truth, attested by Scripture, Fathers, Popes, and Councils, that the Pope has full authority over Councils, and can summon, suspend, or dissolve them at his pleasure.

We must presume that at a period when the most complete theological barbarism prevailed in Rome itself, and there was nothing but scholasticism as represented by some Dominicans like Prierio and Cajetan, the cardinals and bishops of the day did not even know what Eugenius IV., Nicolas V., and Pius II. had so often declared. For they could hardly have expected the autho-

rity of a Leo X., with his hole-and-corner Council of ·
sixty-five Italians, to outweigh the Councils of Constance -
and Basle, and the Popes above named, in the public
opinion of Europe. The *Curia*, however, were further
encouraged by their feeling of complete security, their
consciousness that whatever they undertook, and however threatening or complicated might be the political
situation in Italy, they had nothing to fear in Church
matters. Nor was this confidence disturbed by reproaches
and accusations, however loud; and however often the
cry for a Council was raised, which always and chiefly
meant only a limitation of the Papacy, the *Curia* took
it quietly. So much stronger had the tie become during the last hundred years which bound the clergy to
Rome; every cleric who showed signs of rebelling was
crushed at once, and even the laity could not escape
excommunication and its consequences. Even the bold
Gregory of Heimburg only found a refuge with the
Hussite King in Bohemia, and was at last obliged, even
there, to supplicate for absolution at Rome, when a
sick and broken-down old man, in 1472.[1]

Yet the Christian world had endured, without any revolt worth noting, or even the remonstrance of a Synod

[1] Brockhaus, *Gregor. von Heimburg* (Leipzig, 1861), p. 383.

being raised, the rule of such Popes as Paul II., Sixtus IV., Innocent VIII., and Alexander VI., each of whom had striven to exceed the vices of his predecessor. Paul II., according to the expression of a contemporary, made the Papal Chair into a sewer by his debaucheries.[1] The same witness observes that he had gone to Rome and visited the various ecclesiastical communities, but had nowhere found a man of really religious life. What he says of the lives of the Popes, cardinals, and prelates, is stronger still.

Under Paul II., and still more under Sixtus V., the great clerical market was further extended, and principalities had to be found for nephews, and fortunes for natural sons and daughters. New offices were established in order to sell them, and the cardinalitial dignity was highly priced. Leo X. and Clement VII. sold a number of cardinal's hats, as the unbounded extravagance of the Medici had emptied even the Papal treasury, which before was held to be inexhaustible. From one end of Europe to the other it was again the cry, "Everything is made merchandise of at Rome." That had been said and written, indeed, in and out of Italy, for four centuries, but now, at the beginning of the

[1] Attilio Alessio of Arezzo in Baluze and Mansi, iv. 519.

sixteenth, it was the universal conviction that the venality could not before have been carried on in so gross, open, and shameless a manner as it now was before the eyes of the whole world; the art of turning everything into money could not have been worked up to such perfection. Count John Francis Pico of Mirandola, who wrote a treatise on the misfortunes of Italy as caused by Leo X., mentions, as a symptom of the extent of national demoralization and godlessness, that now ecclesiastical and religious offices were put up to formal and public auction to the highest bidder.[1]

Since 1512 a fresh source of information had been added, in the shape of an official edition, printed in Rome, of the customary taxes in the Roman Chancery and Penitentiary. It was based throughout on the older arrangement of taxes, dating from the time of John XXII., but it was then kept secret, whereas it was now publicly exposed for sale.[2] This publication,

[1] *De Veris Calamitatum Causis nostrorum Temporum* (ed. Colorius Cesius Mutinæ, 1860), p. 24.

[2] The composition of the *Curia* at the opening of the sixteenth century was very different from what it is now. A *Provinciale* of 1518, printed in Rome, contains, somewhere near the end, a list of the "officia Curiæ." Most of them are marked "venduntur." The purchase of such an office was the most profitable investment of capital, which, of course, produced the richest interest. We learn from this *Provinciale* that the referendaries "non habent numerum," that there were 101 *sollicitatores*, 101 masters of the archives, 8 writers of supplications, 12 registrars, 27 clerks

which was soon disseminated in every country, opened men's eyes everywhere to the huge mass of Roman reservations and prohibitions, as also to the price fixed for every transgression, and for absolution from the worst sins—murder, incest, and the like. This tariff of the Chancery was afterwards supposed to be an invention of the enemies of the Papacy, but the repeated editions prepared under Papal sanction leave no doubt about the matter.[1] They show the complete feeling of security in Rome, and what the *Curia* believed it could safely offer to the gaze of the world. For the bitterest enemy of Rome could have invented nothing worse than this exposure of a mechanism systematically developed for centuries, wherein laws seemed to be made only for the purpose

of the Penitentiary, 81 writers of briefs, 104 *collectores plumbi*, 101 apostolical clerks. All these offices were sold. There were besides 13 proctors in the "*Audientia Contradictorum*," 60 abbreviators "*de minori*," 12 *de parco majori*. Most of these also could be bought. We must add 12 Consistorial advocates, 12 auditors of the Rota, who are said to be dependent on gratuities, 10 notaries under the *Auditor Cameræ*, 29 secretaries and 7 clerics of the Camera, with 9 notaries. Think of a well-meaning Pope like Adrian VI. finding himself suddenly, in his old age, with the prospect of only a few years' reign, placed at the head of this gigantic machine, constructed in every part for money-getting; some 800 persons all bent on making the most out of the capital they had bought their places with, and all together forming a serried phalanx united by a common interest! A feeling of hopeless impotence to grapple with such a condition of things must steal over the very boldest heart.

[1] They were afterwards put on the Index, with the comment, "ab hæreticis depravata," but the editions, often indeed provided by Protestants, do not differ from the authentic Roman issues under Leo X. and Julius II.

of selling the right to break them, and both individuals and communities were only allowed the exercise of their natural rights when they had paid for it.[1]

The *Curia* cared nothing for being described by writers as the source of all the corruption in Christendom, the poisoner and plague-spot of the nations. There were indeed outbreaks of indignation here and there, especially when the *Curia* attacked some favourite popular orator. When the Carmelite Thomas Conecte, who had long been labouring in France, Flanders, and Italy, as a travelling missionary, had wrought numberless conversions, and had distinguished himself by the saintliness of his life, at last lashed the vices of the Court of Rome, Eugenius IV. had him tortured by the Inquisition, and burnt alive.[2] And as Eugenius treated him, Alexander VI. treated Savonarola. That famous orator and theologian had called aloud for a reformation of the polluted Church, and had urged the sovereigns to

---

[1] Thus, *e.g.*, cities had to pay a license at Rome for erecting a primary school, and if a school was to be removed, a sum of money had again to be paid for it. Nuns had to buy permission for having two maid-servants for the sick. Cf. *Taxæ Cancellar. Apost.* (Romæ, 1514), f. 10 *seq.*

[2] " Adversus vitia Curiæ Romanæ emergentia nimio quia zelo declamabat, captus pro hæretico habitus est et ut talis combustus." Cosmas de Villiers, *Biblioth. Carmel.* Aurelianis 1752, ii. 814. His brother monk, Baptista Mantuanus (*De Vitâ Beatâ*) pronounces Thomas a martyr, and compares his death with St. Laurence's. Eugenius is said afterwards on his deathbed to have bitterly repented his share in this deed.

Z

lend their aid to the assembling of an Œcumenical Council. For that the Pope excommunicated him, and threatened Florence with an interdict. Papal Commissaries were sent there, and Savonarola, with two brethren of his Order, was executed for heresy, and their bodies burnt. Thus did the crowned theologian overcome the simple preaching monk,—the theologian, for Julius was that, in spite of his children and his "handmaidens."[1] He had done, as Rodrigo Borgia, what was sure to gain him the red hat; he had, besides a gloss on the rules of the Chancery, composed a really learned work in defence of the universal monarchy and infallibility of the Popes.[2] But Savonarola, as even his enemies must admit, was not only one of the most gifted men and best theologians of his day; he also belonged to the most powerful of the Religious Orders, and had many adherents among its members. And thus he came to be honoured as a saint and martyr for the truth, and other saints, like Philip Neri and Catherine Ricci, bore witness to his holiness, and even a later Pope, Benedict XIV., declared him worthy of canonization.[3]

[1] The expression is borrowed from Macchiavelli, "Tre sue famigliari e care auzelle, lussuria, simonia, e crudeltade," J. Decennal. *Opere* (ed. Fiorent. 1843), p. 682.

[2] *Clypeus Defens. Fid. S. Rom. Eccl.* Argentor. 1497.

[3] *De Serv. Dei Canonis*, iii. 25. 17.

§ XXIX.— *The State of Contemporary Opinion.*

Italy was still more thoroughly victimized to the *Curia* than Germany, but the Italians bore the burden more easily, because the sums which flowed in from all parts of tributary Europe to the Court of Rome, through a hundred different channels, were again diffused from Rome, by means of nepotism, throughout the Peninsula, and most of the cardinals and prelates were flesh of their flesh, and bone of their bone. But the very fact of this close neighbourhood and kinship made its moral effects more mischievous. All thoughtful Italians of that age who could make comparisons, regarded their nation as surpassing those of Northern Europe in corruption and irreligion. Macchiavelli says :—"The Italians are indebted to the Roman Church and its priests for our having lost all religion and devotion through their bad examples, and having become an unbelieving and evil people."[1] He adds,—" The nearer a people dwells to the Roman Court the less religion it has. Were that Court set down among the Swiss, who still remain more pious, they too would soon be corrupted by its vices." Nor was a more favourable judgment given

[1] *Discorsi,* i. 12, p. 273, ed. 1843.

by Macchiavelli's fellow-citizen, Guicciardini, who for many years served the Medicean Popes in high offices, administering their provinces and commanding their army ; he observes, on Macchiavelli's words, that whatever evil may be said of the Roman Court must fall short of its deserts.[1] What these statesmen say of the moral corruption introduced into Italy by the *Curia* is confirmed in their way by the prelates. Isidore Chiari, Bishop of Foligno, who had opportunities at Trent of becoming thoroughly acquainted with his episcopal colleagues, says that, in all Italy, among 250 bishops, one could scarcely find four who even deserved the name of spiritual shepherds, and really exercised their pastoral office. "If the Italians are so alienated from Christianity that its profession may almost be said to have died out among us, the fault lies with the bishops and parish priests, for our whole life is a continuous preaching of unbelief."[2]

It is worth showing, that then, in spite of the Inquisition, much could be said in Italy, and many an avowal

---

[1] *Opere Inedite*, i. 27 (Firenze, 1857) :— "Non si può dire tanto malle della corte Romana che non meriti se ne dica piu, perchè è una infamia, uno esemplo di tutti e vituperii e obbrobrii del mondo." In his *Ricordi Autobiografici*, he says again, "A Roma, dove le cose vanno alla grossa, ove si corrompe ognuno," etc.—*Opere*, x. 166.

[2] The passage is cited by Bishop Lindanus in his *Apologet. ad German.* (Antwerp. 1568), p. 19.

made, which would not have been tolerated at a later period, when the Jesuits had got the upper hand, with their system of reticence, hushing up, and excuses. The Popes themselves did not shrink from making confessions which must have offended the majority of the cardinals and prelates of their Court as highly indiscreet. Adrian VI. told the Germans, by the mouth of his legate, Chieregati, that for years many abominations had disgraced the See of Rome, and everything had been perverted to evil; from the head corruption had spread to the members, from the Pope to the prelates.[1] If there was a well-meaning bishop here and there in Italy, he felt himself powerless the moment he tried in good earnest to undertake the administration of his diocese. When Matteo Giberto, the confidant and datary of Clement VII., at last sought out his diocese of - Verona, he found the city itself divided into six different spiritual jurisdictions, and his schemes of reform hopelessly baffled in presence of so many exemptions.[2] His biographer, in describing the state of Lombardy, alleges that the people knew neither the Lord's Prayer nor the Apostles' Creed, and a great part of them did not

[1] Raynald. *Annal.* ann. 1522, p. 66.
[2] " Giberti Vita," prefixed to his *Opera* (ed. Veron. 1733), p. xi.

go once a year even to confession and communion, the best of them not oftener, as a rule.

One evidence of the state of clergy and people in Papal dioceses may be gathered from the writings of Bishop Isidore Chiari, already mentioned. He found in 1550 that not above one or two priests in his diocese even knew the words of the sacramental absolution, and all the rest confused the form of absolving from excommunication with it. He had to send teachers to instruct them how to say mass properly. And they had incurred public contempt by their vices as much as by their ignorance. Most of the beneficed clergy could not even read.[1] In comparison with this state of things, which the *Curia* had produced in its own immediate neighbourhood, the condition of remoter countries was less disheartening. The great diocese of Milan, with 2500 priests, was for sixty years without a bishop. There was nothing in the houses of the clergy but arms, concubines, and children, and it had passed into a common proverb among the people that the priestly profession was the surest road to hell. Here too the use of the sacraments had almost disappeared. These are some features of the terrible picture sketched a few years later by the

---

[1] Isidor. Clar. Episc. Fulgent. *In Serm. Domini* (Venet. 1566), f. 101-125.

Milanese priest, Giussano, of the condition of things there.[1]

When Leo X. was elected in 1513, he had a terrible inheritance to enter upon, which might have made even the boldest shudder. His predecessors since Paul II. had done their utmost to cover the Papal See with infamy, and give up Italy to all the horrors of endless wars. But his first thought was that, now he was Pope, a life of unmixed enjoyment had begun for him.[2]

The Roman prelates bore with great equanimity the knowledge that Rome and the *Curia* were hated all the world over. Giberto, whom we mentioned before, foresaw that, in the event of war, the Germans " would hasten hither in troops to glut their natural hatred against us." Erasmus had repeatedly told them from the first that this hatred supplied its chief nourishment to the schism, daily increasing in strength. And the

---

[1] *De Vit. et Rebus Gestis Car. Borrom.* (ed. Oltrocchi, Mediol. 1757), p. 69.

[2] " Primo Pontificatûs die maximam voluptatem et cupiditatem expressit, dum Florentinâ linguâ palam hoc enuntiavit : ' Volo ut Pontificatu isto quam maxime perfruamur.' " His biographer adds that this could only be understood of physical enjoyments by any one who knew him. The passage is missing in Roscoe Rossi's impression of *Vita di Leone* x. t. xii., but occurs in *Cod. Vat.* 3920, whence a friend copied it for us, with the following, which is also omitted in Rossi, " Eâ tempestate Romæ sacra omnia venalia erant, ac nullâ habitâ religionis aut integræ famæ ratione palam ad Pontificatum suffragia vendebantur, omniaque ambitione corrupta erant."

facts spoke loudly enough for themselves. Even so
thorough-going a partisan as Cornelio Musso, Bishop of
Bitonto, one of the chosen speakers at Trent, did not
shrink from saying that the name of Rome was hated
by all nations, and its friends could only sigh over the
shame and contempt of the Roman Church.[1] And if
at the eleventh hour, as might happen, the bishops
of a country took counsel with a view to stemming
the double tide of corruption and secession from the
Church, they found again that the *Curia* had cut
through the nerves and sinews of their episcopal power.
At the Synod held at Paris in 1528 by the French
bishops of the province of Sens, it had to be actually
inserted in the canons that the bishops could not so
much as keep out the incompetent and unworthy by
refusing them ordination, for the rejected candidate
would at once go to Rome and get ordained there.[2]
Twenty years later the French prelates had again to
protest, at an assembly held at Melun, against the
fatal encroachments of the *Curia*, which had suddenly put in a claim to dispose of the benefices in
Brittany and Provence, and to transplant into France
the whole simoniacal abomination of reservations, ex-

[1] *Sermones,* ii. Dom. v. Serm. 2.   [2] Harduin, *Conc.* ix. 1953.

pectatives, and reversionary rights, with the endless processes they led to, in the teeth of the Concordat of 1517, whereby, as the bishops told the Pope bitterly enough, all hope of reformation was cut off.[1]

When in 1527 that judgment broke upon Rome which, like Rome itself, stands alone in history,—when the city which time out of mind had been absorbing countless sums of money from the whole West, was in its turn plundered by Germans, Italians, and Spaniards, and wrung dry like a sopping sponge, then at last the eyes of many were opened. That very Cajetan or De Vio, who had been Leo X.'s Court theologian and factotum, who had been his instigator in the disgrace of the Lateran Synod, in his decisions against Constance and Basle, in his proclamation of the divine right of every cleric to disobey his sovereign, and had lent his pen to these objects—that same man who, as legate in Germany, had embittered the Lutheran business by his insolence, and who again had induced the Pope to declare it a heresy to disapprove of burning heretics[2]— now in 1527 wrote, after the capture of Rome, "Justly is the life of the pastors of the Church the object of

---

[1] Baluze and Mansi, *Miscell.* ii. 297-300.

[2] [One of Luther's propositions, condemned by Leo x., is, "Hæreticos comburi est contra charitatem Spiritûs."—Tr.]

contempt, and their word neglected. We, the Roman prelates, now experience this, who by the righteous judgment of God have been given up as a prey, not to unbelievers, but to Christians, to be robbed and imprisoned. We are become useless for anything but external ceremonies and the enjoyment of this world's goods, and therefore are we trodden under foot and reduced to bondage."[1]

Whenever the influence of the Papacy on the Church and the religious administration of Rome was discussed in colloquies and conferences between Catholics and Protestants of that period, the Catholic spokesmen were obliged to declare : " Here our apology ceases ; we are conquered here, and can neither deny nor excuse." So spoke in 1519 Bishop Berthold of Chiemsee, Cardinal Contarini, the author of the Roman memorial of 1538, the Abbot Blosius, the French and Belgian theologians, Claudius d'Espense, Ruard Tapper, Gentian Hervet, Bishop Lindanus, and John Hoffmeister. There were moments when even the Popes were obliged to let their most approved servants say what in ordinary times would have led to a process of the Inquisition. Gaspar Contarini, whom Paul III. in his need suddenly

[1] Raynald. *Annal.* ann. 1527, p. 2.

transformed from a secular statesman into a Cardinal, ventured in substance to tell the Pope that the whole Papal system was wrong and unchristian. He said that Luther had good reason for writing his book on the Babylonish Captivity. " Nothing can be devised more opposed to the law of Christ, which is a law of freedom, than this system, which subjects Christians to the Pope, who can make, unmake, and dispense laws at his mere caprice. No greater slavery than this could be imposed on the Christian people."[1] Such utterances indeed produced no effect. Paul III. was not minded to swerve a hair's-breadth from his claim of absolute power, and for one Contarini there were always in Rome hundreds of Torquemadas, Cajetans, Jacobazzis, and Bellarmines.

The two Councils, the Lateran in 1516, and the Tridentine in its earlier period, had this point in common, that the speakers made avowals and charges so outspoken and of such overwhelming force that they cannot but amaze us. These speeches and descriptions reproduce in various forms the same idea : " We Cardinals, Italian bishops, and officials of the *Curia*, are a tribe of worthless men, who have neglected our duties. We have let

[1] *Epist. Duæ ad Paulum* IV. (Colon. 1538), pp. 62 *sqq.* Cf. the Collection of Le Plat, ii. 605.

numberless souls perish through our neglect, we disgrace our episcopal office, we are not shepherds but wolves, we are the authors of the corruption prevalent throughout the whole Church, and are in a special sense responsible for the decay of religion in Italy."

Cardinal Antonio Pucci said publicly before the assembly of 1516, " Rome, the Roman prelates and the bishops daily sent forth from Rome, are the joint causes of the manifold errors and corruptions in the Church ; unless we recover our good fame, which is almost wholly lost, it is all up with us." And Matthias Ugoni, Bishop of Famagusta, who also took part in the Lateran Synod, describes in his work the contempt the Italian bishops had sunk into, so that there was no infamy men did not attribute to them, while they repelled with scorn any one who so much as hinted at the need of reform and of a true Council, as disturbers of peace, and hypocrites. And the worst that had been said before of the Italian prelacy was confirmed in 1546 by the Papal legates at Trent. The German Reformers, when they wished to paint for public view the heinous guilt of the Popes and Italian bishops, had no need to do more than transcribe the words of the legates, and many similar statements and avowals let fall at

the Council. For no words could say more plainly
that the ruinous condition of the whole Church, the
dominant profligacy, the applause with which the neglected and dissatisfied people, in utter perplexity about
their clergy and their Church, universally hailed every
new doctrine or scheme of Church-government, was
ultimately due to the Italian prelacy, concentrated in
the *Curia*, and thence appointed over the dioceses.[1] They
said that all which they suffered at the hands of the
heretics was only a just retribution on their vices and
crimes, their bestowal of Church offices on the unworthy, and the like.

§ XXX.—*The Council of Trent, and its Results.*

The very first speech made at the opening of the
Council by Bishop Coriolano Martorano, of San Marco,

[1] See *Admonit. ad Synodum,* 1546, in Le Plat, *Monum. Coll.* i. 40.
"Horum malorum magnâ ex parte nos causa sumus. Quod lapsam
morum disciplinam et abusus complectitur, hic nihil attinet diu investigare,
quinam tantorum malorum auctores fuerint, cum præter nos ipsos ne nomi-
nare quidem ullum alium auctorem possimus." Cf. Girolamo Muzzio's
Lettre catoliche (Venez. 1571), p. 27, written in 1557, on the "abominazione
introdotta nella Chiesa." The bishops, themselves bad and incompetent,
"danno la cura dell' anima alla feccia degli uomini." Guicciardini describes
in his *Ricordi* how a bishopric was bought at Rome for a fixed sum,
and this was the usual provision for the younger son of an aristocratic
family. His relative, Rinieri Guicciardini, a bastard, but richly beneficed,
bought the See of Cortona of the Pope for 4000 ducats, and with it a dispensation for retaining his benefices.—*Opere,* x. 59.

created astonishment.[1] The picture he drew of the Italian cardinals and bishops, their bloodthirsty cruelty, their avarice, their pride, and the devastation they had wrought of the Church, was perfectly shocking. An unknown writer, who has described this first sitting in a letter to a friend, thinks Luther himself never spoke more severely.[2] What he then heard at Trent gave him the notion that the Council would not indeed accept Protestant doctrine, but would assail the Papal tyranny more energetically even than the Lutherans. How utterly was he deceived in his ignorance of the Italian prelacy! But what was then said in Trent left no doubt that the general absence of the Italian bishops from their dioceses, most of which had never even seen their chief pastor, must be regarded as fortunate, strongly as the Roman compilers of the memorial of 1538, designed for Paul III., insisted on this state of things being intolerable.[3] There is a letter extant of the famous Antonio Flaminio, of 1545, referring to the beginnings

---

[1] See Le Plat, i. 20 ff.

[2] *Fortgesetzte Sammlung von Theol. Sachen.* 1747, p. 335.

[3] " Omnes fere pastores recesserunt a suis gregibus, commissi sunt omnes fere mercenariis" (ed. 1671), p. 114. It was just the same sixty years later, in spite of the pretended reformation of Trent. Bellarmine says, in his memorial to Clement VIII., " Video in Ecclesiis Italiæ desolationem tantam quanta ante multos annos fortasse non fuit ut jam neque divini juris neque humani residentia esse videatur."—Baron. *Ep. et Opusc.* (Romæ, 1770), iii. 9.

of the Council while in process of formation. What, he asked, will a Council, composed of such monstrous bishops, do for the Church? There is nothing episcopal about them except their long robe. He knew of but one worthy bishop in Italy, who was now dead, Giberto of Verona, but nothing was to be hoped from the existing body, who had become bishops through royal favour, through solicitation, through purchase in Rome, through criminal arts, or after long years spent in the *Curia*. If any improvement was to be effected, they must all be deposed.[1]

The appearance of some French and Spaniards at Trent was enough at once to convert the Italian bishops into a herd of slavish sycophants of Rome, acting simply at the beck of the legates. They quietly let themselves be described as wretched, unprincipled hirelings, rude and ignorant men, without a murmur or contradiction interrupting the speaker. An Italian even ventured to say— what would not have been endured from a Cismontane— that all the evils and abuses of the Church came from the Church of Rome.[2] But when they had to testify their

---

[1] See *Quatro Lettere di Gasparo Contarini* (Firenze, 1558). Cardinal Quirini ascribes this letter to Flaminio.

[2] Thus, *e.g.*, Antonio Pucci, afterwards Cardinal Archbishop of Albano, at the Lateran Synod, called " Rome or Babylon, ejusque incolas pastores, qui

devotion to the *Curia*, they rivalled each other in their fervid zeal. " The Italian bishops," says Pallavicini, " knew of no other aim than the upholding of the Apostolic See and its greatness. They thought that in working for its interests they showed themselves at once good Italians and good Christians."[1] When, on one occasion, a foreign bishop mentioned an historical fact which would not fit in with the Papal system, the storm broke out. Vosmediano, Bishop of Cadiz, had observed that formerly metropolitans used to ordain the bishops of their provinces by virtue of their own authority. Cardinal Simonetta promptly contradicted him, and then the Italian bishops raised a wild cry, and put him down by stamping and scraping with their feet. They cried out that this accursed wretch must not speak ; he should at once be brought to trial.[2] That was the Conciliar freedom of speech at Trent !

In Italy, where matters did not come, as elsewhere, to an open breach of communion, and where the great mass of the lower orders remained Catholic, the better-minded were seized with a despondency bordering on

quotidie per universum terrarum orbem animarum saluti præficiuntur, tantorum causam errorum."—*Conc.* (ed Labbé), xiv. 240.

[1] " Non tendevono al altro oggetto che al sostentamento ed alla grandezza della Sede Apostolica."—*Storia del Conc. di Trento*, v. 425 (ed. Milan, 1844).
[2] Psalmæi, *Coll. Actor.*, in Le Plat, vii. ii. 92.

despair. In their speeches and writings about the time of
the opening of the Tridentine Council, they spoke of the
decay of all religion, the last agony, or the actual burial
of the Church, which the bishops were to be present at.
They call the Church a corpse in process of corruption,
or a house on fire, and almost reduced to ashes. So spoke
Lorenzo Giustiniani, Patriarch of Venice, the Cardinals
Ægidius of Viterbo, and Antonio Pucci, and several of the
bishops at Trent. That was the impression made on them
by the state of things in Italy, where the nation seemed
to be divided between unbelief and rude superstition,
whereas the nations north of the Alps were still, on the
whole, believing, though deeply shaken in their allegiance to the Church, which presented itself to them as
a tyrannical mistress, and so terribly disfigured and distorted that it could hardly be recognised. Socinianism
was a national product of Italy ; in Germany and England it found no place.

In Germany, and generally on this side the Alps, it
was long before men grasped the idea of the breach of
Church communion becoming permanent. The general
feeling was still so far Church-like, that a really free
Council, independent of Papal control, was confidently
looked to for at once purifying and uniting the Church,

though of course views differed as to the conditions of re-union, according to personal position and national sentiment. Here, as well as in the Scandinavian countries, in England and in the Netherlands, a *bonâ fide* reformation, by making some concessions about the use of the chalice and clerical marriage, above all, by abolishing the Papal system, might have saved or restored religious unity. If the more moderate Reformers, like Melanchthon, would only recognise the primacy of the Pope as matter of human ordinance, and an institution beneficial to the Church, this was chiefly, as one sees from Luther's statements, because in their minds the notion of the primacy had become inseparably identified with its caricature in the form of an absolute monarchy, which was always held up before their eyes. Just as they could not or would not comprehend the idea of the New Testament priesthood and Eucharistic Sacrifice, because both to their minds assumed only the shape to which they had been perverted and degraded, of a domination over the laity, and a systematic traffic in masses, so was it with the primacy. It could not but be doubly hateful and intolerable to them, both on account of the then occupants of the office, and of the element of tyranny it contained, and the perception that it was precisely the *Curia* which was the source and origin of corruption in the Church.

§ XXXI.—*The Theory of Infallibility formulized into a Doctrine.*

It was above all owing to the Italian devotion to Rome that homage was paid not only to the Papal system, but to the theory of Papal Infallibility which is its consequence. From the time of Leo X. this doc- trine entered on a fresh phase of development. On the whole, during the long controversy between the Council and the Popes from 1431 till about 1450, as to their right of superiority, the question of Papal authority in matters of faith had retired into the background. At the Council of Florence, after the Greeks had summarily rejected the spurious passages of St. Cyril, the subject was not mooted again by the Papal theologians; it was understood that there was no hope of getting that claim acknowledged by the Greeks. At the Council of Basle it was openly said, as a matter of public notoriety, that the Popes, like other people, were liable to error in matters of faith. The theologians of the Papal system, like Torquemada, the Minoritic Capistrano, and the Domini- can archbishop Antoninus, who defended the pet doctrine of the *Curia* about the superiority of Popes to Councils, between 1440 and 1470, devised another method for exempting the Pope from subjection to a Council in matters of faith, which was afterwards adopted by Cardinal Jacobazzi also. They maintained, as Torquemada expresses it, that the Pope can indeed lapse into heresy and propound false doctrine, but then he is *ipso facto* deposed by God himself before any sentence of the Church has been passed, so that the Church or Council cannot judge him, but can only announce the judgment of God ; and thus one cannot properly say that a Pope can become heretical, since he ceases to be Pope at the moment of passing from orthodoxy to heterodoxy.

On this principle they should have said that a bishop or priest never becomes heretical, and cannot be deposed for heresy, because God has already deposed him at the moment of his internal acquiescence in a false doctrine ; for if once such a Divine act of deposition were to be assumed before any human intervention, it is impossible to limit it to the case of the Pope, and to say that God is only so severe against heretical Popes, and milder towards heretical bishops and priests. A theory so obviously devised to meet a particular difficulty could satisfy

---

[1] *Summa*, iv. 2, c. 16 f. 383.

nobody. Meanwhile Torquemada clung to this discovery of his. He repudiates the notion that God would
not allow a Pope to define anything false. What he
knew from Gratian only was enough to exclude this pretext, but then his opinion was that when the Pope acts
thus he has ceased *de jure* to be Pope; he is therefore
but the corpse of a Pope, and the Church can execute
justice upon him at her good pleasure. The contemporaries of Torquemada, St. Antoninus, Archbishop of
Florence, and the canonist, Antonius de Rosellis, highly
as they exalted Papal authority, ascribed infallibility
only to the whole Church and its representative Councils.
Only in union with the Church, and when advised by
it—by a Council—is the Pope, according to the former,
secured from error.[1] And thus there was still no Papal -
Infallibility. The principle was too firmly rooted that -
the Pope may become heretical, and then the Church
or the Council must first tell him to abdicate, and, if he
refuses, proceed to depose him. So Cardinal Jacobazzi
has laid down.[2] And he also applies the prayer of
Christ to the Church, and not to the successor of
Peter,[3] as Thomas Netter or Waldensis had done before

[1] *Summa, Theol.* P. iii. p. 416.
[2] *De Concilio* (ed. Paris), p. 390.   [3] *Ib.* p. 421.

him.[1]   Silvester de Prierio, who was then Master of the
Palace, did not go beyond him.[2]   " The Pope does not
err," he says, " when advised by a Council."   Thomas
of Vio or Cajetan was the first to maintain Papal Infallibility in its fulness.   It was he who first got the
authority of the decisions of Constance and Basle on
the rights of Councils, which had been so solemnly
acknowledged and attested by former Popes, assailed by
Leo X., although the Council of Constance was not once
named, even in the Pope's decree on the subject promulgated at his Italian Synod.

It was now time to crown the edifice of the Papal
system by putting into shape the principle of Infallibility, first sketched out by St. Thomas in reliance on
forged testimonies, which is its natural consummation.
To the decrees of the two Councils were opposed the
well-known forgeries, the spurious passages and canons
of Eastern Fathers and Councils.   The coarsest and
most palpable of these forgeries, where St. Augustine is
made to identify the letters of the Popes with canonical
Scripture, was utilized by Cajetan for his doctrine.[3]
To the fictions he had borrowed from St. Thomas, he

---

[1] *Doctrinæ*, ii. 19.
[2] *Summa Silvestr.* (Romæ, 1516), verbo " Concilium."
[3] *Ad Leon. X. De Div. Inst. Pont.* (Romæ, 1521), c. 14.

added a new fraud of his own, by mutilating the famous censure of Wicliffe's teaching at the Council of Constance, which was very inconvenient for him.[1] Cajetan was a type of that class of sycophantic Court divines afterwards stigmatized by Caraffa and the other compilers of the memorial of 1538, as deceivers of the Pope through their doctrine of absolute supremacy, and authors of the corruption and dissolution of the Church. He was the inventor of that saying, which found its practical comment in the policy of the Medicean Popes and their immediate successors, " The Catholic Church is the born handmaid of the Pope," [2]—he who had seen a Sixtus IV., an Innocent VIII., an Alexander VI.

One cannot say that Cajetan's new doctrine became dominant at Rome. It must have seemed suspicious to many, if at the same time Papal Infallibility had been affirmed, and the long series of Papal Bulls confirming and fixing the chief dogmatic decisions of Constance had been declared erroneous. Innocent VIII. had already, in 1486, acknowledged the orthodoxy of the Paris University, at a time when the theologians Almain and

---

[1] He suppressed the crucial words " (error est) si per Romanam Ecclesiam intelligat Universalem aut Concilium Generale."

[2] *Apol. Tractat. de Comparat. Auctorit. Papæ et Concil.* (Romæ, 1512), c. 1.

Johannes Major declared in its name that it branded as heresy the doctrine of the superiority of the Pope to a Council, and this was universally taught in France and Germany. The Cardinal of Lorraine made a similar statement at the Council of Trent, without its provoking any contradiction. Adrian VI. was elected Pope, although it was notorious that, as professor of theology at Louvain, he had maintained in his principal work that several Popes had been heretical, and that it was certainly possible for a Pope to establish a heresy by his decisions or decretals.[1] The phenomenon of a Pope so wholly destitute of any consciousness of infallibility that as Pope he had his work denying it reprinted in Rome, was not without its effect. Men could still venture in Italy to defend the authority and decrees of the two Councils, and reject the Papal system as untenable on historical and canonical grounds. This was proved by the work of Bishop Ugoni of Famagusta, which received the commendation and assent of Paul III., in spite of his contradicting Torquemada, and maintaining the judicial authority of Councils over Popes.[2] And

---

[1] *Comment. in* iv. *Sent.* Q. de Confirm. "Certum est quod possit errare, hæresim per suam determinationem aut Decretalem asserendo." And he says expressly, "Evacuare intendo impossibilitatem errandi, quam alii asserunt."

[2] *De Concil. M. Ugonii Synodia* (Venet. 1568). The Pope's letter is prefixed to it.

again, it is clear from the whole contents of the famous and outspoken memorial on the state of the Church in Rome and Italy, drawn up by the Cardinals Caraffa, Pole, - Sadolet, and Contarini, with the assistance of Fregoso, Giberto, Aleandro, Badia, and Cortese, that they had very distinctly realized the ecclesiastical errors, mistakes, and false principles of the Popes, and were by no means addicted to the hypothesis of Papal Infallibility. When they describe the misery brought upon the whole Church through the blindness of the Popes, its desolation, nay downfal,[1] caused by the false doctrines of Papal omnipotence and absolutism, they were certainly far from supposing that Christ has bestowed on every Pope the privilege of strengthening his brethren by his dogmatic infallibility, while he is weakening and dismembering the whole Church by his perverse ordinances.

The very men who were most active in disseminating the doctrine of the personal infallibility of the Popes, could not help perceiving that the corruptions and abuses in the Church, which had been introduced and confirmed by the "infallible" Popes themselves, were still further strengthened by this doctrine, and every attempt at improvement made more hopeless. Cajetan,

---

[1] "Collapsam in præceps Ecclesiam Christi."

after he had been rewarded with a cardinal's hat for his services at the Lateran Council, afterwards, under Adrian VI.,—who was open to such representations,—becoming suspicious of the simony of the *Curia*, ventured to complain of the sale of bishoprics and benefices, dispensations and indulgences, which would at last lose all value. Thereupon a general feeling of indignation was kindled against him. What folly! it was said,—did he want to turn Rome into an uninhabited desert, to reduce the Papacy to impotence, and deprive the Pope, who was so heavily involved in debt, of the pecuniary resources indispensable for the discharge of his office? What the Pope had a right to give he had a right to sell.[1] To protect Cajetan, he was sent as legate to Hungary.

The other patron of the Infallibility theory, who laboured hard to naturalize it in Belgium, was the Louvain theologian, Ruard Tapper. He returned from Trent in 1552 cruelly disillusionized. He had had a near view —as his friend Bishop Lindanus tells us—of the manners of the Romans, and the working of the *Curia*, exclusively

[1] " Quid enim aliud esset quam vastam in Urbe facere solitudinem ? Pontificatum ad nihilum redigere ? . . . Ridiculum est quod gratis donare possis, id ipsum vendere non posse."—Joh. B. Flavii, *De Vitâ Th. de Vio Cajetani*, prefixed to *Commentar. Cajetan in S. Script.* (Lugd. 1639), t. i.

directed to filling up an ever hungry and yawning chasm, of the hypocrisy of the heads of the Church, and the venality of ecclesiastical transactions. He now thought this deep-seated corruption and decay of the Church no matter to be disputed about with Protestants, but to be deplored.

The third of the theological fathers of Papal Infalli- bility was Tapper's contemporary, the Spanish Melchior Canus, who, like him, was at the Council of Trent. His work on theological principles and evidences was, up to Bellarmine's time, the great authority used by all infallibilists. But his experience of the effects of that system on the Popes and the *Curia* themselves is thus summed up in a later judgment, composed by command of the King of Spain, " He who thinks Rome can be healed, knows little of her; the whole administration of the Church is there converted into a great trading business, a traffic forbidden by all laws human, natural, and divine."[1]

Out of Italy, the hypothesis of Infallibility had but few adherents even in the sixteenth century, till the Jesuits began to exercise a powerful influence. In

[1] This opinion, which had previously been published in French by Campomanes, may be seen in Spanish, in the new edition of 1855, of Enzinas. *Dos Informaciones,* Appendix, p. 35.

Spain, the subjection of a Pope to a Council, in accordance with the decrees of Constance and Basle, had been maintained, as late as the fifteenth century, by the most distinguished theologian of his country, Alfonso Madrigal, named Tostado. The Spanish bishop, Andrew Escobar, went further in the same direction. It was the Inquisition which first brought the doctrine of the Roman Jesuits into universal prevalence there, by making all contradiction impossible.

In Germany, before the Jesuits had gained the control of the Universities and Courts, the theologians, who were contending against Protestantism, stood entirely on the side of the Councils. They saw with what terrible weapons the adoption of Papal Infallibility armed Protestantism against the Catholic Church, and how it robbed her of her prerogative of dogmatic immutability. Cochlæus, Witzel, and Bishop Nausea of Vienna rejected it. " It would be too perilous," says the latter, "to make our faith dependent on the judgment of a single individual ; the whole earth is greater than the city." [1]

In France, under the powerful influence of the University of Paris, the belief in the superiority of Councils

[1] *Rerum Conciliar.* v. 3.

had been universal, nor was it changed by the abolition, against the popular will, of the Pragmatic Sanction.
So much the more devotedly did the Italian prelates
proclaim their subservience about the time of the Council
of Trent. Bishop Cornelio Musso of Bitonto preached
in Rome on the Epistle to the Romans,—"What the
Pope says we must receive as though spoken by God
himself. In Divine things we hold him to be God;
in matters of faith I had rather believe one Pope than
a thousand Augustines, Jeromes, or Gregories."[1]

When Bellarmine undertook to provide a new basis
for the pet doctrine of Rome, the violence of the intellectual tempest had driven theology into new-made
paths, and compelled theologians to adopt a different
method. The Roman *Curia*, encouraged by the success
of the Jesuits, the powerful European position of the
Spanish Court, which was thoroughly devoted to it,
and the submission of Henry IV., believed at that time
that it could recover its dominion, at least over the West.
The interdict launched against Venice showed what it
was thought safe to venture upon. The favourite institution of Rome was then again the Inquisition, in its
new and enlarged form, with the Congregation of the

[1] *Conciones in Ep. ad Rom.* p. 606.

Index affiliated to it. To be an active inquisitor was the best recommendation and surest road to attaining the cardinalate, or even the Papal throne. Paul IV. had declared the Inquisition to be the one support of the Papacy in Italy. Two remarkable and important documents show what was now aimed at, and how the Gregorian ideas were intended to be adapted to the circumstances of Europe in the sixteenth century.

Paul IV. issued, with peculiar solemnity, and directly *ex cathedrâ*, his Bull, *Cum ex Apostolatûs officio.* He had consulted his cardinals, and obtained their signatures to it, and then defined, "out of the plenitude of his apostolic power," the following propositions :—

(1.) The Pope, who as "Pontifex Maximus" is God's representative on earth,[1] has full authority and power over nations and kingdoms ; he judges all, and can in in this world be judged by none.

(2.) All princes and monarchs, as well as bishops, as soon as they fall into heresy or schism, without the need of any legal formality, are irrevocably deposed, deprived for ever of all rights of government, and incur sentence of death. In case of repentance, they are to

---

[1] " Qui Dei et Domini nostri Jesu Christi vices gerit in terris."

be imprisoned in a monastery, and to do penance on bread and water for the remainder of their life.

(3.) None may venture to give any aid to an heretical or schismatical prince, not even the mere services of common humanity ; any monarch who does so forfeits his dominions and property, which lapse to princes obedient to the Pope, on their gaining possession of them.

(4.) When it is discovered that a Pope has at any previous time been heretically or schismatically minded, all his subsequent acts are null and void.

Such, then, is this most solemn declaration, issued as late as 1558, subscribed by the cardinals, and afterwards expressly confirmed and renewed by Pius v., that the Pope, by virtue of his absolute authority, can depose every monarch, hand over every country to foreign invasion, deprive every one of his property, and that without any legal formality, and not only on account of dissent from the doctrines approved at Rome, or separation from the Church, but for merely offering an asylum to such dissidents, so that no rights of dynasty or nation are respected, but nations are to be given up to all the horrors of a war of conquest. And to all this is finally subjoined the doctrine, that all official and sacramental acts of a Pope or Bishop, who has ever—say twenty or thirty years before—been heretically minded on any single point of doctrine, are null and void! This last definition contains so emphatic and flat a contradiction of the principles on the validity of sacraments universally received in the Church, although mistakes have sometimes been made about it at Rome, that they must have seemed to theologians utterly incomprehensible. The serious inconveniences which at former periods such doctrines had led to in the Church would have been reproduced now, had not even the most decided adherents of the infallibility theory, the Jesuit divines, shrunk from adopting the principle laid down by this Pope and his cardinals, though Paul IV. threatened all who resisted his decrees with the wrath of God. Bellarmine himself, forty years later, said in Rome itself that a bishop or Pope did not lose his power by becoming or by having been a concealed heretic, or everything would be reduced to uncertainty, and the whole Church thrown into confusion.

Far graver and more permanent consequences resulted from the other document, the Bull *In Cœnâ Domini*, which the Popes had laboured at for centuries, and which was finally brought out in the pontificate of

Urban VIII. in 1627. It had appeared first in its broader
outlines under Gregory XI. in 1372. Gregory XII., in
1411, renewed it, and under Pius V., in 1568, it preserved
its substantial identity with certain additions. According to his decision it was to remain as an eternal law
in Christendom, and above all to be imposed on bishops,
penitentiaries, and confessors, as a rule they were to
impress in the confessional on the consciences of the
faithful. If ever any document bore the stamp of an
ex cathedrâ decision, it is this, which has been over and
over again confirmed by so many Popes.

This Bull excommunicates and curses all heretics
and schismatics, as well as all who favour or defend
them—all princes and magistrates, therefore, who allow
the residence of heterodox persons in their country. It
excommunicates and curses all who keep or print
the books of heretics without Papal permission, all—
whether private individuals or universities, or other
corporations—who appeal from a Papal decree to a future
General Council. It encroaches on the independence
and sovereign rights of States in the imposition of
taxes, the exercise of judicial authority, and the punishment of the crimes of clerics, by threatening with excommunication and anathema those who perform such

acts without special Papal permission; and these penalties fall not only on the supreme authorities of the State, but on the whole body of civil functionaries, down to scribes, jailers, and executioners. The Pope alone can absolve from these censures, except *in articulo mortis.*

No wonder that Sovereigns and States resisted such a manifesto, forbade its publication, and declared it null and void. The French Parliament ordered, in 1580, that all bishops and archbishops who promulgated the Bull should have their goods confiscated, and be pronounced guilty of high treason. The bishops themselves opposed it in the Netherlands. Nor was the King of Spain, who saw in it an encroachment on his rights, any readier to allow its introduction into his territories, nor the Viceroy of Naples. Rudolph II. protested solemnly against its publication in Germany, and especially in Bohemia. Nor could the Archbishop of Mayence be induced to admit it, nor Venice. But the theologians and canonists, above all the Jesuits, inserted the Bull in their doctrinal treatises, and wrote commentaries on it; many confessors went so far as to make it a ground for refusing absolution. Even in 1707, Clement XI. ventured to excommunicate Joseph II.

and all his adherents on the strength of this Bull, for his proceedings about Parma and Piacenza, over which Rome claimed rights of suzerainty; but the Emperor strenuously resisted, and the Pope had to yield. When, still later, in 1768, Clement XIII. once again invaded the sovereign rights of the Duke of Parma by excommunication, it caused a general commotion in the Catholic States. Even so rigid a Catholic as Maria Theresa energetically repulsed the Papal encroachments from Austrian Lombardy, and forbade the Bull being acted upon, remarking in her edict that it contained decisions unsuited to the priestly character, wholly incapable of justification, and very prejudicial to the royal power. As this Bull was annually published in Rome on Maundy-Thursday for 200 years, the ambassadors of the Catholic Powers who were present could each time report that their Sovereigns and Governments, who did not allow the Papal claims to be carried out in practice, had been excommunicated on that day. And if it has ceased to be read out on Holy Thursday, as before, since Clement XIV.'s time, still it is always treated, as Cretineau-Joly states, in the Roman tribunals and congregations, as having legal force.

It was wholly inconsistent with the character and

objects of the Jesuit Order to acquiesce in any half-
and-half views on the question of Papal infallibility, or,
like the older infallibilists from St. Thomas to Cajetan,
to oscillate between the possibility of an heretical Pope
and the duty of unconditional submission to his decisions. The Jesuit sees the perfection of piety in the
renunciation of one's own judgment, the passive surrender of intelligence and will alike to those whom he
recognises as his rulers. The sacrifice of one's own
understanding to that of another man is, according to
the teaching of the Order, the noblest and most acceptable sacrifice a Christian can offer to God.[1] The Jesuit
who is entering upon his novitiate is at once admo-
nished to quench the light of his understanding so far
as it may interfere with blind obedience. He is therefore to be tempted by the novice-master as God tempted
Abraham.[2] In the Exercises it is inculcated that if
the Church decides anything to be black which to our
eyes looks white, we must say that it is black.[3] The
Order considers itself the most exact copy of the

---

[1] " Obedientia tum in executione, tum in voluntate, tum in intellectu sit
in nobis semper omni ex parte perfecta omnia justa esse nobis persuadendo,
omnem sententiam ac judicium nostrum contrarium cæcâ quâdam obedientiâ abnegando."—*Instit. Soc. Jesu* (Pragæ, 1757), i. 408.   Here conre the
well-known comparisons of a corpse and of a staff.

[2] *Instit.* i. 376.   [3] *Excrcit. Spirit.* (ed. Reg. 1644), pp. 290, 291.

ecclesiastical hierarchy, the General being for it what the Pope is for the whole Church.[1] As the Jesuit obeys his General, every Christian should obey the Pope—as blindly, and with as complete a sacrifice of his own judgment.

Every Jesuit therefore must be the advocate of the extremest absolutism in the Church. In his eyes every restriction is an abomination, every legal ordinance attempting to maintain itself against any one arbitrary act of the one almighty lord and master is an assault on him, and matter of high treason. When the Pope speaks on a doctrinal question every one must sacrifice his understanding and submit blindly, and first of all the bishops, singly or in union, as patterns to their flocks. And yet this is but little; the Jesuit, as the most perfect being, makes the offering twice. He first sacrifices his judgment to the Pope, and secondly to his General. For, according to the notion which had haunted some minds previously, but was first reduced to consistency by the Jesuits, and expressed by Cardinal Pallavicini, the collective Church is a body, inanimate when alone and without the Pope, but informed by the

---

[1] "In hâc religione quæ hierarchiam ecclesiasticam maxime imitatur."
—Suarez, *De Rel. Soc. Jesu*, pp. 62), 725.

Pope with a soul.[1] To this soul therefore, *i.e.*, to the
Pope, belongs dominion over the whole Christian world ;
he is its monarch and lord, and his authority is
the foundation, the uniting bond and moving intelligence of all ecclesiastical government.[2] And Gregory
XIV., in his Bull of 1591, recognised the pre-eminence
of the Jesuit Order as an excellent instrument, which,
from the despotic power of its General, can the more
easily be applied to various purposes by the Pope.

The Papal system, when raised to this level, displays
itself with a perfection and consistency even Trionfo
and Pelayo had not conceived of. The absolutists of
the fourteenth century had not yet risen to the idea of
the whole Christian world having but one thinking,
knowing, and willing soul, and that soul the Pope.
Such a notion could only be formed in the minds of
men who had grown up under the discipline of the
Holy Office.

Bellarmine further developed the ideas of Cajetan, in
which he generally concurs, but he rejects decisively
Cajetan's hypothesis of an heretical Pope being deposed

[1] " Non meriterebbe più la Chiesa nome di Chiesa, cioè di Congregazione,
mentre fosse disgregata per tante membra senza aver l'unità di un anima
che le informasse e le regesse."—*Storia del Con. di Tr.* i. 103 (ed. 1843).
[2] *Ib.* i. 107.

ipso facto by the judgment of God. An heretical Pope is legitimate so long as the Church has not deposed him. If Cajetan said the Church was the handmaid of the Pope, Bellarmine adds that whatever doctrine it pleases the Pope to prescribe, the Church must receive; there can be no question raised about proving it; she must blindly renounce all judgment of her own, and firmly believe that all the Pope teaches is absolutely true, all he commands absolutely good, and all he forbids simply evil and noxious. For the Pope can as little err in moral as in dogmatic questions. Nay, he goes so far as to maintain that if the Pope were to err by prescribing sins and forbidding virtues, the Church would be bound to consider sins good and virtues evil, unless she chose to sin against conscience;[1] so that if the Pope absolve the subjects of a prince from their oath of allegiance—which, according to Bellarmine, he has a full right to do—the Church must believe that what he has done is good, and every Christian must hold it a sin to remain any longer loyal and obedient to his sovereign. In Bellarmine's eyes it must have been a perverse act of presumption in Councils to submit

[1] "Si autem Papa erraret præcipiendo vitia vel prohibendo virtutes, teneretur Ecclesia credere vitia esse bona et virtutes mala, nisi vellet contra conscientiam peccare."—*De Rom. Pont.* iv. 5 (ed. Paris, 1643), p. 456.

Papal declarations on matters of faith to their own examination.[1]

After Cajetan and Canus, Bellarmine so widely extended the range of Papal Infallibility, and so completely subordinated Councils, and indeed the whole Church, to the Pope, that only one method of conceiving the relations between them was possible. God does nothing superfluous. He does not give the Christian world the infallible authority it requires twice over, once to the whole body of the Church, and again specifically to the Pope. And as it is certain that it belongs to the Pope, it follows that the Church has not received it for herself, but only through the Pope, as an illumination proceeding from him and residing in his person, —in other words, that active infallibility belongs to the Pope, and only passive infallibility to the Church. Hence, according to the teaching of this party, every decision of a Council is doubtful till it has received the Papal confirmation, which first imparts to it complete certainty. On the other hand, a Papal utterance cannot be confirmed by any earthly power or community,—it is in itself of binding force and divine certainty.

The spurious character of the Isidorian decretals had

---

[1] [As, *e.g.*, St. Leo's Tome on the Incarnation was examined in detail, and finally approved by the Council of Chalcedon. Cf. *supr.* p. 72.—Tr.]

been exposed by the Magdeburg Centuriators, and no one with any knowledge of Christian antiquity could retain a doubt of their being a later fabrication. But the growth cf the Papal system had been so inseparably associated with these forgeries, that the theologians of the *Curia* and the Jesuit Order were resolved to defend them, and make further use of them for proving the infallibility and monarchy of the Popes. The Jesuit Turrianus composed an elaborate apology for the decretals. Bellarmine acknowledged that without the forgeries of the pseudo-Isidore, and of the later anonymous Dominican writers, it would be impossible to make out even a semblance of traditional evidence; the three leading authors of the new doctrine—St. Thomas, Cajetan, and Melchior Canus—had grounded it exclusively on these fictions. Moreover, the new and extremely vigilant censorship had now been established, and hopes were entertained in Rome that by its aid in suppressing and condemning every work which pointed out or admitted that these testimonies were spurious, their authority and influence might be upheld.

Bellarmine then made copious use of the Isidorian fictions. To his mind, enlightened by these letters of the earliest Popes, it is abundantly clear that all the principles of the Papal system were in full bloom in the first and second centuries of the Church, that Christendom already formed an absolute monarchy, and that even then the Popes had exempted the clergy from the jurisdiction of civil courts.[1]   St. Thomas's favourite witness, the spurious Cyril, is also an invaluable authority with Bellarmine, and he thinks the Greek text exists, only it has not yet been discovered and printed.   What Greek testimonies for Papal monarchy and infallibility could have been cited from the first thousand years of Church history if all the forged or corrupted passages had been set aside ?

It is impossible to maintain the entire good faith and sincerity of Bellarmine, for such blind credulity would be inconceivable in a man like him, the more so as Rishton states that he is reported to have said in his lectures at Rome that he considered the Isidorian decretals spurious in spite of Turrianus's defence ;[2] and in fact, in a moment of forgetfulness, he has distinctly hinted, in his great work on the Pope, his disbelief in their genuineness.[3]   But of course the most transparent

---

[1] Cf. especially *De Rom. Pont.* i. 2. c. 14.

[2] *Colloq. Rainold. cum Harto.* p. 94.

[3] *De Rom. Pont.* ii. 14, in speaking of the second epistle of Calixtus and Pius.   He says he dares not affirm that they are undoubtedly genuine.

fictions were welcome to him if they served the great
end of supporting the universal monarchy of the Pope.
Even Pope Innocent's letter excommunicating the Emperor Arcadius was accredited, and the legend of the
Popes appointing the German Electors was expressly
vindicated. This dishonesty is shown again in his
attempts to get rid of the fact he was perfectly acquainted with, that the whole Church, with all universities and theologians of any weight in the sixteenth
century, had rejected the Papal system in its two leading principles of absolute monarchy and infallibility.
He knew from the writings of Pius II. (Æneas Silvius)
that in his time the superiority of Councils was the
dominant view;[1] yet he spares no pains to make his
readers believe that this doctrine was represented only
by two isolated theologians, who were universally condemned.

It seems to have been really believed in Rome that
the *Curia*, with the help of the Inquisition, which had
been more effectively organized since Paul V.'s time, and
the *Index prohibitorum Librorum*, could again suppress

[1] *Hist. Conc. Basil.* p. 773: "Illud imprimis cupio notum, quod
Romanum Papam omnes, qui aliquo numero sunt, Concilio subjiciunt."
Only some, "sive avidi gloriæ, sive quod adulando præmia expectant,"
then defended the opposite opinion, according to Æneas Silvius.

criticism and Church history, or at least keep the mass of the clergy in ignorance of them. The *Index* was just then so rigorously worked that scholars were reduced to despair, and many had to abandon their theological studies. In Germany, matters had come to such a pass, under the influence of the Jesuits in 1599, that Catholics had to give up studying altogether, for they could no longer venture to use lexicons, compendiums, or indexes.[1] Even the bishops were forbidden to read any book condemned at Rome; they too were to be kept in ignorance of the true state of things on so many points which had been now cleared up. The publication of works revealing the very different condition of the Church and the Roman See in earlier days, like the *Liber Diurnus* and Agnellus' History of the Bishops of Ravenna, was forbidden under the severest penalties, and impressions of them already in print were destroyed.

This explains how it was that in the new edition of the Breviary a whole series of Popes of the first three centuries was introduced, with proper offices and lections, of whom no one knew anything, and who have left no trace behind them, who are found in none of the

[1] Jodocus Græs wrote to Baronius, " Præter infinitos alios libros neque Lexico aut Thesauro aut Indice aliquo tute licet uti."—See *Briefe des Cardinals*, i. 474 (ed. Alberic. Rom. 1759).

ancient martyrologies, and were taken no particular notice of in Rome for 1500 years. The only ante-Nicene Popes in the ancient unreformed Breviaries were Clement, Urban, Marcus, and Marcellus. But Bellarmine and Baronius introduced into the new Breviary, under Clement VIII., Popes Zephyrinus, Soter, Caius, Pius, Calixtus, Anacletus, Pontianus, and Evaristus, with lections taken from the pseudo-Isidorian decretals. The older lections, taken from the legends, were even turned out to make room for the pseudo-Isidorian, and the clergy were obliged to nourish their devotion on the reading of such fables as that without the Pope no Council could be held, that he is the sole judge of all bishops, that no clergyman can be cited before a civil court, and the like. And Cardinal Baronius, the author of the Annals, co-operated in this work, although he had there spoken with indignation of the fraud of the pseudo-Isidore.

The new Breviary, moreover, was mutilated as well as interpolated. The name of Pope Honorius was struck out of the lection for Leo II.'s feast, in the passage where his condemnation by the sixth Œcumenical Council had been related, for since the Popes wanted to be infallible, this inconvenient fact ought at least to

be obliterated from the memory of the clergy.[1] Even
the fable of the apostasy of Pope Marcellinus and the
Synod of Sinuessa was now for the first time incorporated in full into the Breviary, in order to keep constantly before the eyes of bishops and priests that darling maxim, in support of which so many fictions had
already been invented at Rome, that no Council can
judge a Pope. Then the word "souls" had to be expunged from the Missal and Breviary in the collect for
the feast of St. Peter's Chair. It was now held scandalous at Rome, that the ancient Roman Church should
have restricted Peter's power of binding to souls only,
whereas the full right was claimed for the Pope to
bind bodies also, and to put them to death.[2] One of
these enrichments of the Breviary was the putting
Satan's words to our Lord in the Temptation, "I will
give thee all the kingdoms of the world," into the
mouth of Christ, who is made to address them to

---

[1] The Breviaries we have compared are a Roman edition printed at Venice
in 1489, the Augsburg Breviary printed in Venice in 1519, and the new reformed edition printed at Antwerp in 1719.

[2] "Deus, qui B. Petro . . . *animas* ligandi et solvendi pontificium tra-
didisti" (Jan. 18, Fest. Cath. S. Petr.) "Animas" is now struck out.
In the old Roman missal of the eleventh century, edited by Azavedo in
1754, it occurs at p. 188. Bellarmine maintained that the reformers of the
Breviary had mutilated this collect under Divine inspiration. *Resp. ad Ep.
de Monit. contr. Venet.* resp. ad 3. prop.

Peter.[1] These forgeries and mutilations in the interest of the Papal system were so astonishing, that the Venetian Marsiglio thought in course of time no faith would be reposed in any documents at all, and so the Church would be undermined.[2]

Thus Baronius and Bellarmine worked together to pour out a new stream of inventions and corruptions of history, in the interest of the Papal system, from Rome, over the countries and Churches of the West which had retained their allegiance to her, or had been forcibly reclaimed. Besides his Annals, which contain a vast repertory of spurious passages and fictions, Baronius availed himself for this purpose of his commission to re-edit the Roman martyrology. His object here was to attest the fables that Peter, as bishop of Rome, had sent out bishops to the cities of the West, and that thus Rome was strictly the Mother Church of all the rest. It was merely stated, for instance, in the older editions of the Roman martyrology, for August 5, that Memmius was the first bishop in Chalons. Baronius made him into a Roman citizen whom St. Peter had himself consecrated for that See. So again with Julian of Le Mans,

---

[1] *Brev. Rom. Fest Petr. et Pauli resp. ad lect.* 5.
[2] *Defens. contr. Bellarm.* c. 6.

on January 27. Baronius knew what the ancient Roman martyrology was ignorant of, that St. Peter had consecrated him to that See. His treatment of Bishop Dionysius of Paris is still more audacious. The oldest accounts, which were well known to him, represented Dionysius as first preaching in Gaul after the middle of the third century, but Baronius relates that he was first consecrated bishop of Athens by the Apostle Paul, and afterwards sent from Rome by Pope Clement as bishop to Gaul. And thus two points were gained for Rome : first, it was proved that the Pope could remove a bishop appointed even by the apostle Paul; and, secondly, that Paris was the immediate spiritual daughter of Rome. And as with interpolations and inventions, so it fared with criticism at Rome. Baronius and Bellarmine pronounced all documents concerning the sixth Council fabricated or falsified which mentioned the condemnation of Pope Honorius.

It is clear that within a few decades after the spread of the Jesuit Order, the Infallibility hypothesis had made immense strides. The Jesuits had from the first made it their special business to suppress the spirit of historical criticism, and the investigation of Church history. They had rivalled one another in taking under their charge the pseudo-Isidorian decretals, as well as both the earlier and later Roman fabrications. Thus Maldonatus, Suarez, Gretser, Possevin, Valentia, and others. That same Turrianus, who expressly defended the decretals, had come to the aid of the Roman system with fresh patristic forgeries, for which he appealed to manuscripts no human eye had seen. At the same time the Jesuit Alfonsus Pisanus composed a purely apocryphal history of the Nicene Council, adapted simply to the exaltation of Papal authority. Others, like Bellarmine, Delrio, and Halloix, defended the writings of the pseudo-Dionysius as genuine; Peter Canisius produced forged letters of the Virgin Mary.

But the chief affair was the maintenance of the authority of the Isidorian decretals, Gratian, and the forgeries accepted by St. Thomas. For a long while no one in the Catholic Church dared to expose the latter. French scholars were the first, about 1660, to tell the truth about them. Gratian's *Decretum* had gained new authority through the revision and correction ordered by the Popes, in the course of which many forgeries must doubtless have been detected. The pseudo-Isidore was still for a long time protected by the Index. When the famous canonist, Contius, brought forward the evidence of its spuriousness, the Preface in which this is contained was suppressed by the censorship. On the appearance of the famous work of Blondel, which completely dissected the pseudo-Isidore, the last doubts about the true nature of the fraud were exploded. But it too was placed on the Index. About the time of the Declaration of 1682,[1] the Spanish Benedictine, Aguirre, made the last attempt worth mentioning to rehabilitate the pseudo-Isidore. It could now no longer be denied that with this forgery disappeared the whole historical foundation of the Papal system for any one acquainted with history. Aguirre was rewarded with a cardinal's hat. But in the course of the eighteenth century it came to be perceived at Rome that it was impossible to maintain any longer the genuineness of this compilation, and thus at last the fraud was admitted in the answer given by Pius VI., in 1789, to the demands of the German archbishops. In recent times the Jesuits in Paris have gone still further. Father Regnon now confesses that " the impostor really gained his end, and altered the whole discipline of the Church as he desired, but did not hinder the universal decay. God blesses no fraud ; the false decretals have done nothing but

---

[1] [The Declaration of the French clergy containing the Four Gallican Articles.—Tr.]

mischief."[1] The crucial importance of this admission does not seem to have been understood in the Order.

One difficulty resulted from the formulization of the doctrine of Infallibility, for the solution of which a variety of hypotheses have been invented, without any unanimity among theologians in accepting some one of them being secured. Every theologian, on closer inspection, found Papal decisions which contradicted other doctrines laid down by Popes or generally received in the Church, or which appeared to him doubtful; and it seemed impossible to declare all these to be products of an infallible authority. It became necessary, therefore, to specify some distinctive marks by which a really infallible decision of a Pope might be recognised, or to fix certain conditions in the absence of which the pronouncement is not to be regarded as infallible. And thus, since the sixteenth century, there grew up the famous distinction of Papal decisions promulgated *ex cathedrâ*, and therefore dogmatically, and without any possibility of error.

The distinction between a judgment pronounced *ex cathedrâ* and a merely occasional or casual utterance is, indeed, a perfectly reasonable one, not only in the

---

[1] *Etudes de Théol., par les PP. Jésuites à Paris,* Nov. 1866.

case of the Pope, but of any bishop or professor. In other words, every one whose office it is to teach can, and will at times, speak off-hand and loosely on dogmatic and ethical questions, whereas, in his capacity of a public and official teacher, he pronounces deliberately, and with serious regard to the consequences of his teaching. No reasonable man will pretend that the remarks made by a Pope in conversation are definitions of faith. But beyond this the distinction has no meaning. When a Pope speaks publicly on a point of doctrine, either of his own accord, or in answer to questions addressed to him, he has spoken *ex cathedrâ*, for he was questioned as Pope, and successor of other Popes, and the mere fact that he has made his declaration publicly and in writing makes it an *ex cathedrâ* judgment. This holds good equally of every bishop. The moment any accidental or arbitrary condition is fixed on which the *ex cathedrâ* nature of a Papal decision is to depend, we enter the sphere of the private crotchets of theologians, such as are wont to be devised simply to meet the difficulties of the system. Of such notions, one is as good as another; they come and go, and are afterwards noted down. It is just as if one chose to say afterwards of a physician who had been consulted, and had given his opinion on a disease, that he had formed his diagnosis or prescribed his remedies as a private person, and not as a physician.   As soon, therefore, as limitations are introduced, and the dogmatic judgments of the Popes are divided into two classes, the *ex cathe-drâ* and the personal ones, it is obvious that the sole ground for this arbitrary distinction lies in the fact that there are sure to be some inconvenient decisions of Popes which it is desirable to except from the privilege of infallibility generally asserted in other cases.   Thus, for instance, Orsi maintains that Honorius composed the dogmatic letter he issued in reply to the Eastern Patriarchs, and which was afterwards condemned as heretical by the sixth Œcumenical Council,[1] only as " a private teacher," but the expression *doctor privatus*, when used of a Pope, is like talking of wooden iron.   Others, like Gonet, have pronounced the decision addressed by Nicolas I. to the Bulgarian Church, that baptism administered simply in the name of Jesus is valid, to be a judgment given by him as a private person only.[2]

Several theologians said that for the Pope to be infallible, he must understand something of the things he is

---

[1] [Cf. *supr.* p. 74.]
[2] *Cursus Theol.* Disput. I. No. 105.

to pronounce sentence upon infallibly, and it must
therefore be made a condition of his infallibility that
he should first have been duly informed about the
matter in hand, and should have consulted bishops and
theologians. " For it is notorious," said the Spaniard
Alphonsus de Castro, " that many of the Popes knew
nothing of grammar, not to speak of the Bible.   But one
cannot decide on dogma without a knowledge of the
Bible."[1]   That is to say, the Pope is infallible when he
decides *ex cathedrâ*, but that implies that he should
first have made careful inquiry, and have informed
himself, and acquired certainty by his own study, and
by consulting others.

Others, especially Jesuits, replied that the Church
would be ill served with such an infallibility as this.
Most of the Popes have attained this supreme dignity as
jurists or administrators, or sons of distinguished families,
and would no longer be able, even if they wished it, to
prosecute theological studies at so advanced an age. Most
of them do not even know how to set about it.   The
spiritual gift of infallibility must be so regulated as to
enlighten for the moment even the most ignorant Pope,

[1] " Constat plures eorum adeo illiteratos esse ut grammaticam penitus
ignorent.   Qui fit, ut Sacras literas interpretari possent ?"—*Adversus Hœ-
reses* (ed. 1539), f. 8b.

and secure him from any error. When a Pope proclaims a doctrine, when he decides on dogmatic and
moral questions, his decision is final, whether it be the
result of lengthened deliberation or pronounced at once.
The seat of infallibility is only in the innermost workshop of his mind. Why consult others, who are liable
to error, while he is not ? Why bring in the feeble light
of a few oil-lamps, when he himself possesses the full
radiance of the spiritual sunlight streaming from the
Holy Ghost ?

Bellarmine most strictly limited the Papal prerogative
of dogmatic infallibility. He would know nothing indeed of the concurrence of a Council, or of consulting
the episcopate ; only when the Pope issues a decree
addressed to the whole Catholic Church, or when he
proclaims a moral law to the whole Church, is he to be
held infallible.[1] This limitation seemed rather to be
framed with a view to the future than the past, for no
single decree of a Pope addressed to the whole Church
is known for the first thousand years of Christian history, and even after the twelfth and thirteenth centuries
the Popes usually decided at Councils on doctrinal
questions. Boniface VIII.'s Bull *Unam Sanctam*, in 1303,

---

[1] *De Rom. Pont.* iv. 3, 5. So his fellow-Jesuit, Eudæmon Johannes.

- is the first addressed to the whole Church. Why the Pope should be held fallible when addressing himself to a part of the Church, but infallible when he addresses himself to the whole, the Cardinal has omitted to state. His opinion therefore has been almost suffered to drop.

Other theologians of his Order, like Tanner and Compton, assumed that a Papal decree was to be considered *ex cathedrâ* and infallible only when certain formalities had been complied with, when it had been affixed for some time to the door of St. Peter's, and in the Campofiore. But most were not satisfied with this. Some, like Duval and Cellot, maintained that the Pope was only infallible when he anathematized all who rejected his teaching.[1]

The general opinion was that very little depended on such points, but yet they could not make up their minds to affirm an absolute and simply unconditional infallibility. The Jesuits Francis Torrensis and Bagot thought the infallibility of a Papal decree could not be reckoned on without a Council, including at least the cardinals, prelates, and theologians resident at Rome. So, again, Driedo, Lupus, and Hosius wanted to make

[1] Duval, *De Supr. R. P. in Eccl. Potest.* (Paris, 1614), Q. 5 ; Cellot, *De Hierarch.* (Rothom. 1641), iv. 10.

infallibility dependent at least on a Council being previously consulted. And hence arose a fresh controversy, -
as to whether the assent of the Council were required for -
a decision *ex cathedrâ*, or whether it were enough for -
the Pope to hear the assembly, and then decide according to his own good pleasure. To make the assent of
the Council a condition were in fact to overthrow the
principle of Papal infallibility. Why call an assembly
of bishops, said others, when the cardinals are there for
that very purpose, who, as belonging to the *Curia*, outweigh a whole host of bishops? But then a new difficulty came in,—is it of the essence of an *ex cathedrâ*
judgment that the Pope should first take the opinions
of the whole college of cardinals? or does it suffice, as
Gravina and Cherubini maintain, if he consults two
cardinals only, and leaves the rest unnoticed, among
whom he presumes a contrary opinion to prevail? This
question has become a crucial one since 1713, when
Clement XI. issued his famous Bull *Unigenitus*, which
he had drawn up with the assistance of two cardinals
only, like-minded with himself. This gave the Jesuits
a new light on the knotty point of how to differentiate -
a definition of faith *ex cathedrâ*. They seem to have -
perceived that it was better to set aside altogether the -

conditions of a previous consultation and questioning of others, and to make the Pope alone the immediate organ of the Divine Spirit; but to introduce two other limitations, viz., Bellarmine's, that his decree must be addressed to the whole Church, and Cellot's, that he must anathematize all who dissent from his teaching. According to this doctrine, which is taught by Perrone,[1] and received by pretty well the whole Order, the Pope is liable to err when he addresses an instruction to the French or German Church only, and, moreover, his infallibility becomes very questionable whenever he omits to denounce an anathema on all dissentients. Meanwhile, as Perrone's theology has not obtained the character of a confession of faith in the Church, nor even attained equal authority with the *Summa* of St. Thomas, there is no hope of his exposition of the term *ex cathedrâ* forming a common point of agreement. And thus, notwithstanding the immense importance ascribed to it, the meaning of the term is still among the dark and inexplicable problems of dogmatic theology. It remains open to every infallibilist to make his own definition of an *ex cathedrâ* decision for his own private use.

[1] *Prælect. Theol.* (Lov. 1843), viii. 497.

§ XXXII.—*Infallibility of the Church and the Popes compared.*

A personal infallibility evidently extends far beyond the inerrancy of a great corporation, like the Catholic Church, or of a Council representing it. The Church in its totality is secured against false doctrine; it will not fall away from Christ and the Apostles, and will not repudiate the doctrine it has once received, and which has been handed down within it. When a Council passes sentence on doctrine, it thereby gives testimony to its truth. The bishops attest, each for his own portion of the Church, that a certain defined doctrine has hitherto been taught and believed there; or they bear witness that the doctrines hitherto believed involve, as their logical and necessary consequence, some truth which may not yet have been expressly formulized. As to whether this testimony has been rightly given, whether freedom and unbiassed truthfulness have prevailed among the assembled bishops,—on that point the Church herself is the ultimate judge, by her acceptance or rejection of the Council or its decision.

Here, therefore, the certainty and infallibility rest entirely on the solid ground of facts. The Church does

not go on to disclose new doctrines,—she does not want
to create anything, but only to protect and keep the
deposit she has inherited.   The meaning of a judgment
passed by the assembled bishops is simply this,—thus
have our predecessors believed, thus do we believe,
and thus will they that come after us believe.   A great
community, a whole Church, is not exposed to the
danger of self-exaltation and presumptuous pretensions
to special Divine illumination.   It makes no attempt
to establish some particular subjective view or opinion
of its own.   Being left to itself, it naturally keeps
within the limits of the traditional faith which has
been constantly and everywhere received.   But matters
assume a very different shape when a single individual is made the organ of infallibility.   The whole
Church, as long as its representatives at a Council
preserve their apostolic independence, cannot be forced
or cajoled into giving a wrong testimony, or proclaim-
ing the view or doctrine of a particular school or party
as the constant and universal belief of all Catholic
Christendom ; but an individual Pope is always exposed to the danger of falling under the influence of
sycophants and intriguers, and thus being forced into
giving dogmatic decisions.   Advantage is taken of his

predilection for some theological opinion, or for some
Religious Order and its favourite doctrines, or of his
ignorance of the history of dogma, or of his vanity and
ambition, for signalizing his pontificate by a memorable
decision, and one supposed to be in the interest of the
Roman See, and thus associating his name with a great
dogmatic event which may constitute an epoch in the
Church. Nor is anything easier for a Pope than to keep
all contradiction at arm's length; as a rule, no one who is
not expressly consulted ventures even to make any representation or suggest any doubts to him. The flatter-
ing conviction, so welcome to the old Adam, grows up
easily within his soul, that his wishes and thoughts are
Divine inspirations, that he is under the special grace
and guidance of Heaven, and that by virtue of his office
the fulness of truth and knowledge, as of power, is his,
without effort of his own. He will the more believe,
and the more quickly catch at this idea, the smaller is
his information and the less suspicion or knowledge he
has of the doubts and difficulties which restrain learned
theologians from adopting a particular doctrinal opinion.
And thus even a well-meaning Pope may come to imagine
that he is far removed from all self-exaltation, and is
simply the humble organ of the Holy Ghost, who speaks
through him.

One of the Popes whose government is of most inauspicious memory, Innocent X., himself confessed that, having been all his life engaged in legal affairs and processes, he understood nothing of theology. But that did not hinder him from originating, by his condemnation of the Five Propositions on grace, a controversy which lasted above a century, and has never found a solution.[1] He told the Bishop of Montpellier that he had received so great an enlightenment of soul from God, that the sense of Holy Writ had become clear to him, and he had suddenly attained a comprehension of the intricate subtleties of scholasticism. The presence of the Holy Ghost, as he expressed it to another clergyman (Aubigni), had become palpable to him. He needed no Synod, nor even any advice of the cardinals, but only the opinion of some regular clergy selected by himself. "All this depends on the inspiration of the Holy Ghost," he said to the theologians who had come to him from Paris.[2]

To speak of a Pope of very recent date, a statesman

[1] [The Five Propositions, said to be extracted from Jansen's *Augustinus*, and condemned by Innocent X. in 1653. His successor, Alexander VII., pronounced further, that they were condemned "in sensu auctoris," which gave rise to a fresh dispute about infallibility extending to "dogmatic facts." Clement IX. somewhat modified the sentence.—TR.]

[2] "Tutto questo dipende dall' inspirazione dello Spirito Santo."— Arnauld, *Œuvres,* xxii. p. 210.

resident in Rome related " that Gregory XVI., in his naïve manner, enjoyed his high position on the express ground that he believed by virtue of it he must always be in the right. When Capaccini discoursed with him on financial affairs, and neither the refined and ingenious statesman could convince his master, nor he with his home-baked arguments convince his minister, Gregory used to exclaim from time to time that he was Pope, and could not err, and must know everything best."[1]

All absolute power demoralizes its possessor. To that all history bears witness. And if it be a spiritual power, which rules men's consciences, the danger of self-exaltation is only so much the greater, for the possession of such a power exercises a specially treacherous fascination, while it is peculiarly conducive to self-deceit,—because the lust of dominion, when it has become a passion, is only too easily in this case excused under the plea of zeal for the salvation of others. And if the man into whose hands this absolute power has fallen cherishes the further opinion that he is infallible, and an organ of the Holy Ghost,—if he knows that a decision of his on moral and religious questions will be

[1] *Politische Briefe und Charakt.* (Berlin, 1849), p. 248.

received with the general, and, what is more, *ex animo* submission of millions,—it seems almost impossible that his sobriety of mind should always be proof against so intoxicating a sense of power. To this must be added the notion, sedulously fostered by Rome for centuries, that every conclave is the scene of the eventual triumph of the Holy Ghost, who guides the election in spite of the artifices of rival parties, and that the newly elected Pope is the special and chosen instrument of Divine grace for carrying out the purposes of God towards the Church and the world. The whole life of such a man, from the moment when he is placed on the altar to receive the first homage by the kissing of his feet, will be an unbroken chain of adorations. Everything is expressly calculated for strengthening him in the belief that between himself and other mortals there is an impassable gulf, and when involved in the cloud and fumes of a perpetual incense, the firmest character must yield at last to a temptation beyond human strength to resist.

It is related of Marcellus II. that at his election he was full of alarm, lest that should also happen in his case, which had been observed in most of his predecessors, who had been completely changed after their accession, and had carried out nothing of their previous good intentions. So injurious, he thought, was the influence on a Pope's character of the change of position, the swarm of sycophants, and the spirit of partisanship.[1] Even the Jesuit General Oliva, about 1670, observes that the character of the newly elected Pope is generally so deteriorated by his elevation, that no one desires such an elevation for a good man, and no one expects that the very best cardinal will retain as Pope the good and holy resolutions he cherished at the time of his accession.[2]

Cardinal Sadolet, who was his intimate friend, said of Clement VII., that he had the Bible constantly in his hands, and thus entertained good resolutions, yet his pontificate was but a series of mistakes, a perpetual dodging to evade the Council which he hated and feared. Sadolet is obliged to admit that Clement, "misled by his minister," departed widely from his former character, and the goodness of his nature.[3]

Paul IV. (Caraffa) before his election was a warm friend of Church reformation, and left the Papal Court because there was no hope of obtaining any help towards it under Clement VII. When he became Pope

---

[1] Pollidor. *De Vit. Marcell. II.* (Rom. 1744), p. 132.

[2] *Lettere* (Bologna, 1705), ii. 214.

[3] *Epistolæ Sadoleti, Omphalii et Sturmii* (Argentorati, 1539), p. 9.

himself nothing was to be seen of his former zeal for reforming the Church. At a time when almost every post brought fresh news of the advance of Protestantism, he left the Church in its helpless condition; he did not so much as think of continuing the Council which had for some years been suspended. His chief concerns were the advancement and enrichment of his nephews; his favourite institution, the Inquisition; and the quarrel with the two only champions the Papal system then had, Charles v. and Philip ii., for it is the office of the Papacy to tread under foot kings and emperors.[1]

His contemporary, Onufrio Panvinio, paints in the most glaring colours the complete transformation which took place in Pius iv. (John Angelo de Medici, Pope from 1559 to 1565). Before his elevation he had shown himself humane, tolerant, beneficent, gentle, and unselfish; but as Pope he was just the reverse—passionate, covetous, and jealous. Especially after he had freed himself from the hated Council of Trent, he abandoned himself to vulgar sensuality and lusts, ate and drank immoderately, became imperious and crafty, and withdrew himself from Divine service in the chapel.[2]

---

[1] *Relaz. di Bernardo Navagero*, in *Relazioni degli Ambasciadori Veneti*, vii. 380.

[2] Panvin. *Vit. Pontif. post Platinam* (Colon. 1593), pp. 463, 477. With

So was it afterwards with Innocent X. (Pamfili), who had previously passed for a blameless and honest man, but who as Pope gave the world the spectacle of an administration guided and made pecuniary capital out of by an imperious and covetous woman, his sister. So again with Alexander VII. (Flavio Chigi), who as Cardinal was an able and gifted man of business, but as Pope soon let himself be readily persuaded by the fawning Jesuit Oliva that it was a mortal sin not to bring his nephews to Rome and make them rich and great.[1] His chief care was to get rid of all business, and lead an easy and quiet life. Of later Popes we say nothing here.

§ XXXIII.—*What is meant by a Free Council.*

The experiences of the non-Italian bishops at the Council of Trent, its results, which fell so far short of the reforms desired and expected, the conduct of Rome in strictly prohibiting any explanations or commentaries on the decrees of the Council being written, and reserv-

this agrees the statement of the Venetian ambassador Tiepolo, *Relazioni*, x. 171.

[1] What has so often been observed of the Popes, that in audiences and official intercourse they had behaved without any scruple, and with habitual dissimulation, the Florentine ambassador expresses shortly in these words, in his report about Alexander VII. : " We have a Pope who never speaks a word of truth."—See the *Chronol. Hist. des Papes* of the Benedictines of St. Maur (Paris, 1783), p. 341.

- ing to herself the interpretation of them, while she
- quietly shelved many of its most important decisions
- (*e.g.*, on indulgences, and many others), without even
- any semblance of carrying them out—all this led to
- the call for a new Council, so often repeated previously,
- being silenced from that time forward. In countries
- subjected to the Inquisition, the mere wish for another
- Council would have been declared penal, and have ex-
- posed to danger those who uttered it. The Roman See
had no doubt suffered considerable losses of privilege
and income in consequence of the Tridentine decrees,
and still more from the opposition of the different
Governments; but, on the other hand, those decrees, the
activity of the Jesuits, and the establishment of standing
congregations and of the nunciatures, which had been
previously unknown, had very materially increased the
power and influence of Rome. But at Rome Councils
were always held in abomination; the very name was
strictly forbidden under penalties there. When in the
controversy about grace in 1602 the Molinists spoke of
its being decided by a Council, the Dominican Peña
wrote that in Rome the word Council, at least in matters
of dogma, was regarded as sacrilegious, and excommunicated.[1]

---

[1] In the letter in Serry, *Hist. Cong. de Grat.*, (Antwerp, 1709), p. 270.

And thus it has come to pass that three centuries have elapsed without any earnest desire for a Council making itself heard anywhere—a thing wholly unprecedented in the past history of the Church. It is commonly taught in theological manuals, schools, and systems, that the Councils of the Church are not only useful but necessary. But this, like so much else in the ordinary teaching, was held only in the abstract. It was at bottom universally felt that Councils as little fitted into a Church organized under an absolute Papal monarchy, as the States-General into the monarchy of Louis XIV. The most faithful interpreter of the Roman view of things, Cardinal Pallavicini, put this feeling into words, when he said, " To hold another Council would be to tempt God, so extremely dangerous and so threatening to the very existence of the Church would such an assembly be." In that point, he thinks his History of the Council of Trent will make the same impression on the reader as Sarpi's.[1] Even National Synods, he says, the Popes have always detested.[2]

But the chief reason why nobody any longer desired a Council, lay in the conviction that, if it met, the first and most essential condition, freedom of deliberation and voting, would be wanting. The latest history

[1] *Storia del Conc. di Tr.* iv. p. 331, ed. 1843.   [2] *Ib.* p. 74.

showed this as much as the theory. In the Papal system, which knows nothing of true bishops ruling independently by virtue of the Divine institution, but only recognises subjects and vicars or officials of the Pope, who exercise a power lent them merely during his pleasure, there is no room for an assembly which would be called a Council in the sense of the ancient Church.[1] If the bishops know the view and will of the Pope on any question, it would be presumptuous and idle to vote against it ; and if they do not, their first duty at the Council would be to ascertain it and vote accordingly. An œcumenical assembly of the Church can have no existence, properly speaking, in presence of an *ordinarius ordinariorum* and infallible teacher of faith, though, of course, the pomp, ceremonial, speeches, and votings of a Council may be displayed to the gaze of the world. And therefore the Papal legates at Trent used at once to rebuke bishops as heretics and

---

[1] Cardinal de Luca says (*Relat. Curiæ Rom.* Diss. iv. n. 10), it is the " opinio in hâc Curiâ recepta " that the Pope is " Ordinarius Ordinariorum, habens universum mundum pro diœcesi," so that bishops and archbishops are only his " officiales," or, as Benedict XIV. observes (*De Synod. Dioces.* x. 14 ; v. 7), the Pope is " in totâ Ecclesiâ proprius sacerdos—potest ab omni jurisdictione episcopi subtrahere quamlibet Ecclesiam." In Merlini's *Decis. Rot. Rom.* ed. 1660 (Dec. 830), we read, " Papa est dominus omnium beneficiorum." In a word, this system leaves nothing which can be said to belong to bishops of right. The Roman theory allows the *Curia* to rob them, wholly or in part, of their rights, to hand over their rights to others, etc.

rebels who ever dared to express any view of their own.[1]
Bishops who have been obliged to swear " to maintain,
defend, increase, and advance the rights, honours, privileges, and authority of their lord the Pope "—and every
bishop takes this oath—cannot regard themselves, or be
regarded by the Christian world, as free members of a
free Council; natural justice and equity requires that.
These men neither will nor can be held responsible for
decisions or omissions which do not depend on them.
There have certainly been the weightiest reasons for
holding no Council for three hundred years, and avoid-
ing such a "useless hubbub," as the infallibilist Cardinal Orsi calls Councils.[2]

Complete and real freedom for every one, freedom
from moral constraint, from fear and intimidation, and
from corruption, belongs to the essence of a Council.
An assembly of men bound in conscience by their oaths

---

[1] Numberless instances of this may be found in the letters of the Spanish ambassador Vargas, and the autobiography of Bishop Martin Perez de Ayalas, in the appendix to Villanueva, *Vida Liter.* ii. 420.

[2] Bossuet has brought forward the question, so often asked and never answered : to what purpose were so many Councils held in the Church, with so much trouble and expense, if the infallible Popes could have finally set-tled every doctrinal controversy by a single utterance of their own? To this Orsi answers, and we have his reply in Count de Maistre's trans-lation, " Ne le demandez point aux Papes qui n'ont *jamais* imaginé qu'il fût besoin de conciles œcuméniques pour reprimer (les hérésies d'Arius, etc.) Demandez le aux empereurs qui ont absolument voulu les conciles, qui les ont convoqués, qui ont exigé l'assentiment des Papes, qui ont excité *inutile-ment tout ce fracas* dans l'église."

to consider the maintenance and increase of Papal power their main object,[1]—men living in fear of incurring the displeasure of the *Curia*, and with it the charge of perjury, and the most burdensome hindrances in the discharge of their office—cannot certainly be called free in all those questions which concern the authority and claims of the See of Rome, and very few at most of the questions that would have to be discussed at a Council do not come under this category. None of our bishops have sworn to make the good of the Church and of religion the supreme object of their actions and endeavours; the terms of the oath provide only for the advantage of the *Curia*. How the oath is understood at Rome, and to what reproaches a bishop exposes himself who once chooses to follow his own conviction against the tradition of the *Curia*, there are plenty of examples to show.

In Rimini and Seleucia (359), at Ephesus (449) and at Vienne (1312), and at many other times, even at Trent, the results of a want of real freedom have been displayed. In early times, when the Popes were as yet

[1] The more important passages of the oath are :—" Jura, honores, privilegia et auctoritatem S. Rom. Ecclesiæ Domini nostri Papæ et sucessorum prædictorum conservare, defendere, augere et promovere curabo. . . . Regulas sanctorum Patrum, decreta, ordinationes seu dispositiones, reservationes, provisiones et mandata apostolica totis viribus observabo et faciam ab aliis observari."

in no position to exercise compulsion or intimidation
upon Synods, it was the Emperors who sometimes
trenched too closely on this freedom. But from
Gregory VII.'s time the weight of Papal power has
pressed ten times more heavily upon them than ever
did the Imperial authority. With abundant reason were
the two demands urged throughout half Europe in the
sixteenth century, in the negotiations about the Council,
—first, that it should not be held in Rome, or even in
Italy, and secondly, that the bishops should be absolved
from their oath of obedience. The recently proclaimed
Council is to be held not only in Italy, but in Rome
itself, and already it has been announced, that, as the
sixth Lateran Council, it will adhere faithfully to the
fifth.[1] That is quite enough—it means this, that whatever course the Synod may take, one quality can never
be predicated of it, namely, that it has been a really
free Council.

Theologians and canonists declare that without complete freedom the decisions of a Council are not binding, and the assembly is only a pseudo-Synod. Its
decrees may have to be corrected.

[1] [Cf. *supr.* pp. 197, 198, 348.]

EDINBURGH : T. CONSTABLE,
PRINTER TO THE QUEEN, AND TO THE UNIVERSITY.

www.ingramcontent.com/pod-product-compliance
Lightning Source LLC
Chambersburg PA
CBHW031826270326
41932CB00008B/559